DEVILS, LUSTS AND
STRANGE DESIRES

To Ames

DEVILS, LUSTS AND STRANGE DESIRES

The Life of Patricia Highsmith

Richard Bradford

BLOOMSBURY CARAVEL
LONDON · OXFORD · NEW YORK · NEW DELHI · SYDNEY

BLOOMSBURY CARAVEL
Bloomsbury Publishing Plc
50 Bedford Square, London, WC1B 3DP, UK
29 Earlsfort Terrace, Dublin 2, Ireland

BLOOMSBURY, BLOOMSBURY CARAVEL and the BLOOMSBURY CARAVEL logo
are trademarks of Bloomsbury Publishing Plc

First published in Great Britain in 2021
This paperback edition published in 2023

A catalogue record for this book is available from the British Library

ISBN: PB: 978-1-4482-1822-6; HB: 978-1-4482-1790-8; eBook: 978-1-4482-1791-5

2 4 6 8 10 9 7 5 3 1

Typeset in Perpetua by Deanta Global Publishing Services, Chennai, India
Printed and bound in Great Britain by CPI Group (UK) Ltd. Croydon, CR0 4YY

MIX
Paper | Supporting
responsible forestry
FSC® C171272

To find out more about our authors and books visit www.bloomsbury.com
and sign up for our newsletters

CONTENTS

ACKNOWLEDGEMENTS

Firstly, I wish to express my thanks to Andrew Wilson and Joan Schenkar for their fine achievements in their biographies of Patricia Highsmith, details of which will be found in 'Suggested Further Reading'.

The editorial advice provided by Patrick Taylor and Claire Browne has been invaluable, and thanks are due to Jayne Parsons who set it all in motion. To Dai Howells: diolch yn fawr.

Lisa Verner has done a great job, as has Mark Sampson.

Dr Amy Burns made it possible.

INTRODUCTION

Leaving aside one's personal opinions of her work, it has to be accepted that Patricia Highsmith was an incomparable individual. Where to begin? She was born Mary Patricia Plangman in Fort Worth, Texas on 19 January 1921. She was an animal lover – largely because she regarded them as superior to human beings. On one occasion, she declared that if she came upon a starving infant and a starving kitten, she would not hesitate to feed the latter and leave the child to fend for itself. Why, she once asked, should domestic pets be expected to consume material that we might find unpalatable? She recommended that as a mark of respect to dogs and cats they should be fed carefully prepared foetuses from human miscarriages or abortions. We care nothing for the dignity of bulls and other animals when we eat their testicles, so why shouldn't we compensate mammals similarly with our own bodies? For some time when in France she enjoyed eating beef as it came from the butcher, uncooked. Not tartare, but in a bloody lump. Again, she appeared to think that eating dead cattle unadorned accorded them some respect. She had a particular affection for snails – regarding the French, who ate them, as cannibals. In several of her homes she created space in her garden for her private snail 'colonies' and when she moved from England to France she smuggled out a handful of her favourites in her bra. Her obsession with them began, apparently, when she watched two mate with one another. The spectacle appealed to her because the participants seemed devoid of pleasure or emotion. We should not, however, regard her as a forerunner of animal rights or Green activism. Once, she shocked her guests by swinging her pet cat around in a sack apparently to see how animals would cope with being drunk.

On the matter of drink, Highsmith was a record-breaker. From college days she enjoyed everything from beer to spirits and by middle age she worked hard at remaining drunk from breakfast until bedtime. She was most fond of gin, but would counterpoint her intake of this with quarter-pint shots of whisky. When she lived in Suffolk she once attended an event at a hotel, and sat alone in the hall with her drink. She drew the attention of another guest, who'd never met her before but who commented to a friend that she was in his opinion insane, dangerous and someone who should be committed. He was a psychiatrist, and was struck by her facial expression, which he claimed never to have encountered outside of a mental institution.

Perhaps a psychiatrist might be able to explain her claim that 'I am a man and I love women'. In basic terms, she wasn't and she did, and her record as a lover might be treated as a triumph for lesbianism, gay sexuality and even women's rights in general. Compared to Highsmith, the likes of Casanova, Errol Flynn and Lord Byron might be considered lethargic – even demure. She seemed to enjoy affairs with married women in particular, but breaking up lesbian couples came a close second. Had she lived in our era, one could imagine her taking great delight in adding breaking up lesbian marriages to her repertoire. On six occasions, at least on record, she choreographed ménages à trois, ensuring that she was the only member of the threesome who was aware of what was going on, and twice she involved a fourth participant. She found time during her busy career as a nymphomaniac to fall deeply in love, becoming enchanted by five women in particular. More intriguing than what Highsmith said or did with them were the entries on how she felt in her private diaries and *cahiers* (notebooks) – she was a prolific diary keeper, her diaries alone coming to more than 8,000 pages.

The beginning of each relationship is recorded in terms of other-worldly ecstasy, but the hyperbole of infatuation is always accompanied by predictions of murder and death, which usually turned out to be accurate. Not literally, but in terms of the butchery of emotions or the extermination of love. Typically: 'Beauty, perfection, completion – all achieved and seen. Death is the next territory, one step to the left.' One of her long-term lovers did attempt suicide and failed, but only just. Highsmith watched as her girlfriend washed down half a bottle of high-strength barbiturates with gin and then left for supper with friends, one of whom Highsmith had had sex with the day before.

One of Highsmith's closest friends commented on her disposition as a whole: 'She was an equal opportunity offender ... You name the group, she hated them.' Her hate list was impressive in its diversity: Latinos, black people, Koreans, Indians (south Asians), 'Red Indians', Portuguese, Catholics, evangelicals and fundamentalists, and Mexicans, among others. In 1992, she visited her erstwhile girlfriend, Marijane Meaker, in America and, glancing around a diner, remarked on how the vast majority of customers were African American. Meaker assumed that she was acknowledging how things had changed since their youth when discrimination was routine, but no. To Highsmith, there were so many of them because of their 'animal-like breeding habits', that it was common knowledge that black men became physically ill without a regular diet of sex and were too stupid to realise that unprotected intercourse led to pregnancy.

Despite, or perhaps because of, spending ten years as a permanent resident of France, Highsmith cultivated a loathing for all Gallic customs and persons. While she occasionally displayed nostalgic feelings for her native land of America, these were aberrations from her long-standing contempt for the place. She disliked Arabs, mainly for, in her opinion, their poor standards of hygiene, but she made an exception with the Palestinian cause. It was not so much that she sympathised with this small Middle Eastern nation of the dispossessed; rather, her support for Palestine reflected her feelings about another group of people which she abhorred far more than any other: Jews.

She regretted that the Nazis had only succeeded in exterminating less than half of the globe's Jews and even coined a term to describe their negligence: 'Semicaust'. Another of her contributions to the linguistics of genocide was 'Holocaust Inc.' In Highsmith's view the Holocaust was by parts an exaggeration in terms of the number slaughtered and an enterprise employed by Jews – Israel in particular – to exploit the collective conscience of the rest of the world and squeeze money from it. She once confessed to a friend that she enjoyed the rural areas of Switzerland, where she spent her final years, because they seemed like Europe as envisioned by the Nazis after the successful completion of the Final Solution. Jews, if they existed at all, were certainly somewhere else. And yet, three of the women to whom she declared her unbounded love were Jewish. With one woman in particular, Marion Aboudaram, Highsmith took a particular interest in her physiognomy and the hair distribution on the rest of her anatomy, along with the experiences of her mother who had survived the Nazi occupation of Paris.

As I will show, Highsmith's novels are a lifelong autobiography, though certainly not in the sense that all of her characters are modelled either on herself or on those she knew. She was not, like Ripley, a murderous psychopath, but he was shaped by her personality, often as a means of rewriting her life and opinions as a special form of masochism. Few things that happen in her novels relate directly to her immediate experience, but each bears her view of the world and how she understood her role in it. One of her editors suggested to her that although her books commanded immense respect in America, many ordinary readers would feel alienated as all of her characters lacked decency or humanity. She agreed, and added: 'Perhaps it's because I don't like anyone.'

Her writing varies immensely in terms of its artistic qualities. Some novels, especially *Strangers on a Train*, *Carol* (originally published as *The Price of Salt*) and *The Talented Mr. Ripley*, will endure as works of genius, while others will continue to fascinate us in their refusal to fall into the category of genre pieces or 'serious' fiction. And a number are, simply put, bad. Above all, I argue, Highsmith has done more than anyone to erode the boundaries between crime writing as a recreational sub-genre and literature as high art, books that contribute to our understanding of who we are and how we behave. This came about more by fortuitous accident than as the realisation of a lifelong aesthetic enterprise on her part. She never killed anyone or committed a serious criminal offence, but she regarded those who did as honest representations of the sheer wickedness of human nature.

THE BEGINNING

Patricia Highsmith took pride in the history of her maternal grandparents and great-grandparents, the Coats, or later the Coates. Gideon Coats, her great-grandfather, was born in South Carolina in 1812, and rumour had it that his father was just old enough to be involved in the War of Independence. Gideon resettled in Alabama in 1842, purchased 5,000 acres of wild bush and forest from the Cherokee Indians for an undisclosed sum and set up a plantation producing mainly cotton and corn. Patricia later boasted that his 110 slaves were 'not unhappy'. She enjoyed comparing her ancestor with figures from Margaret Mitchell's *Gone with the Wind*, 'a true novel about the South'. Mitchell's novel was published in 1936 and at one point was only slightly behind sales of the Bible in US bestseller lists, largely because it ferociously sanitised and distorted the true nature of slavery and institutionalised racism in the Southern States. Patricia saw her great-grandfather as a version of Major Ashley Wilkes, the perfect gentleman who would in any event have freed his slaves had the Northerners not forced him to do so after the Civil War. Gideon built a neo-classical colonial residence and refused to sully the purity of local oak with nails, instead employing local craftsmen to fit the timbers together using joints and pegs. It had fourteen main rooms, six downstairs and eight bedrooms above; all were spacious and well-lit with French windows opening onto beautifully finished lawns.

It was a very handsome plantation house and Patricia kept a photograph of it, taken before her grandfather left Alabama in the

1880s, with her throughout her life. Gideon and his wife, Sarah, had eight children who were dispersed across the South after he and his wife died and the plantation was broken up.

Patricia's grandfather, Daniel Coates, married Willie Mae Stewart in 1883. They moved to Fort Worth, Texas, in the same year, to a lifestyle much less gentrified than that of Gideon in Alabama. They opened their wood-framed home to boarders, 'young gentlemen of talent and sensibility', a coded reference to white, mostly manual workers, who would be forbidden from bringing drink onto the premises.

Willie Mae's father, Oscar Wilkinson Stewart, might also have been invented by Mitchell, had she thought of introducing a dour puritanical counterpart to Ashley Wilkes and Rhett Butler. He was a surgeon, also from Alabama, who served for the Confederates in the Civil War. It was said that the rugs in his bedroom carpet carried holes from his 'frequent and protracted kneeling in the act of prayer'.

It was in Fort Worth that Mary Coates, Daniel and Willie Mae's only daughter, met and married Jay Bernard Plangman, or 'Jay B', as he preferred to be called. The Plangmans lived only two streets from the Coates and were given grudging respect but generally regarded as coming from a lower point on the social order. They were descended from German immigrants of the mid-nineteenth century. Every Euro-American came from immigrants, but the older Anglo-Saxon generation saw themselves as the aristocracy of the New World, whereas those who had fled from Europe in the nineteenth century due to discrimination or poverty were looked down upon as second-class incomers.

Highsmith was not ashamed of her father's Lutheran, artisan background because until her teens she knew nothing of it. Her parents separated and divorced shortly after she was born but she only learned of what had happened between them while she was still a youngster. In 1988 she told an interviewer in the *New York Times Magazine* that her mother had said to her when she was a teenager, 'It's funny how you adore the smell of turpentine, Pat', going on to explain that when she became pregnant, Plangman had urged her into a DIY abortion using the substance, as it was believed to clean out the womb. In 1971, shortly after his daughter's fiftieth birthday, Plangman wrote to her and confessed that 'I did suggest an abortion as we were just getting started in the art field in New York and thought it best to postpone a family until sometime later.' He continued: 'The turpentine was suggested by a friend of Mary's and tried with no results' (Plangman to Highsmith, 30 July 1971).

The rather gruesome detail of his description was prompted by Highsmith, who had written to him two weeks earlier commenting that 'I believe in abortion, and the decrease of the population, so you must not think for a moment I am annoyed by this idea' (Highsmith to Plangman, 15 July 1971). She went on to demand a detailed account of why the attempt to end her pre-natal existence had failed and which of them, her mother or father, had thought it necessary.

Jay Bernard Plangman and Mary Coates were married on 16 July 1919. They had met in Fort Worth little more than six months earlier and their incipient careers as commercial artists had convinced them that they could be a 'modern' couple, sharing their incomes rather than playing the traditional roles of breadwinner and housewife. A year into their marriage they decided to move to New York, hoping to find jobs in the booming magazine and advertising industries. Illustrators could retain a sense of themselves as artists while earning a secure living, in a business where there was an almost limitless demand for freelancers. Mary discovered she was pregnant shortly before they were due to take the train north and the prospect of rearing a child would have ruined their dream of well-paid bohemianism. The botched abortion played a part in the collapse of their relationship. Neither of them wanted the child but now they could do nothing about it. They were divorced around six months before their second wedding anniversary in 1921 and soon after the birth of their daughter. Two years later Mary met Stanley Highsmith, an illustrator and professional photographer. As with Plangman, the period between their first encounter and their marriage, engagement included, was brief: less than four months. The recently married Highsmiths moved into one of the unappealing bungalows from which Mary's parents were earning a living. The others were let out to African Americans whose behaviour and activities Willie Mae controlled as if they were still pre-abolition – as her possessions rather than her tenants. A small, seemingly inconspicuous woman, she could force her black tenants to hand over stocks of illicit drinks and at her command fist fights would cease immediately.

Patricia was only three years old when her mother married Highsmith. She made an entry in an early *cahier* of her first recollection of her stepfather. She describes a rather sinister stranger who, without introduction, walked into her room, bent over her and asked her to pronounce a particular phrase in a book she was reading. 'Open see-same!', she responded, but Stanley corrected her: 'Sess-a-mi!', and insisted that she repeat his pronunciation. She did so and recalled that he smiled 'indulgently' at her, 'his red heavy lips tight together and spread wide below his black moustache'. The sexual undertones of this image are rather menacing, and it is clear enough that in 1941, aged twenty, Highsmith already had a feel for the way in which language could create unease. But this also raises the question of whether the account is authentic. When she first met Stanley Highsmith, she had only just reached her third birthday. In her *cahier* of 3 August 1948 she returned again to her childhood and this time took a step into a third-person account of 'a small, dark figure ... an alert, anxious-faced child over whom hangs already the grey-black spirit of doom, or foreordained unhappiness, the knowledge of which made this child weep often'. In 1941 she projected herself backwards into her imagined three-year-old presence and seven years later she adjusts this trick so that the infant can foresee a melancholic state that awaits her in later life.

In 1925 she allegedly contracted Spanish flu, a virus estimated to have resulted in more than half a million deaths in America alone. She told the journalist Duncan Fallowell of this in an interview published in the *Daily Telegraph* in 2000, explaining that this virus was so widely feared that the doctor who had first attended her at the Coates's house decided that it would be best to leave her to deal with the condition herself, rather than risk spreading it further via contact with his friends, family and other patients. She 'made it through' because her grandmother, 'who was the daughter of a doctor, gave me calomel, which is a kind of laxative with mercury in it'. Out of ignorance or politeness, Fallowell did not comment on the fact that there were no vaccines for Spanish flu and that by its onset in America calomel was, by consensus, regarded by the medical profession useless as a cure for anything. Its hideous side-effects undermined claims by its nineteenth-century advocates that it was a miracle drug for everything from syphilis to cancer. Highsmith's interviewer also remained silent on the anachronism of her contracting Spanish flu three years after the pandemic had come to an end: no new cases of the virus were reported in America after 1921.

In a private notebook from 1974 called 'An American Bookbag', now in the Bern archive, Highsmith tells of how in the same year that she contracted influenza, she also became obsessed with a nationwide media event that shifted between the exhilarating and the prurient. In January 1925, the explorer Floyd Collins was trapped by a large rock that fell on his foot when he was exploring the so-called Mammoth Caves in Kentucky. Floyd spent fifteen days underground as rescuers tried to reach him. He died from a combination of freezing temperatures and starvation and almost three months after his death, the rotting corpse was brought out. Highsmith wrote of how she would rush downstairs every day to pick up a copy of the Fort Worth *Star Telegraph* to keep up with this story of Floyd, decomposing underground while the authorities deliberated over when it would be safe to remove what was left of him. Her fascination with this morbid tale reflected her own flu-afflicted confinement, abandoned by her doctor and suffering, seemingly the last person in America living with the virus.

Psychologists are still uncertain about the exact nature of what is commonly referred to as childhood amnesia, but empirical evidence disclosed by surveys shows that while children are able to recall more and more of their past as they progress from the ages of four to eleven, the onset of early and full adulthood diminishes the clarity of these early life remembrances. Our childhood memories do not fully disappear, but they become clouded and distorted by the aggregations of maturity. When we look back on our early experiences, for example, direct recollection is sometimes overwhelmed by our acquired perception of the environment in which we grew up, the background and activities of our parents and so on. The clash between lateral perceptions during childhood – what we thought and felt when we were, say, six years old – and our notion of our past at twenty-six, hardly concerns most of us. However, one has to wonder if Highsmith intuited childhood amnesia as a means of rewriting her past. She would later become a fan of psychologists who produced bestsellers in effortless self-diagnosis.

After Highsmith's death, Vivien De Bernardi, whom the author had known during the last decade of her life, told of how her friend had confided to her that 'she thought she might have been sexually abused at her grandmother's house ... [when] she was a small child, around four or five, and remembered two men, whom she thought could have been salesmen, coming into the house'. She recalls being lifted onto a counter or kitchen sink and though she was reluctant to state that she had been raped, 'She had a sense of being violated by these two men in the way she did not really understand' (interview between De Bernardi and Andrew Wilson, July 1999).

In 1968 Highsmith wrote an article for *Vogue* magazine and told of how, around roughly the same time that she may have been sexually abused, she was plagued by a particular nightmare. She would be lying on a table but the atmosphere was so 'gloomy' that it was impossible for her to tell if the room was an operating theatre or some routine domestic space. She was more precise about the individuals who stood over her. Three doctors and four nurses were present, though she does not explain how she recognised them as members of the medical profession. They seem about to perform an operation but instead they speak and 'nod in solemn agreement over some unspeakable defect in me … It is an irrevocable pronouncement, worse than death because I am fated to live' (*Vogue*, September 1968).

Two years later she wrote to her stepfather, 'My [sexual] character was essentially made before I was six' (29 August 1970). What prompted her to confide such intimate details to a man she had loathed since she first encountered him? He was hardly a figure she had come to treat with grudging respect, as one might a confessor who despises the priesthood. In her *cahier* (16 October 1954) she recorded that from around the time she was eight she had regularly entertained 'evil thoughts of murder of my stepfather'. Throughout her *cahiers* and diaries from the early 1940s until her death in 1995 she records her infanthood – roughly the period from the age of three, when she attains a sense of selfhood, to around eight – as involving a blend of fear, self-loathing and hatred for her close family, primarily her grandmother, her mother Mary and most of all Stanley. This hatred was based on 'sex primarily and my maladjustment to it as a result of suppressed relations in the family' (Diary, 11 June 1942). 'I learned to live with a grievous and murderous hatred [for her family members] very early on' (*Cahier*, 12 January 1970).

Aside from relatively inconsequential facts such as her birthdate, where she lived and with whom, the story of Highsmith's childhood is based on observations and anecdotes she offered as an adult in public interviews and articles, and privately in her *cahiers* and diaries. She generally reserved the more traumatic and grotesque for the confidential notebooks, but was fully aware that, in presenting them to the open archive in Bern, they would be pored over by biographers and others determined to locate the woman behind the books. There is considerable evidence to suggest that she was playing games with these scrutineers, creating some narratives that are contradicted by others and making claims upon events and their traumatic outcomes that often seem incredible. It seems odd, for example, that she should have spoken to no one of the alleged act of sexual abuse until she confided in Vivien De Bernardi. Why her? It is common for trauma to be suppressed until later in life but we should also wonder if Highsmith was carefully choreographing disclosures for other reasons. She had already decided to appoint De Bernardi as her testamentary executor, a magnet for biographers and researchers.

The copies of letters she sent to figures such as her mother and Stanley seem to be part of a one-sided dialogue. There is little doubt that she wrote and posted the originals, but we have no record of what her mother and stepfather wrote to her. Often it seems that she was responding to questions that might never have been asked or implying that she needed answers to questions based on no more than her own speculations. One of her earliest *cahiers* includes an entry that stands out as more transparent and authentic than the rest. 'I cannot remember as much of my childhood as I should like, or even remember myself a few years back. I hope to do better when I grow older' (*Cahier*, 29 August

1940). Aged nineteen she confesses that her childhood is a blur, but she feels confident that later in life 'I hope to do better'. This is cautiously phrased. Some might treat it as an early version of what we now call 'recovered memory' while others could regard it as her looking forward to a time when she felt more confident about making things up.

As we will see, Patricia Highsmith had two careers as a fiction writer. Both began around the time she wrote *Strangers on a Train*. As well as writing books featuring invented characters she decided that her own life should become the equivalent of a novel, a legacy of lies, fantasies and authorial interventions.

In 1927 Stanley and Mary Highsmith moved from Fort Worth to New York, repeating the endeavour of the Plangmans six years earlier to better themselves in the city. They took an apartment in the centre of town on West 103rd Street and enrolled Patricia, aged six, at a primary school nearby on West 99th Street. Mary began work, successfully, as a freelance illustrator for advertising agencies and magazines while Stanley took on a more mundane though secure job doing layout and lettering for the Yellow Pages telephone directory. Much later, Highsmith recalled that at first she felt isolated at school, primarily because of her Southern accent, and always found a seat for herself at the back of the room. She claimed to know nothing of segregation in the South since she had never been to school there. 'It was no surprise to me, it was indeed a pleasure, to find black children in the New York schools.' She added that 'I had romped and played in my grandmother's "alley" ever since I could walk, with the black kids of the families to whom my grandmother rented houses.'

At the end of her first day, when her mother came to collect her, she walked down the front steps of the building hand-in-hand with a black boy. Patricia formed a close friendship with the boy, at least until her grandmother Willie Mae intervened, albeit by post and from a distance of about 1,500 miles. Patricia's grandmother appeared to tolerate mixed-race 'romping' in the alley but the forming of what appeared to be an attachment was too much. Had Mary informed her mother of this, and if so, why? Mary herself was of a liberal mindset, and was not, as far as it is known, unsettled by the skin colour of her daughter's new friend, so it seems odd that she should tell Willie Mae of it, knowing it would provoke her racism. According to Highsmith, she was soon moved to a more 'respectable' private school – i.e. one that only whites could afford – on Riverside Drive, all at the behest of the long-distance matriarch Willie Mae. The story is riddled with improbabilities, not least the fact that Mary had, for much of her life, tried to distance herself from her mother, whom she felt was a bully who treated her with a disregard that bordered on contempt. Why would she take orders from her on Patricia's schooling?

I mention this story because its only source is an essay by Highsmith called 'A Try at Freedom', which is unpublished but available in the Swiss Literary Archives (SLA). References to other events in the essay suggest that it was composed at least four decades after the time it describes. There is no evidence that Highsmith attempted to get it into print, which would not have been difficult, given that magazines and newspapers would have been eager to offer their readers an intriguing insight into the early life of one of the world's most celebrated writers. She knew that at some point the archived manuscript would be read and quoted from, but that by then anyone who might dispute its authenticity – principally her parents and grandparents – would not be around to do so. The piece is extraordinarily detailed and includes a reference to the mixed-race school on West 99th Street, which, as the papers of the New York Historical Society show, never existed.

The Highsmiths moved back to Fort Worth in February 1929 and for almost a year they lived with the Coates. The reason for their return to Texas is undocumented, but we might surmise that because of the precarious and often transitory nature of their jobs, they found themselves unable to afford living in New York. Oddly, Patricia makes no mention of this in her various private notebooks. She finds space to recall completing her first school assignment, called 'How I Spent My Summer Vacation', based on a trip with her mother and stepfather to the Endless Caverns near New Market, Virginia, where she developed an interest in the lifestyle and history of Native American Indians. Later they visit her grandmother, who shows her the Fort Worth city centre (involving her first encounter with a Latino shanty town), followed by a visit to the cinema. She even writes of how she developed a crush on 'a certain little red-haired girl in a lower class than mine' (*Cahier*, 23 June 1942). It is a beguiling entry, but not once does its author refer to the question of why she seems perpetually rootless, shifting 1,500 miles from one part of the US to another.

In January 1930 the Highsmiths moved to Astoria, Queens, a suburb of New York that was becoming popular with white-collar workers who commuted to and from Manhattan, but could not afford to live there. There is a picture of Patricia standing outside what appears to be a spacious brick-built house of the kind favoured by families whose breadwinners would be only a fifteen-minute subway ride from the centre of the city. The question of whether this was the Highsmith residence remains unanswered. Similarly, we know nothing from Highsmith's recollections or elsewhere of the kind of jobs and salaries that Mary and Stanley had secured to enable them to move to this reasonably affluent district. In contrast, Patricia provides abundantly detailed records of her ongoing fascination with the psychologically 'abnormal'. One of the bestsellers in the US in 1930 was Dr Karl Menninger's *The Human Mind*. It sold 70,000 copies within three months of its publication and it proved attractive to readers who had never previously shown interest in psychology or psychiatry, because it concentrated almost exclusively on 'deviant' behaviour.

By the close of 1930, Menninger had become the equivalent of today's media don, a figure with a respectable background in the arts or sciences who offers up user-friendly, sometimes dumbed-down access to specialised research. Menninger's qualifications and record as a psychiatrist were authentic enough, but *The Human Mind* was a shameless exercise in populist hucksterism. The scientific ranking of psychoanalysis is used by him as respectable padding for the prurient attractions of case studies, involving a happily married woman who murders her children while claiming to recall nothing of the incident, a student who has an uncontrollable sexual attraction to her roommate, a wealthy businessman addicted to theft seemingly for the sake of it, and so on. Menninger's prose reminds one of Hemingway's: clipped, unadorned and designed to allow the reader direct access to gory detail.

References to the volume made much later in Highsmith's life show that the nine-year-old Patricia took a precocious interest in Menninger's tales of 'deviant' behaviour. In 1989, a year before his death, she wrote to him: 'To me [aged nine] they were real, of course, consequently more stimulating to my imagination than fairy tales or fiction would have been.' There is no record of Mary or Stanley ever mentioning the author or the book, but according to Highsmith, throughout her childhood she was intrigued by stories of deranged, murderous individuals who would later become the mainstays of her fiction.

In 1990, she wrote to her Swiss publisher, Diogenes Verlag, of another book that in the early 1930s got 'under my skin': George Bridgman's *The Human Machine: The Anatomical Structure and Mechanism of the Human Body*. It was a medical textbook used by artists as a guide to drawings of the human anatomy. Highsmith told her publisher that her parents, illustrators, kept a copy for this purpose and implies that its availability to her was in some way connected to her obsession with Menninger's volume. Menninger offered examples of how human beings destroyed each other while Bridgman provided a map of how muscles, organs and other vital features of physical existence were available for those who might wish to damage them. Did the nine-year-old Highsmith read it? Or did the mature writer cause it to become part of a mythology she had manufactured: a child – unsettled and slightly disturbed – whose childhood would in some way explain, perhaps justify, the curious nature of her later years? Was she, as an adult, rewriting her past?

Patricia was ten when Mary told her the truth, that Stanley was not her biological father. Much later in interviews (notably with Ian Hamilton in 1977 and Craig Brown in 1991) she observed that she was not particularly surprised at the disclosure. She had seen drawings in her grandparents' house signed by one Mary Plangman, recognising the handwriting as her mother's, and she had often wondered why Stanley's dark hair and complexion differed so significantly from the blonde-brown hair and light skin tone of her mother, her grandparents and herself. On the *South Bank Show* (14 November 1982) she linked this moment of truth-telling with the onset of a kind of neurosis in which she felt that sleep would lead to death. Sometimes she would simply force herself to stay awake and when exhaustion set in she began a bizarre procedure of breathing water up her nose so that if she started to doze off the retching in her throat and nasal cavities would force her back to consciousness.

According to her recollections from middle age, Highsmith started to menstruate when she was eleven. Having no knowledge of sexual biology, she feared that the bleeding was the indication of some fatal illness. Understandably she asked her mother for advice and bizarrely Mary replied with a question: "'Don't you think that a man has something to do with it?" I replied, "No – I don't know."' That was the end of the talk on the facts of life. She should be complimented on her extraordinarily accurate memory given that she wrote of this four decades after the exchange with her mother, but even more striking is the fact that she chose to share the recollection

with her long-absent stepfather Stanley in a letter she sent to him on
1 September 1970.

By the close of 1932 the relationship between Stanley and Mary
had become precarious, or so we have been led to believe. In early
summer 1933 Highsmith spent a month at a girls' camp near West
Point in New York State and, while there, made notes for what
would become her first piece of published writing.

In July 1935, *Woman's World* published a piece called 'Girl
Campers' by Patricia Highsmith, which was made up of letters
written by a girl in her early teens to her parents on her experiences
in an all-female summer camp. It was an almost verbatim version
of letters that Highsmith had sent to Mary and Stanley in 1933,
with some corrections by copyeditors on the magazine. Those
who have scrutinised it are taken by her references to the joys
of what she calls 'Diana Swimming', a term made up by the girls
and their supervisors to describe swimming, collectively, 'without
any clothes on at all'. Most treat this as evidence of her early
inclinations towards lesbianism. She seemed to exult in these
experiences. She also refers to 'Campers–Councillors Day', when
pupils and staff swapped clothes and, she implied, roles as adult
and early teenage females.

All of this is indeed intriguing, but even more so is the manner
in which she addresses her parents in these letters. There is no hint
that she will be unhappy to return to the family home once the
summer camp is over. She enjoys telling Mary and Stanley of her
experiences and the mood of her account is informally affectionate.

At the close of the *Woman's World* article she informs her parents of
how she feels about the imminent prospect of returning to Astoria.
'I'm packing tonight for going home. Oh joy, oh joy.' Was a twelve-
year-old capable of an act of calculated disingenuousness in the hope
of getting her letters into print? The question arises because her later
accounts of this same period tell a very different story of how she
felt about her life with Mary and Stanley. In 1973, she wrote to her

mother that 'I remember quarrels constantly, he was not my father, you threatened separation, packed (and sometimes unpacked) your suitcases, threatened departure and so forth' (16 March 1973). She is referring to the period shortly before she set off for her summer camp. 'The Highsmith house was a house divided if ever I saw one, on the brink of collapse,' and she goes on to describe the distress this caused her. Was this the atmosphere which prompted her to write of the 'joy' she felt at returning to it? Barely a month after her return the marriage broke down completely, at least in the sense that Mary left Stanley and returned with Patricia to the Coates's house in Fort Worth.

The discrepancies between the *Woman's World* piece and what was actually happening are significant, and it was not that Patricia censored and improved on the reality of the Highsmith household to present a respectable picture to the reading public. The letters she actually sent to her parents from the camp are all but identical to the versions that went into print. Perhaps she was pretending to herself that all was well at home, or at least that the situation might soon repair itself. If so, what followed would be even more traumatising for the naively optimistic girl.

Mary and Patricia had been in Fort Worth for only a few weeks when Stanley arrived and took his wife back to New York. Patricia spent a year with her grandparents, but during this period it was not explained to her whether the separation from her mother and stepfather was permanent or if they hoped simply to repair their marital problems. Much later she wrote to Stanley of how she felt, particularly regarding Mary's failure to tell her why she appeared to have been abandoned. 'She never said in regard to the (to me) appalling year 12–13 which I spent in Texas, "We parked you with grandma because we were broke." Or "I decided to go back to Stanley. I am so sorry because I told you we were going to be divorced, but it is not so." Either of these situations would have made the situation easier to bear' (29 August 1970). She had written to her biological father, Plangman, two weeks earlier of this 'devastating betrayal of faith to me' (8 August 1970). Plangman, who had been divorced from Mary for more than twelve years, knew nothing at all of the state of the relationship between his ex-wife and Stanley Highsmith, but by the 1960s and 1970s Patricia was prone to sending out enquiries more or less at random regarding her unusual childhood.

What we do know is that in summer 1934 Mary returned to Fort Worth, asked her daughter to pack her clothes and took her back to New York by train. Stanley and Mary had moved to an apartment in Greenwich Village, an area of nineteenth-century terraces occupied in the early twentieth century largely by destitute Italian immigrants. By the 1930s its antique aspect – some of its houses dated from the 1830s – had made it attractive to bohemians and artists and the Highsmiths, though dependent on commissions from commercial agencies of various sorts, saw themselves as part of this creative niche.

. Soon after her arrival in Greenwich Village Patricia realised that Mary and Stanley had not reconciled their differences. In her diary she wrote that 'M will never leave S, and never know real happiness' (*Cahier*, 1935; otherwise undated). Much later she wrote to Mary that 'the broken promise when I was 12 ... marked the turning point in my life' (26 March 1966).

In 1969 she expanded on this: 'Her "abandonment" of me to my grandmother, when I was aged 12, when my mother took me to Texas, with a promise that she would divorce my stepfather ... I never got over it. Thus I seek out women who will hurt me in a similar manner ...' (Letter to Alex Szogyi, 18 February 1969). This seems a rather simplistic case of self-diagnosis. If she was hurt so much by her mother's apparent act of betrayal, why would she wish to continue to repeat the experience in her adult relationships? Moreover, the exact cause of her distress seems to come from the reluctance of anyone involved, Mary in particular, to explain what was happening or what the outcome would be for Patricia. In her 1970 letter to Stanley she complains persistently that neither her mother nor her stepfather would provide a convincing explanation for their break-up and makes it clear that the worst aspect of the whole experience was that no one had told her anything, even expedient lies. Highsmith's claim to Szogyi that she caused pain to her lovers because of the trauma of her parents' marriage seems to me the form of huckster psychology promoted by Menninger and his kind. As we will see, her taste for turning relationships into sado-masochistic catastrophes was contrived.

This might go some way to account for the assembly of very curious incidents that are generally accepted as the truth regarding that year in Fort Worth. In an interview with Naim Attallah in *The Oldie* (3 September 1993), little more than a year before her death, she tells of how she met her natural father Jay B. Plangman for the first time in her grandmother's front room. Apparently he took her hand, seemingly as a symbol of their biological connection, and walked her to and from school several times. She describes it all as 'brusque and formal'. Nowhere else, in her *cahiers*, her diaries or her letters to her family – Plangman included – does she refer to this. Nor does anyone else. The Coates had not remained in contact with Plangman after the divorce and Highsmith does not tell of who arranged this introduction. Also, again much later, she beguiled guests with the story of how she obtained two Confederate swords which she displayed prominently on the walls of her private homes. She told of how she had bought them during her year of involuntary exile in Fort Worth. Both carried the trademark of a manufacturer in Massachusetts – Union territory – and if a guest questioned this apparent anomaly, Highsmith declined to comment. Did she buy them later as an adult, from another part of America? Who knows, but she continued to delight in the mystery that surrounded her account. Everywhere she lived, the instruments were hung in a crossed duelling position, until Mary's death when she separated them.

Throughout this traumatising period she was lied to or misled by omission, principally by her mother. So why should she not, in later life, revisit it with her own falsifications? A year after her mother took her back to New York, her letters to Mary and Stanley on the summer camp of 1933, infused with an idyll of a home life to which the youngster longed to return, appeared in *Woman's World*. Who knows what she felt when she read her own completely false version of the Highsmith home life of two years before. Shame? Further anger at her mother in misleading her? Her own credulity in accepting these stories? She seemed to encounter repeated clashes between truth and betrayal, and one suspects that between the ages of twelve and thirteen she had begun to treat fabrication as a standard feature of life. Long before Highsmith had written her first adult fiction, she viewed reality as something that could be routinely manipulated and distorted.

After her return to New York in late 1934, she enrolled at the Julia Richman High School on 317 East 67th Street, where she would remain until 1938. At the age of fifteen, after less than a year at school, Highsmith began recording her observations and thoughts in the first of her *cahiers*. Her earliest entry involved the trial and eventual execution in the electric chair of Bruno Richard Hauptmann, who had been found guilty of the murder of the child of aviator Charles A. Lindbergh. She collected details from the comprehensive reports of the kidnapping and later the conviction of Hauptmann in the newspapers, but she also inserted pieces of dialogue which enabled her to take part in these events. At one point she implores Hauptmann to '"Stop lying"...' (*Cahier*, 1935; no other date). By the time Highsmith wrote *Strangers on a Train*, twelve years later, Lindbergh's public image as a national hero and victim of a hideous crime had been eroded by his display of support for Nazi Germany, his antipathy towards Britain as the last of the European democracies capable of defending itself against Hitler's forces, and his suspected antisemitism. The man whose child had allegedly been murdered by a foul individual was showing himself to be undeserving of sympathy. As a result, Highsmith reincarnated Lindbergh and the kidnapper/murderer Hauptmann as a hybrid: Charles Anthony Bruno.

Richman was a single-sex girls' school. Sixty per cent of pupils were second-generation Italian, thirty per cent were Jewish and the majority of the remaining ten per cent were from Polish, Irish or German families which had arrived in the US within only a generation. 'Non-Catholics and non-Jews were not invited from fourteen onward to parties given by Catholics or Jews ... there were never enough Protestants to throw a party' ('A Try at Freedom', SLA). Highsmith felt like an outsider and the alienation she felt manifested itself in an obsession with her weight. She reports that while she usually shared seats with girls of similar size, individual chairs were reserved for the larger Germans and Jews. Evidently it was not necessary to allocate single seats to Protestants. When she entered Barnard College in 1938 she felt that this correlation between size and ethnicity had followed her from school to university.

> Here for the first time in three years I saw the brothers of the [Jewish and Italian] girls I had been going to high school with, and I couldn't face it ... everyone seemed to weigh two hundred pounds and to be covered with hair, and I knew what it was to be bumped by one of them while walking in a hall or climbing a stairway. ('A Try at Freedom')

As well as feeling slightly relieved at being self-evidently different, physically, from these 'repulsive' Judeo-Germans, she allows herself a sliver of indignation at being excluded from their clubbish grotesqueness by virtue of belonging to a WASP minority. One must assume that the hairy, overweight 'brothers' of her one-time school friends were visitors to Barnard.

'Books in Childhood' is an undated and unpublished essay, though it is evident that Highsmith wrote it in her adult years. For one thing, its first-person manner closely resembles her novels. She tells of how she became particularly fascinated by two authors, Edgar Allan Poe and Joseph Conrad. Both were misfits, the first voluntarily and the second by accidents of birth and history, and each is seen as being dissociated from their fictional universes. Poe was committed to inventing stories both grotesque and unbelievable while Conrad always seemed an uninvited visitor in the Anglophobic settings of his fiction. Highsmith tells of how she visited Poe's cottage in Fordham, fifteen miles from New York City, which had by then become a museum. She looked at the manuscripts on display and once followed the route he took, on foot, to deliver a manuscript to his publisher in Manhattan. A few miles from the Highsmith apartment were the docks of the Hudson River, through which Highsmith would wander, looking at the various flags of the merchant ships, covering virtually all the major countries of the globe, and fantasise about climbing aboard one of them, at random, simply to 'escape from school and family'. The parallels between Highsmith as a perpetual itinerant, never fully committed to a particular nation or continent, and Conrad, are clear enough, as are the similarities between her fiction and Poe's radical preoccupations with the macabre.

This story of her as part of the legacy of two great, though very different, writers is beguiling. Highsmith the novelist does indeed seem to have inherited aspects of Poe and Conrad.

One of the most unusual periods of Highsmith's early life occurred after she left Richman High School and was waiting to enrol as an undergraduate at Barnard College, the women-only branch of the prestigious Ivy League Columbia University. In February 1938 she decided to visit her grandparents in Fort Worth. There are no records, even in her intimate diaries and *cahiers*, of her reasons for doing so, only that she booked a steamer ticket from New York to Galveston and took with her two books: *Sir Roger de Coverley*, a wry, satirical portrait of an eighteenth-century country gentleman, and Adolf Hitler's *Mein Kampf*, the Nazi leader's quasi-autobiographical rant which returns again and again to the threat posed to global civilisation by the Jews. She did not explain her choice of reading but left conspicuous records of it later, probably as evidence of a seventeen-year-old's precocious eccentricity. On reaching Fort Worth she remarked in her diary that her grandparents' house was 'looking more neglected' and she seemed ill-disposed towards the other permanent guests, her cousin Dan Coates and his wife and child.

. Four days after her arrival she made arrangements to once again meet her biological father, Jay B. Plangman. How she did so, let alone her motive, remains a mystery. Apparently Plangman 'shows me pornographic pictures (to my mingled disgust and fascination, and shame for him)'. Also, 'And now to my father. There were some lingering kisses when I was seventeen in Texas, not exactly paternal. This is all I meant. I do not want to make a big thing out of it. The word incestuous is a strong one.' Both reports are treated by Highsmith's biographers as part of the same narrative, but they were written thirty-two years apart. The first appeared in her *cahier* of 1938 and the second in a letter she sent to her stepfather Stanley Highsmith on 29 August 1970. This does not mean that they were untrue, but it does invite us to look again at their contexts. In the *cahier* entry of the seventeen-year-old, the reference to her father's displaying of pornography appears in a list of largely inconsequential reports on, for example, her visit to Dallas, where she drank whiskies in a bar.

The description of the non-paternal kiss with Plangman seems to be part of a dialogue. It was 'all I meant', indicating that she had referred to it in an earlier exchange of letters, and 'the word incestuous' seems similarly to suggest that she and Stanley had already discussed a potentially disturbing encounter between herself and her natural father. The problem is that there are no other letters or copies of letters to or from Highsmith and Stanley on these matters. It is as if we have overheard one statement from an individual involved in a conversation, while remaining deaf to the rest of it. It is possible that letters to and from Highsmith and Stanley relating to this have disappeared, but at the same time one has to be aware of the fact that the only one that survives includes the most disturbing and ultimately unanswerable questions. It is also worth noting that this letter was sent to Stanley in 1970, during a period when Highsmith was bombarding him with enquiries on what really happened between him and her mother. Why would she assume that he knew anything of Plangman? They had never met and there is no evidence that she had told him anything previously of her uncomfortable encounter with Jay B. in 1938. The letter that survives in the archive is a copy of the one she allegedly sent to Stanley, and there is significant evidence to suggest that she forged it as part of her long-term rewriting of her past. The trope of a phrase misheard or a tone of voice mimicked appears again and again in Highsmith's fiction; Tom Ripley is made up of such fakeries and illusions.

Towards the end of her life she confided in Vivien De Bernardi that she first had sex with a man shortly before her departure for Texas. 'It wasn't at all pleasurable ... she was just curious. Like a medical experiment' (De Bernardi to Wilson, p. 59). Neither the moderately incestuous encounter with Plangman nor her first experience of sex with the unnamed male teenager appear in her contemporaneous *cahiers*. She does, however, give a detailed account of her feelings for four of her female contemporaries at the Julia Richman school: Helen and Elaine (both remain unidentified, with no known surnames); Mickey Goldfarb (Mickey was a popular shortening of the Jewish female name, Michaela); and Judy Tuvim. We know most about Tuvim who in her twenties became an actress and changed her conspicuously Jewish surname to Holliday. She would win an Oscar for Best Actress in 1950 for her performance as the scatter-brained Billie Dawn in *Born Yesterday*, beating Bette Davis, Anne Baxter and Gloria Swanson. Four years later she starred alongside

Jack Lemmon in his first feature film, *It Should Happen to You*, and the film's director, the legendary George Cukor, later praised her as a comic genius. Highsmith's entries for all four girls are scattered with references to 'love', 'the two of us', 'together forever', 'kisses' and 'dates'. It is clear that Judy is her favourite and on one occasion she admits that 'I tell Judy I lie always' implying that she thinks less of the others in never confessing that she lies to them.

It is clear enough that Highsmith is aware of her lesbian inclinations – 'I observe the pickings at Barnard,' she discloses a little later, referring to female students – but one remains enthralled and perplexed by her tendency to include self-disclosures in her contemporaneous private journals while quietly memorising significant incidents, all involving sex, for exposure in letters and conversations decades later. Some insight into this is offered by her first attempt at literary fiction, begun shortly before the opening of her first *cahier* in 1937. Highsmith was seventeen when she wrote 'Crime Begins', a seemingly innocuous short story about the theft of a book. It was, Highsmith later admitted, based on her experience of several of her peers attempting to 'get at' the one history book in the library that was relevant to their ongoing studies and examinations. 'It occurred to me to steal it, so I wrote a story about a girl who did. I never stole the book' (*South Bank Show*, 14 November 1982). Her emphasis on the difference between thinking about doing something bad and doing it is notable, given that it foreshadows the career of a woman whose disturbing private inclinations manifested themselves in novels where murderous behaviour is routine. What happens thereafter in the story is revealing. The girl who steals the book does so by cutting out a section of her very thick private notebook, big enough to hide the valuable work, while she removes it from the library. A single book contains information sought by everyone – essential knowledge, truth if you wish – but Highsmith has her proxy steal it by concealing it within a similar text, a notebook that surrounds it, enmeshes it and silences it for others.

As we have already seen, her notebooks, *cahiers* and diaries promise disclosures and confessions while simultaneously confusing and misleading the reader. It is evident from the SLA archive that Highsmith in her later years gave almost as much attention to embedding as many insoluble mysteries in her autobiographical legacy as in her novels. Often, she cross-references entries in her *cahiers* with references to comments in diaries or correspondences, enchanting the researcher with the offer of a solution to the enigma of Patricia Highsmith. But as we attempt to make sense of these internal back-and-forth narratives on how one event or emotion relates to another, we begin to realise that the sole purpose of her emendations is to create a fog of bewilderment.

'Crime Begins' is not necessarily an important piece of fiction in its own right, but for Highsmith it is probably her most honest and prescient.

2

BARNARD

Highsmith enrolled at Barnard College, Columbia, in September 1938; its campus was situated in central New York, adjacent to Broadway. It was the equivalent of the women's colleges of Oxford and Cambridge which were established during the late nineteenth century in response to the admission of women to the ancient universities and whose separateness reflected the refusal of the male-only colleges to allow them in.

During her four years there, Highsmith exhibited personality traits by parts eclectic and exhibitionist. Those of her contemporaries who spoke of her later gave primary attention to her physical appearance: 'She dressed up and wore very, very tailored clothes'; 'My image of Pat is wearing riding clothes and starched white shirts'; 'Pat always had an aura about her, there was something special'; 'My vision of her is with a cigarette hanging out of the corner of her mouth. And the camel hair coat, the high white collar and I think she wore an ascot. I mean she was stylish' (Schenkar, pp. 114–17). In the *cahier* started when she enrolled at Barnard, there is a striking description of a girl of around Highsmith's age dancing to the music of Tchaikovsky in an otherwise empty room. In her account of the girl Highsmith states that she becomes indistinguishable from the music, as if the sounds seemed to become part of the girl's presence. Barnard's English curriculum was commendably up to date, including poems by W. B. Yeats, and it seems almost certain that Yeats's enigmatic line from 'Among School Children', 'How can we know the dancer from the dance?', was the unacknowledged inspiration for Highsmith's passage. We have to wonder if she is acknowledging her own performance among her peers at college as, like the dance, something that obscures any clear perception of the actual Patricia Highsmith.

Her affiliation with ideals and beliefs was ambivalent. When she started at Barnard it was already clear that the Republican, democratic forces in Spain were on the brink of defeat by Franco's fascists. Highsmith abandoned her previous interest in Hinduism and committed herself to communism. In 1939, she joined the Young Communist League and in her later *cahiers* claimed that she read a considerable number of works by Marx and Engels as well as post-Marxist texts such as Stalin's *Foundations of Leninism*. Why exactly she decided to commit herself publicly to the hard-left remains a matter for speculation, but it should be noted that during this period Barnard and its undergraduates maintained a comfortably conservative stance towards US and international politics. The vast majority of undergraduates were from middle-class families and only two of Highsmith's year confessed to sympathising with the Democrats; the rest were, like their parents, Republicans, and none was associated with any kind of political radicalism, let alone communism. Again, Highsmith was making an exhibition of herself. The moody, stylish figure with the cigarette dangling from her mouth, dressed like a character in a noir movie, had now committed to a political party which promised to expose liberal democracy and capitalism as covers for mass exploitation and to undermine the government of the United States. Quite soon, though, she grew tired of this new performance. 'A meeting this evening of the League ... I feel uncomfortable with them ... I wonder if I should tell them I am degenerate and be expelled' (Diary, 1 September 1941).

The degeneracy she was referring to? In 1940 she went to a bar in Greenwich Village, along with several of her undergraduate friends, and there met Mary Sullivan, a short and stocky middle-aged lesbian, who often dressed in trousers and the kind of jackets favoured by

men. She ran a bookshop near the Astoria Hotel and according to
Highsmith's diary entry (13 June 1941) Sullivan invited her back
to her apartment for drinks and offered her the divan bed for the
night. Highsmith then took the initiative, suggesting that Sullivan's
bed was big enough for both of them: 'Mary accepted with alacrity.
Quickly. And then well, we barely slept, but what does that matter?
She is marvellous, kind, sweet, understanding.' There is no doubt
about the existence of Mary Sullivan. She features in Margaretta
Mitchell's biography of Ruth Bernhard (2000) as a rather squat,
socially active bookshop manager. But beyond that we have to take
it on trust that Highsmith had a brief affair with Sullivan and that
this was, as she later claimed, her rite of initiation as a lesbian.
Bernhard was a wealthy New York socialite and photographer and as
Highsmith's biographer Joan Schenkar states, 'perhaps it was Mary
who introduced Bernhard to Pat' (p. 230). The 'perhaps' is pertinent
because we have no conclusive evidence, aside from her diary entry,
that Highsmith knew Sullivan at all, let alone had an affair with
her. Indeed, Schenkar interviewed Bernhard six months before her
death and she stated that 'I never knew anyone that Mary Sullivan
had a relationship with,' and conceded that if she had slept with
Highsmith she had not made a 'bad choice'. But her observation was
prompted solely by Schenkar's suggestion that the two women had
an affair. Bernhard had no knowledge that Highsmith and Sullivan
had ever met.

Tracking through the interviews and statements made by
Highsmith's contemporaries, such as Bernhard, on what happened
during this period, and comparing these comments with the
entries in Highsmith's diaries and *cahiers*, there are few outright
contradictions. But at the same time, there are two completely
separate narratives that intersect only when her biographers,
notably Schenkar, cause them to do so.

There is then the mysterious presence of 'Virginia', the woman
without a surname who Andrew Wilson, Highsmith's first

biographer, regards as her first serious lover, following her brief dalliance with Sullivan. First of all, we have an account in her diaries (28 July 1941) of how Sullivan was so distraught by Highsmith's abandonment of her for Virginia that she sent regular deliveries of gardenias to her at Mary and Stanley's apartment. Highsmith recorded in her diary that she stored the flowers in the refrigerator with the label of the sender prominently displayed: 'Mike Thomas'. The 'sender' was apparently the host at the party where they had first met. He did not exist and Highsmith had not met Sullivan at a party.

Highsmith refers to Sullivan's replacement in her diary: 'I know in the way of intelligence, fidelity, dependability, and intensity, Mary is superior to Virginia. Perhaps I shall live to regret it – breaking with her' (6 July 1941). Of all the women who were at college with Highsmith at this time and who were interviewed later (five by Schenkar, three by Wilson), none refer to, or seem able to recall, an individual called Virginia or even someone who might have been her and for whom the name was invented for the sake of propriety. Bernhard has no knowledge of her and nor has Highsmith's closest friend in college, Kate Kingsley, or anyone from among the growing circle of Highsmith's friends outside Barnard. Yet she features in Highsmith's diaries as a figure both erotically real and in other respects chimerical, with behavioural and temperamental features that are erratic to say the least. For example, she comments that 'Va [her abbreviated version of Virginia] criticises me always ... was terrible to me as always on the phone,' while at other times she characterises her as consistently kind and generous. How can she be 'always' terrible and critical while being otherwise benign and tolerant? Perhaps 'Va' was indeed capricious and irresolute. Equally possible, however, is that these irregularities result from the fact that Highsmith has created a hybrid between the mysterious real woman and the fantasies of her notebooks. A further irregularity arises from the fact that 'Va' first features in Highsmith's *cahiers* in 1938 around the time she first entered Barnard and three years before she began to see Sullivan. Can we really accept that Kate Skattebol, née Kingsley, whose friendship with Highsmith endured from their first meeting at Barnard in 1938 until the author's death, never met or was never told anything of the woman with whom Highsmith was supposedly having an intense affair during the four years of her time as a student? Perhaps Kate did know of someone who Highsmith was seeing but was unaware of a very different version of her, the fictitious counterpart that appears in the *cahiers*. Barely six months after her first encounter with Virginia, Highsmith wrote that 'I miss Va., can't end it' (March, 1939). Did she mean that she was thinking of finishing their relationship? Perhaps, but the subsequent sentence suggests that by putting an 'end' to 'Va' she meant that she was thinking of disposing of her as an invention: 'Must write something good to calm and satisfy myself.'

In 1942 Highsmith met Rosalind Constable, a verifiably real woman with whom she would have her first serious relationship. At that point 'Va' disappears for ever from her *cahiers*. When 'something', or rather some*one*, 'good' entered her life she no longer needed to rely on fantasy.

Highsmith graduated from Barnard in June 1942 and for the next few years her life followed two trajectories. The first involved her search for secure employment and the second took her through a sequence of encounters that can best be described as social climbing.

The social climbing began around a year before her graduation. Through Bernhard's circle of mostly European expatriates Highsmith met Buffie Johnson who, in 1941, had returned to New York from what amounted to the Grand Tour undertaken by artistically and intellectually ambitious Americans – Hemingway and Fitzgerald included. Johnson, a painter, had lived in Paris before and during the German occupation, in the house of the acclaimed soprano Mary Garden and, like many others, attended the literary salons of Gertrude Stein and Alice B. Toklas. Through Johnson Highsmith also formed an attachment, seemingly platonic, with the journalist and writer Janet Flanner, another veteran of Paris in the twenties and thirties, who fascinated her new young friend with stories of Stein, Hemingway, Fitzgerald, Dos Passos and Pound. Once America had entered the war after the attack on Pearl Harbor, New York became more and more a replica of what Paris had been a decade before. Europe was now out of bounds and while sea battles were raging in the Pacific, the US East Coast offered a refuge for those who enjoyed the exoticism that the European fascists and Japanese imperialists seemed intent on eradicating. Through Bernhard she also formed a friendship with the photographer and painter, Rolf Tietgens. German-born, Tietgens had fled Europe shortly before the Second World War not least because, as a practising homosexual, he feared for his fate if the Nazis succeeded in their military ambitions. She and Tietgens enjoyed each other's company and the lack of tension created by the confiding of their sexualities erased the complications of mutual attraction. His photographs of her as a naked twenty-one-year-old have become art objects in their own right, irrespective of Highsmith's later eminence as a writer.

She seemed particularly attracted to those associated with the visual arts. Madeleine Bemelmans, ten years older than Highsmith and a mature student at Barnard, invited her to parties which she co-hosted with her husband Ludwig, an Austrian-born writer who was enjoying acclaim as the author and illustrator of the first *Madeline* (1939) children's book, which would eventually become a major classic of the genre. At one of these parties Highsmith was introduced to Berenice Abbott, a celebrated photographer and pioneer in the development of new apparatuses designed to improve and expand photography as an art form. Abbott shared a hallway with Elizabeth McCausland in an apartment building on Commerce Street in Greenwich Village. Their respective apartments occupied the entirety of the fourth floor and they were effectively live-in lesbian lovers. McCausland and Buffie Johnson were responsible for introducing Highsmith to figures in the New York literary and publishing establishment. In July 1941, just less than a year before she graduated, Highsmith was taken to a party in Greenwich Village attended largely by authors and commissioning editors from the New York literary set. Buffie was a close friend of Tennessee Williams, Truman Capote and Paul and Jane Bowles, though there is no evidence to suggest any of them were at the party. Buffie does remember, however, in her unpublished memoir that 'Without even saying goodnight, Patricia had left with the group of editors.' One of these people was Rosalind Constable, a decade older than Highsmith and well established as a member of the New York intelligentsia. She was strikingly good looking and despite being born in England, was regarded as quintessentially Scandinavian due to her posture, bone structure and shiny blonde hair. Her principal job was as a researcher for and occasional contributor to *Fortune* magazine. She also acted as a consultant within the literary circuit of book publishers, in which everything from individual submissions to market trends were discussed. The day after the party they went for dinner and drinks, Highsmith spent the night at Rosalind's apartment in a spare bedroom, and for the subsequent ten years Highsmith remained obsessed with her.

They never had sex, at least according to Constable, but the fact that Highsmith was obliged to deny herself a physical union with a woman who she regarded as a goddess is significant. This was a reversal of her sexual relationship with the ethereal Virginia. Previously she had imagined sex with a woman she had turned into a myth, and now she had to endure the perpetual denial of sex with an actual woman she adored. Think ahead to the plot of *Strangers on a Train*. Bruno, the disturbed predatory figure, tries to draw handsome, socially respectable Guy into a foul conspiracy. He fails, but both characters face appalling consequences. Nothing quite like this happened with Highsmith and Rosalind but there are eerie resemblances between the real-life stalker, Highsmith, and her horrid creation, Bruno.

Highsmith's ascent into the metropolitan bohemian elite was accompanied by her more humdrum trajectory through the job market. Rosalind Constable used her connections to get Highsmith interviews at *Fortune*, *Good Housekeeping*, *Mademoiselle*, *Time* and *Vogue*. For each, she failed, and Constable later informed her this might have been because 'you looked like you'd just got out of bed'. Kate Kingsley Skattebol later revealed that she was amazed her friend managed to attend lectures and seminars, given that she spent most of her free time at parties, drank for entire days and was often incapable of standing up, let alone speaking coherently. A few weeks after the disastrous interview at *Vogue* in June 1942 she met William Shawn, managing editor of *The New Yorker*, and again Constable was responsible for persuading Shawn to see her. He looked at pieces she'd contributed to the *Barnard Review* and asked her to submit some sample copy for the 'Talk of the Town' column, but she did not hear from him again.

Her mother had paid her college fees – considerable given that Columbia would soon be ranked as one of the elite Ivy League schools – and she lived without cost in the various apartments rented by Stanley and Mary. As a graduate, she aspired to the kind of independence she had encountered in her new circle of professional women, notably Constable. At the close of 1942, she was obliged to settle for a poorly paid job as editorial assistant to Ben Zion Goldberg who ran F.F.F. Publishers, the largest US agency for Jewish newspapers and journals. Goldberg was a mostly secular Zionist who went on to research and write about the fate of Jews in the Soviet Union and the post-war Soviet bloc. Highsmith's work was partly administrative, but Goldberg largely utilised her as a researcher for pieces that commissioned authors were preparing for F.F.F.'s various outlets. In her December diary of 1942 she wrote that it was 'a lousy journalistic job' and complained that 'I'm frankly bored and ashamed of it. Why wouldn't it be the scarabs of Tutankhamen? Why not the history of the Dalai Lamas? ... Why not the story of the philosopher's stone?' The angry 'Why not?' sequence is prompted by what she actually has to do, involving 'kikes'. The entries are laced with antisemitic comments, some particularly vile, and she comments that Goldberg 'would try to Jew me down to eighteen [dollars] a week'. In reality, she had been earning twenty dollars a week since her appointment and Goldberg raised it to twenty-four some time prior to this note that she expected him to 'Jew' her 'down' to eighteen. Also, she was contradicting the June 1942 diary entry describing when she was first appointed, where she states that on being offered twenty dollars, 'I didn't haggle ... being poor at haggling', unlike 'kikes'. In the December entry she writes of Goldberg 'he seems to be of some repute – somewhere', in the full knowledge that his *The Sacred Fire* (1931) on sex and organised religion was one of the most controversial books of the previous decade. But given his ethnicity she found it easy to blind herself to his considerable reputation.

Fifty years later, in 1993, Highsmith published an article called 'My First Job' in the London-based *Oldie* magazine. She described her first period of employment after Barnard as a street-corner advertiser for the Arrid Deodorant Company, involving her standing in front of Bloomingdale's and Macy's department stores questioning customers as to their opinion of Arrid's possible list of advertising phrases. 'How do you feel about Arrid is the fastest selling underarm deodorant in America and around the world?' she would ask exasperated shoppers. This was partially true in that Highsmith did earn some cash in hand as a pavement promoter for several months after she left F.F.F. in early 1943. But for *The Oldie* she erased any reference to Goldberg and F.F.F. By then she had earned herself a reputation as a pro-Palestinian whose antagonism towards Israel was a poor façade for visceral antisemitism, though she hardly bothered to disguise her loathing for Jews per se as some form of idealism regarding Israel's military and political activities.

She excised records of Goldberg from her life, while in truth she remained on good terms with him after she left F.F.F. They travelled to Mexico together in 1944 and in her diaries she tells of how Goldberg would come to her room and suggest that they might be well suited, sexually. At the time, being courted by a middle-aged Jew might, one would have thought, have been particularly repulsive to her, as an antisemitic lesbian. But she describes his visits dispassionately, because she knew that he was well connected in the New York publishing business. He would, four years later, offer her constructive advice on how to make *Strangers on a Train* a saleable novel.

In December 1943 she found a job that paid her, in terms of commissions, three times more than her salary at F.F.F. She became a scriptwriter for the Sangor-Pines Comics Shop at 10 West 45th Street. During the forties in America, comic books were seen as irredeemably low culture despite their sales outnumbering those of popular and mainstream fiction by around 30 per cent. At the end of the 1940s there were more than forty US comic-book publishers producing at least 250 titles monthly for an estimated seventy million readers. Highsmith provided the text and dialogue for *Black Terror* and *The Fighting Yank*. *The Fighting Yank* was largely a propaganda tool, offering readers an account of the heroic exploits of American servicemen in the Pacific and Europe.

Today the graphic novel is treated as a respectable cousin of the conventional word-on-page text, but opinion will remain divided as to whether the mid-century comic book was populist fantasy or something more insurgent, an artefact that brought together the immediacies of the movie with the more complex demands of narrative fiction. Gertrude Stein was a fan, and placed a standing order for a monthly delivery of up to fifty comics to her Paris salon, where she would enthral her friends with a taste of something largely unknown in Europe. Pablo Picasso regarded the fantastic stories and images of humans defying the laws of nature and gravity as comparable to surrealism.

By contrast, many of those who saw the comic book as a debased, transitory form of mass consumption were its practitioners. Stan

Lee was the most prominent. He was responsible for the characters of Captain America and Spider-Man, but he later disclosed in his autobiography that he had changed his name from Stanley Lieber because he did not wish to leave a detectable trace of himself on works that would make him enormously wealthy. His true ambition was to write the Great American Novel. Highsmith too felt slightly ashamed at having to sacrifice her true vocation, writing, to a form of disposable mass entertainment. Lee and Highsmith occasionally worked together in that they did scripts for one of the best illustrators in the industry, Vince Fago. He noticed similarities between them and arranged a blind date in Lee's apartment, which came to nothing. Significantly, he thought that they might be well matched as two people disillusioned with their line of work.

One has to wonder if her experience in comic books had some residual effect on Highsmith as a writer of mainstream fiction. Comic scriptwriters were obliged to strip their prose of stylistic conspicuousness. It had to be plain and transparent and Highsmith's novels are most effective when they allow for the particulars of events and dialogue to come directly to the reader without the messy decorations of literariness. At the same time, we should take note of her preoccupation with characters who feel that they are immune from moral and legal strictures on what may or may not be done, notably Ripley. This is mirrored in the culture of comic-book villains, which feeds the appetite of readers who enjoy the fantasy world of the impossible, often the illegal.

In the meantime, Highsmith continued her unconsummated relationship with Rosalind Constable. Whether Constable was the woman she truly loved or the figure she thought would open a door for her to mainstream literary culture remains open to question. Throughout this period, she continued to send short stories to *The New Yorker* and other major outlets and, consistently, received rejection slips or was not even replied to. The contrast between her chimerical desire for Rosalind and her actual dance of promiscuity with others is striking.

Allela Cornell was a painter of considerable talent whose work, tragically, has never received full recognition. Perhaps because there is so little of it; she committed suicide by swallowing nitric acid in 1946. She was slim, plain, with short light-brown hair and an unassuming manner. 'I love Allela, and the God within her ... she is the best' (Diary, 19 August 1943), commented Highsmith, in the hyperbole that would come to mark the beginning of her significant relationships. Cornell's boyish appearance at once excited and repulsed her, blurring any clear sense of whether she was having sex with a man or a woman. 'This morning I thought so much about Allela that I had to go to the bathroom to relieve myself of a big erection. Is this disgusting? Am I a psychopath? Yes, but why not' (Diary, 7 January 1943). In the *OED*, all cited uses of the word 'erection' in print, beginning with Sir Hugh Platt in 1594, refer to the male organ, implying in every instance that men are uniquely the proactive, dominant figures in sex. While Highsmith's note was private it can be credited as the first by a woman which goes against this.

According to her diaries, Highsmith also became involved with Allela's lover, 'Tex'. Schenkar states that Tex's surname, though missing from Highsmith's notebooks, is Eversol. It is surely not a coincidence that Wilson interviewed one Maggie Eversol, who was a close friend of Allela but certainly neither her lover nor Highsmith's. The likeliest explanation is that Highsmith knew, or knew of, Eversol but reinvented her as Tex in her diary as part of a sex triangle. Soon afterwards Patricia began an affair with a woman called 'Ann T' who, like Tex, had no surname and whose recorded existence is limited exclusively to entries in her diaries. Which brings us to the legendary Chloe. Blonde, extremely attractive and an occasional model for the Hattie Carnegie fashion and jewellery house, she was also married, a closeted lesbian and an alcoholic. They met at a party held by Angelica de Monocol and thereafter saw each other regularly at launches at Julien Levy's art gallery.

We have a detailed history of Highsmith's relationship with her via Highsmith's diaries. They regularly spent Saturday nights together in Highsmith's small apartment which her comic-book job had enabled her to rent and thus free herself from Mary and Stanley. For several weeks there was kissing and touching, but no genital contact. When they did have sex, Highsmith observed that '[T]he earth didn't move' (Diary, 29–30 October 1943). This phrase, regarding the satisfying or unsatisfying nature of a sexual act, was invented by Hemingway in *For Whom the Bell Tolls* (1940) and entered common discourse almost always as a form of self-mockery.

Chloe is a puzzling figure because she has been effectively brought to life by Highsmith's biographers who relied entirely on entries in her diaries for corroborative evidence. Rosalind knew of her, but only because Highsmith allowed Rosalind to read accounts of their relationship in her diary, and even here we have to take this on trust. Rosalind never spoke of Chloe to anyone. Again, we only know that she was fascinated by Highsmith's relationship with her from records in Highsmith's notebooks. We learn from Wilson that in November 1943 Highsmith sublet her apartment on East 56th Street, sold her wireless and record player to her parents and added the amount they paid her to the $350 she had saved for a trip to Mexico. She knew that the country had been a magnet for writers such as D. H. Lawrence, Aldous Huxley, Hart Crane and Tennessee Williams, and she wanted to experience something of its allure. It was a region that was the US backdated, where Europe seemed only recently to have left its footprint. In December she and Chloe took the train to San Antonio, Texas, and then on to Mexico City. She spent Christmas evening drinking with Teddy Stauffer, a jazz musician and club owner, and later entered in her journal that her relationship with Chloe was disintegrating. Significantly, Chloe did not accompany her on her drinking session with Stauffer.

Of all the individuals who gave accounts of Highsmith's life and activities in the early 1940s, in interviews and elsewhere, not one mentions Chloe. If she had a husband, who was he? What was his name? The records of Hattie Carnegie involve no model called Chloe, but perhaps it was a pseudonym. Just as puzzling is the party held by Angelica de Monocol at which they met. The name Angelica de Monocol – hinting at Spanish gentry – sounds like that of an expatriate Manhattan socialite but no record of her existence can be found, except in Highsmith's diary. Julien Levy certainly had an art gallery but Highsmith's account of her liaisons there with Chloe are questionable, given that there is no record of Levy ever having been in contact with the author, apart from stories in her diaries. Is it not strange that neither Chloe, nor her husband, spoke to anyone after the conclusion of her relationship with Highsmith in 1943?

Both of Highsmith's biographers, Andrew Wilson and Joan Schenkar, tell of how she set out alone for the remote town of Taxco in January. Taxco was largely unchanged, at least architecturally, since its foundation in the sixteenth century, following the discovery of silver deposits nearby. Its most notable building is the cathedral-size church of Santa Prisca, which some regard as extraordinarily beautiful and others as a display of Baroque excess. Americans greatly enjoyed the region's atmosphere of indulgence. Bars were open from early morning onwards and the local custom seemed to be to begin the day with alcohol and continue drinking until they had reached, as Highsmith put it, 'total oblivion'. She embraced this socio-cultural routine and regularly remonstrated with herself in her diary for its effects on her attempt to write a novel, one that would remain unfinished and unpublished. She rented a house called *La Casa Chiquita*, a spacious villa with a pretty red-tiled pitched roof, which might have been imported from one of the more affluent areas of southern Spain. It cost her a great deal of money and it remains unclear how she managed to support herself in this fashion on what she had saved for the trip.

She remained alone in Taxco until March, save for a recently acquired cat, but telegrammed her previous employer Ben Goldberg, indicating that she would welcome a visit from him if he would offer guidance on her novel. He replied that he would be happy to do so and arrived in mid-March, spending three weeks in Mexico, mostly in Taxco aside from a few days he and Highsmith spent together in Acapulco. They flirted – he as a rehearsal for a serious attempt to seduce her, she as an act of heterosexual self-caricature – and he expressed polite but constructive reservations about her book. In this respect, we might treat his restraint as an indication of his hope that she might submit to his advances because by any standards the novel, *The Click of the Shutting*, is irredeemably bad. The dialogue is leaden and inauthentic, but worse are the descriptive passages, in which syntax circles its subject and eventually loses contact with it. The plot, however, is revealing. It involves two young men: the privileged George Willson, and Gregory Bulick from much further down the social scale, with an alcoholic father and a life that involves the cultivation of fantasies – the most prominent being that he can become a version of George, whom he observes from a distance. Gregory follows George to his prestigious apartment block and utters to himself: 'I'll pretend that I live there.' It is clear to see the bizarre relationship between Ripley and Greenleaf was initiated here, involving degrees of empathy, envy and displaced self-loathing. Ripley is a stalker who wants to become part of Greenleaf's elevated social circle, and so it is with Gregory and George. But just as significantly the novel, which was never published, tells us a great deal about Highsmith's rather uneasy perception of herself. We can see how she would refine the George/Gregory interaction to something more specific and dynamic in *Strangers on a Train* and *The Talented Mr. Ripley*. However, while in Mexico, she allowed herself numerous digressions involving Gregory's fantasies about two of his school friends, Charles and Bernard, who seem to be in a homoerotic relationship – or so Gregory imagines – and the mysterious figure of Paul, whom he idolises and fears.

It also becomes evident that Highsmith had lost control of the relationship between invention and credibility, and to this extent her attempt at writing a novel mirrors her diary entries. According to these she received letters from Chloe saying that she wanted to visit her in February and from a lover of Chloe's, male, who asked for a report on her current mental health and drinking habits. We must take her account of the former on trust but the letter from Chloe's previously unknown lover defies credibility. Aside from the fact that he is nameless, we have to wonder how he obtained Highsmith's postal address. Perhaps Chloe supplied it, but if she did, why did he write to Chloe's separated lesbian lover rather than Chloe herself? The diary, like the unfinished novel, seems to be spun out of projections and imaginings. Gregory is the fictional proxy of Highsmith the diary writer, creator of a composite universe of what he perceived and what he invented. Notably, when Highsmith returned to America at the end of March 1944, she wrote in her diary of how she met up again with Chloe, 'my alcoholic beauty ... in Mexico City. She ... is staying on. Her hands still shake as they did in New York – and for the same thing' (20 March 1944).

In May Highsmith sent a letter to Kate Kingsley Skattebol giving an account of her meeting with Chloe in Mexico City, which is identical, verbatim, to the one which can be found in her diary. Skattebol later remarked that apart from Highsmith's references to Chloe neither she nor anyone else of her acquaintance had any knowledge of her, anecdotal or otherwise. She was distributing the story of her 'alcoholic beauty' as liberally as she could, so that the presence of Chloe would survive in her letters. The fact that none of her correspondents had ever met her is intriguing. Blending the real with the invented to the extent that no one could disentangle the two might well be a suitable programme for a radical creative writing course, patented by Patricia Highsmith.

3

BOARDING THE TRAIN

In 1946 Highsmith allowed Stanley to officially adopt her, though why she (then twenty-five) or he (then fifty-five) saw this as necessary or suitable remains a mystery. She continued to think of him as someone whose presence she must wearily accept while regarding him with contempt. Perhaps, privately, she saw it as a darkly comic overture to another case of what might happen when a parent is loathed sufficiently enough. Ten months later in 1947 she would begin the draft of her first published novel, *Strangers on a Train*, the plot of which is driven by Bruno's determination to kill his father and get away with it. Throughout the two and a half years prior to this, following her return from Mexico, she existed in a state between limbo and exhilaration. As a writer she went nowhere, but in terms of her sexual and social life, frenetic is an understatement.

On 29 September 1944, her main diary entry was on her love life over the previous five months. 'Loves by the dozen, love affairs by the dozen are all very well. But oh God, when they overlap! If one could merely be clear with one before beginning another, all would be well. It is the overlapping, the overlapping, until where one's love heart is, is so thickly padded, nothing can any longer be felt.' Clearly she is troubled, but the clogged self-contradictory phrasing makes us wonder about the nature of her dilemma. Is she contrite regarding her seemingly insatiable promiscuity, or does she simply feel irritated by her apparent inability to keep things in order ('the overlapping, the overlapping...'), rather like a distracted dealer who fumbles with the pack of cards?

Most of her lovers of that year cannot be properly connected with women whose presence is recorded elsewhere, with the notable exception of Natica Waterbury. The *New York Times* of 21 September 1937 gives a lavish account of a dinner party held at Lynnwood Lodge in Elkins Park, Pennsylvania, to honour the coming out of debutante Miss Natica Waterbury. Very few residents of Elkins Park were worth less than ten million dollars. Lynnwood Lodge (now called Lynnewood Hall) is a sprawling 110-room neo-classical residence then owned by the multimillionaire Widener family, neighbours of Waterbury's widowed mother, who was herself enormously wealthy. Natica would in the 1950s go on to earn fame as a pilot, photographer, associate of Sylvia Beach (of the legendary Shakespeare and Company) in Paris and one of the few figures of her generation who made no secret of her gay sexuality. Natica's background is worth noting because it singles her out as a near replica of Virginia Kent Catherwood, who Highsmith first met at a party roughly a month and a half after her diary entry on the 'overlaps' between affairs with Waterbury and others. Virginia's debutante ball was held four years before Natica's but only a few miles away at the Bellevue-Stratford Hotel in central Philadelphia. Allegedly, the sixty-piece orchestra alone cost close to $10,000. Earlier in the year Virginia Tucker Kent, as she was then known, was presented at Court to King George V and Queen Mary as an intercontinental deb.

It is difficult to imagine that Highsmith had not seen George Cukor's Oscar-winning *The Philadelphia Story* (1940), the most popular movie in the US in 1940–41. It was an adaptation of a Broadway play by Philip Barry, who based it on reports of the 1930s activities of immoderately wealthy families in Pennsylvania/Philadelphia, who seemed to exist in a world of their own. Their lifestyles were more like those of the degenerate Regency aristocracy, plus swimming pools, than the America of the Depression.

Highsmith, like Barry, had a taste for these other-worldly figures. Katharine Hepburn's Tracy Samantha Lord could have been modelled on Virginia and Natica. For Highsmith they were fantasies made real. Her own existence during this period was far more mundane. She continued to work in comic books, producing more paintings and drawings than attempts at literary writing, and many regard her visual art as important. After her death, Diogenes Verlag brought out a book called *Patricia Highsmith Zeichnungen* (1995) offering a small selection of her works. She had admirable talents as a draughtswoman but seemed uncertain of whether to make use of this in representational sketches and paintings or as an anchor for more avant-garde pieces, largely surrealist. One of her 1948 works brings to mind Dalí, with a woman's trunk mutated into facial expressions: the breasts are eyes, a nose extends from the navel and the waistline carries a pair of smiling lips. She later admitted that during 1944 and 1945 she had considered exchanging her literary ambitions for a career as an artist. In her *cahier* she wrote that 'Painting could never have been sufficiently complex and explicit to please me' (4 December 1947).

It is evident from her entries on painting and drawing that what eventually alienated her from these genres was the absence of a narrative. And in December 1946 she entered into her *cahier* (16 January 1946) the first whispers of a plot for *Strangers on a Train*. She was walking by the Hudson with her mother and Stanley, and we must assume that the antagonism between them had some influence on what she wrote as soon as she returned to her own apartment. She imagines a meeting between two figures, and one speculates that 'An exchange of victims would clear us both by eliminating all possible motivation.' And she goes on. 'Yes, we shall let ourselves be caught for the crime, but the police will find no motivation. We shall go free!' This is the voice of the figure who would become Bruno, who wants Guy to kill his father, in return for Bruno's murder of Guy's ghastly wife, Miriam, who is intent on complicating their divorce and preventing his marriage to Anne Faulkner.

In the completed novel, there are insinuations that Bruno is homosexual – Highsmith tells us he has no interest in sleeping with women – and his approach to Guy on the train carries homoerotic undertones, which Hitchcock picked up on and emphasised in his film adaptation. Soon, however, our suspicions that Bruno might in some way be attracted to Guy are sidelined by their mutually destructive pact as murderers. Immediately after he has killed Bruno's father, Guy's reflection encapsulates the novel as a noir murder mystery: 'love and hate ... good and evil, lived side by side in the human heart.' Less than a month after the book was published Highsmith entered the following in her *cahier*:

> I am interested in the murderer's psychology, and also in the opposing planes, drives of good and evil (construction and destruction). How by a slight defection one can be made the *other*, and all the power of a strong mind and body can be deflected to murder or destruction! It is simply fascinating! (1 July 1950)

The parallels with this passage and Guy's sense of good and evil as mutually attractive are striking. One has to wonder why she dwells on this and personalises it even after the book has been published. It is not as though she is still struggling with the moral dilemmas of writing the novel.

Highsmith continues:

> How perhaps even love by having its head persistently bruised, can become hate. For the curious thing yesterday is I felt close to murder, as I went to see the house of the woman who almost made me love her when I saw her a moment in December 1948. Murder is a kind of making love, a kind of possessing ... To arrest her suddenly, my hands upon her throat (which I should really like to kiss) as if I took a photograph, to make her in an instant cold and rigid as a statue. (1 July 1950)

This was written in 1950, but it begs comparison with the description of how Bruno killed Miriam, which she wrote almost two years earlier. The woman in her *cahier*, Kathleen Senn, was real and would become the inspiration for Highsmith's second novel. It is bizarre that Highsmith was capable of visiting upon an actual individual, if only in her imagination, the horrible fate to which she condemned her invention.

> He sunk his fingers deeper, enduring the distasteful pressure of her body under his so her writhing would not get them both up. Her throat felt hotter and fatter. Stop, stop, stop! He willed it!

Kathleen Senn shopped at the upmarket department store Bloomingdale's under her husband E. R. Senn's account, which specified a prestigious address in New Jersey. Kathleen's father was the millionaire owner of Wiggins Airways and her husband a well-paid executive who worked in New York City. Kathleen would be reborn in Highsmith's ground-breaking novel about lesbian relationships, *The Price of Salt* (1952), but Kathleen's impact on Highsmith as an individual and a writer was overwhelming long before she began to write the book.

In early 1948 Highsmith had taken a job at Bloomingdale's to supplement her income from her (largely freelance) comic-book output, and to sustain herself in her small Greenwich Village apartment. One day a woman of striking beauty and wealth entered the store and bought several items from her. Highsmith would later reinvent this moment in *The Price of Salt*. In 1950 Highsmith went out to New Jersey to look for the house of Kathleen Senn, having nurtured the desire to do so for the previous two years. She went through the Bloomingdale's files to track down this fascinating woman and in effect stalked her, as the two women never actually met again. One cannot ignore the parallels between this and Bruno's pursuit of Miriam.

For years Highsmith had been obsessed by brief and possibly life-changing encounters between people who had completely different backgrounds – those who would not usually belong in the same social circuit and whose meeting would result in something explosive – emotionally, sexually and often physically. It happened for her with Natica Waterbury, Virginia Kent Catherwood and, for a brief moment, with Kathleen Senn.

Ostensibly, *Strangers on a Train*, Highsmith's debut novel, has little in common with her second, *The Price of Salt*, which was published in 1952 under the nom de plume of Claire Morgan and was reissued in 1990 as *Carol*, under Highsmith's name. This was because the novel is a lesbian love story with a happy ending and Highsmith's agent, Margot Johnson, advised her that it would damage her career to admit to being its author. It was entirely different from the book that had made her name as a writer capable of evoking the horrific and the grotesque. What links the two books, however, is the *cahier* entry which replicates the feelings and actions of Bruno as he tracks down Miriam, but which refers specifically to Highsmith's fascination with a woman she'd met for only a few moments. In it she admits that her 'love' for Kathleen Senn could mutate into a form of hate and, even worse, to thoughts of murder – specifically strangulation. Highsmith would never physically assault any of her lovers, but her associative confession in the *cahier* regarding love and hate, making love as a kind of murder and of the 'cold rigid' body of the woman about whom she simultaneously fantasised as a sexual partner and a fatal victim, is key to understanding her as a woman and an author.

Not all lesbians of the 1940s and 1950s lived in abject fear of disclosure. In the US and Britain, sexual relations between women were regarded as falling into a grey area between affection and impossibility. Anti-homosexuality laws were targeted at men, specifically at sodomy as a form of violence; women were regarded as incapable of acts of penetration. In the US, many states passed laws in the nineteenth century which specified sexual acts that were regarded as 'against nature' and therefore illegal. These laws exclusively involved men as participants. Technically lesbianism was never a criminal offence, because the male-dominated political hierarchy and judiciary were incapable of envisioning sex between women. At the same time, monogamous relationships between women, of whatever type, were treated as a form of social and moral degradation. A publicly exposed lesbian might not, like a gay man, be subject to prosecution and imprisonment, but she might be open to prejudice and alienation. In *The Price of Salt* the relationship between Carol (Senn) and Therese (Highsmith) is plagued by the activities of a private detective, hired by Carol's husband to prove that she is a lesbian. This would not send her to prison, but it would weaken her claim to custody of their child.

Highsmith's affair with Virginia 'Ginnie' Kent Catherwood began in 1946, two years after they had first met at Rosalind Constable's party. Virginia's own family was outstandingly wealthy but she supplemented this in her marriage to Cummins Catherwood in 1935. Catherwood had inherited fifteen million dollars in 1929 and despite the Depression he maintained an income from deposits of more than one and a half million per year. The *Philadelphia Evening Bulletin* of 24 April 1935 reported that the bride wore a 'shimmering white satin' dress, with 'three widths of tulle, seven and a half yards long, the veil completely enveloped the satin train'. Less than six years later the couple were divorced and while there is no official documentation of the reason for their separation, Highsmith later told her friend Ann Clark that 'Virginia lost custody of her child after a recording made in a hotel room and exposing a lesbian affair was played in court' (Wilson, p. 132).

While the account of the trial is based on Ann Clark's testimony, a version of it features in the relationship between Therese and Carol. In her diary (11 October 1950) Highsmith wrote that 'I worry that Ginnie may feel Carol's case similar to her own' adding that 'Ann [Clark] knows another woman in the same predicament now.'

A mutual friend of Highsmith and Allela Cornell, David Diamond, informed Highsmith in September 1946 of what had happened to Allela. Following her return from an unhappy trip to Alabama with another woman, unnamed, Allela drank approximately half a pint of nitric acid. She spent two weeks in hospital in excruciating pain (nitric acid burns away the surface of the throat, lungs and stomach) and decided that she did not want to die, telling one of the doctors that she hoped to paint a portrait of him once she recovered. According to Diamond, the doctor put his face into his hands and cried, aware that the damage that she had done to herself was irreversible. She died two days later and following Diamond's report, Highsmith entered in her *cahier* (14 October 1946) that '[I am] an evil thing.' This was four years before her much more considered and lengthy reflections on the relationship between love and murder that appeared in her *cahier* of 1 July 1950. She was building towards these. In September 1947 her relationship with Ginnie began to deteriorate, as Highsmith visited her apartment unannounced and found her in bed with a photographer called Sheila (surname unknown). On 4 September she scribbled a poem in her *cahier* called 'Murder Fills My Heart Tonight' and on the 23rd of the same month she recorded that 'In the night, alone, awake after sleep, I am insane ... without discretion, judgement [or] moral code, there is nothing I would not do, murder, destruction, vile sexual practises [sic] ...' Quite soon afterwards she would channel this combination of sexual and homicidal energy into *Strangers on a Train*:

Today is a great day; I have written the Murder, the raison d'être of the novel [*Strangers on a Train*] ... something happened today, I feel I have grown older, completely adult ... completely satisfied, very happy. I don't want to marry. I have my good friends ... and girls? – I always have enough. (Diary, 22 December 1947)

Months before Highsmith discovered Ginnie in bed with Sheila, she and Ginnie were arguing vehemently and sometimes violently, in that Ginnie had attacked her with her fists. She caused her no injury and Highsmith hardly needed to defend herself, since her lover's outbursts were fuelled by bouts of drinking. Highsmith wrote that Ginnie was incapable of landing a punch because her hands were shaking so uncontrollably. Below is a description of Bruno's attack of nerve paralysis following days of drinking.

> His face was white, flat around the mouth as if someone had hit him with a board, his lips drawn horribly back from his teeth. And his hands! He wouldn't be able to hold a glass any more, or light a cigarette. He wouldn't be able to drive a car. He wouldn't even be able to go to the john by himself!

Bruno's murderous instincts were in part a determination to demonstrate his ability to exert power, despite his pitiful, self-destructive failings.

The events in Highsmith's private life between 1946 (the beginning of her relationship with Ginnie and the death of Allela) and 1950 (the publication of *Strangers on a Train*, with *The Price of Salt* in progress) made a significant impression on her as a writer. It would be simplistic to regard actual characters as models for fictional ones, but what is clear is that issues such as guilt, hatred, self-loathing and unfulfilled longing which Highsmith endlessly contemplated without resolution became the cocktail for her fictional narratives and characters – by parts dreadful, fascinating and vile.

On 9 February 1968 she wrote in her diary: 'Where is Ginnie – without whom *The Price of Salt* would never have been written ...' The question was rhetorical given that, as she knew, Ginnie had died two years earlier, aged fifty-one, from the long-term effects of alcoholism. But 'where is she' is pertinent. Highsmith had spent much of her life as a writer siphoning the emotional catastrophes she prompted, encountered and experienced. So did Ginnie survive for her as a memory or an invention?

4

YADDO AND CONSEQUENCES

In March 1948 Highsmith applied to become a member of the colony of artists and writers at Yaddo in upstate New York. She had heard of the place from Truman Capote, whom she'd met at a book launch in February. Capote was the newest literary celebrity in New York, having established his reputation with a series of short stories, notably the eerie 'Miriam' (from which Highsmith borrowed the name for Guy's wife) and the novel *Other Voices, Other Rooms* (1948). He was openly homosexual and during his conversation with Highsmith he suggested that she should spend time at Yaddo, where he had stayed while writing his novel. He explained that the colony, or refuge, provided writers with 'unconventional inclinations' the opportunity to exempt themselves from the pressures and prejudices of mainstream society.

Highsmith, on Capote's recommendation, was accepted and arrived at Yaddo on 10 May 1948. *Strangers on a Train* was in progress but directionless and unfocused. Three years earlier she had come across Margot Johnson, an influential literary agent, who to her credit had taken the time to read some of Highsmith's work and sent samples of her fiction-in-progress to the major New York publishers. All had been rejected, including the early first-draft chapters of *Strangers on a Train*. Yaddo's influence on her progress, at least in her view, can be judged in terms of her bequest to the institution of three million dollars shortly before her death, which seems generous given that she spent only two months there. During this short period she pressed her sprawling debut draft into a narrative that would horrify and entertain for decades to come.

Originally Yaddo had been a Queen Anne-style country house, built in the mid-nineteenth century – the British Georgian architectural mode endured for wealthy East Coast Americans as a badge of distinction. When it was bought by Spencer and Katrina Trask in the 1880s it was derelict, and they replaced it with a building that blended Tudor, medieval, gothic and Victorian excess. It was a grotesque melange of styles that calls to mind a vastly expanded version of the Bates residence in Hitchcock's *Psycho*.

Highsmith remembers it as a place where artists and writers variously addicted to drink, drugs and sex went to dry out, only to find that it encouraged excess. Katrina Trask, who decided that their country retreat should become a hub for artistic inspiration, told her husband that 'the future is clear to me ... At Yaddo they will find the Sacred Fire, and light their torches at its flame. Look Spencer! They are walking in the woods, wandering in the gardens, sitting under the pine-trees, creating, creating, creating!' (M.P. Waite, *Yaddo, Yesterday and Today,* p. 22). Substitute 'staggering', 'falling' and 'collapsing' for 'walking', 'wandering' and 'sitting' and one has a more accurate picture of Yaddo and its residents in the summer of 1948. Among Highsmith's contemporaries were the novelist Flannery O'Connor, the English fiction writer Marc Brandel and the black crime writer Chester Himes. Its director, Elizabeth Ames, was, according to Highsmith, 'a strange, creepy sort of woman, silent and sinister like Mrs Danvers in *Rebecca*', and while Ames perpetually spied on her guests, she did not seem to care what they got up to. She installed a dormitory-style routine of breakfast at 8.00, lunch at an equally specified time and a general expectation that guests should spend around eight hours in their rooms in the unremitting pursuit of artistic fulfilment. The result was mass rebellion, led largely by Highsmith, involving in-house drinking sessions and even more chaotic group excursions to nearby Saratoga Springs. Highsmith began this maniacal ritual of evenings out in Saratoga two days after her arrival, apparently laying down a challenge to Himes and Brandel by downing ten Martinis and Manhattans, alternately, adding a dash of gin to each. She wrote to Kate Kingsley Skattebol that she suffered a '48-hour hangover' but carried on undeterred. The newcomer Flannery O'Connor declined invitations to join these self-destructive excursions – she was a devout Roman Catholic with strong opinions on the morality of alcohol – but one night Highsmith left her a bottle of bourbon. A tremendous thunderstorm had been forecast and when the drinkers returned, they found her kneeling on the porch, pointing at a knot in the beam of the porch wood. '*What* are you doing?' asked Highsmith and O'Connor replied, '*Look*, can't you see it?! … Jesus's face.' The bottle was half empty and Highsmith later commented that 'ever since then I've not liked that woman' (Interview between Phyllis Nagy and Schenkar, 13 October 2002). Why? Perhaps because in the *cahiers* and diary entries during these years Highsmith appends her murderous fantasies, vivid descriptions of sexual desire and alcoholic abuse with variations on the phrase 'then read the Bible'. One suspects that, in her case, recourse to the good book involved a mixture of self-caricature and masochism.

The impact of Marc Brandel on the completion of *Strangers on a Train* is significant, though it should be stressed that this was unintentional on his part. Brandel's real name was Marcus Beresford. He was born in London in 1919, the son of the novelist and esteemed patron of the arts J. D. Beresford. Educated at Westminster School, one of England's major public schools, he went on to St Catherine's College, Cambridge. By the time he met Highsmith at Yaddo he had published two acclaimed novels, *Rain Before Seven* and *The Rod and the Staff*. Tall, athletically built, with light-brown hair and chiselled cheekbones, he was by anyone's standards an attractive prospect, which begs the question of why he declared his love for Highsmith, and more importantly why she, for around six months, took his proposals seriously. He asked her to marry him on four occasions and it was not as though she had misled him regarding her prevailing sexual inclinations.

In the course of their first proper conversation during an afternoon together on the banks of the lake at Yaddo she explained to him that she had, for as long as she could remember, been a lesbian and that, at twenty-seven, she had been sexually involved with an extraordinarily large number of women, and that she was having an ongoing affair. On two occasions she spent nights away from Yaddo at a hotel with a woman from New York called Jeanne. She commented later that his response to her disclosures was 'amazingly tolerant', which is commendable, but does not explain why he thought he could treat her as something she was not. They had sex before they left Yaddo and her account of this in one of her confessional letters to her stepfather more than two decades later is vividly honest, to say the least. Sex with him, she wrote, felt like 'steel wool in the face, a sensation of being raped in the wrong place – leading to a sensation of having to have a, pretty soon, a boewl [she meant 'bowel'] movement' (1 September 1970). Highsmith's notebook entries on sex with women focus exclusively on mutual clitoral stimulation, not vaginal penetration, so we must assume that in this instance she regards heterosexual/penetrative sex as something so foul as to stimulate a bowel movement.

Nonetheless, she agreed to stay with Brandel later that summer in a house he had rented in Provincetown, Cape Cod, an attractive coastal resort that had earned the reputation as a kind of Greenwich Village-on-Sea, at least for those New York bohemians wealthy enough to rent or purchase a property there. Highsmith arrived in early September to find that Brandel was taking drinks with Ann Clark, who was vacationing from New York at a nearby house. He planned to use Ann as an antidote to the abnormalities of Yaddo. She was cosmopolitan: a painter, designer and ex-*Vogue* model who would, he assumed, help create an atmosphere of civilised interaction, at least until he and Highsmith were alone. But within a day, Ann, who had previously only had heterosexual relationships, agreed to meet Highsmith for a date as soon as the two of them returned to the city. However, even before they left Provincetown, 'on a little wharf near my deck ... we were making love and I was going absolutely out of my mind. I'd never felt anything like that in my life' (Clark to Wilson, 12 April 2000). Later that month when they met at Ann's apartment: 'Considering I'd been in bed with more men than I could remember, I couldn't believe what was happening. The next morning I said, "I just lost my virginity." She couldn't believe I'd never been in bed with a woman before.' It is not surprising that in the same account to Wilson she treats Brandel with contempt. 'He was unattractive because of being a sneering and nasty drunk ... He launched into his great successes in England with his first novel ... [I took] an instant dislike to him.' The woman who had fallen in love with Highsmith within hours of meeting her regarded her new lover's suitor as vile. It therefore seems odd that Highsmith herself should continue to countenance Brandel's obsession with her. In her letter to Stanley she reported that she had sex with Brandel 'many times ... [t]wenty–thirty'. While considering this we should bear in mind the fact that while she was having affairs with Brandel and Ann (and Jeanne) she was also choreographing an equally bizarre relationship, between Guy and Bruno in *Strangers on a Train*.

Things entered a new level of strange in November 1948 when Highsmith, following the advice of her composer friend David Diamond, enrolled on a course of therapy with the New York psychoanalyst Eva Klein Lipshutz. Lipshutz, a graduate of Columbia, specialised in the analysis and correction of deviation: alcoholism, other forms of addiction and, most prominently, non-heterosexual inclinations and desires. She was well qualified and respected in her profession, which should cause us wonder if, at least in the 1940s, the boundary between expertise and quack diagnosis was secure. After Highsmith explained to her that she had spent virtually all of her adult life sexually involved with other women, Lipshutz informed her patient that like those addicted to violence, alcohol or drugs, a 'cure' was available. Lipshutz was a crude Freudian and she spelled out to Highsmith that her relationships with women involved a persistent ritual of loving and leaving them because she was recreating and compensating for her irresolutely mixed feelings of love and hatred for her mother, Mary.

Highsmith was incapable of maintaining a happy relationship with a woman, Lipshutz continued, because in truth she hated all of them, in part subconsciously in that her 'unnatural' lesbianism had forced her to sublimate her genuine desire to enter into a conventional heterosexual relationship with a man. Lipshutz's theory was a distortion of Freud's ideas on homosexuality which predated pro-gay liberalism by around a century. Freud acknowledged that homosexuals were 'different' but that their sense of undergoing an 'illness' was due to societal prejudice rather than the nature of their sexuality. He believed that therapy must enable them to come to terms with who they are rather than to treat gay sexuality as something that might be remedied through a psychoanalytical cure. Lipshutz, like many others in the largely conservative psychoanalytical establishment of mid-twentieth-century America, shamelessly refashioned Freud's theories into a model for conformity, believing it her duty to rectify all manner of deviant inclinations which might threaten the ideals of law, order, patriotism, religion and the secure family.

In her diary Highsmith left sardonic comments following her sessions with Lipshutz. The therapist at one point recommended that she should begin group therapy with four married women who were displaying latent lesbian tendencies and who had come to her for, as they saw it, treatment for feelings that aroused in them a sense of horror and dismay, comparable to homicidal inclinations towards their husbands and children. Highsmith might, Lipshutz indicated, benefit from contact with women who knew they were ill and were terrified of the potential consequences of what they'd become. In her diary she wrote, 'Perhaps I shall amuse myself by seducing a couple of them' (6 May 1949).

There is no evidence to suggest that Highsmith regarded her lesbianism as a deformity or a state from which she wished to free herself. She had sometimes had sex with men, but largely out of curiosity and certainly not because she wanted to reconcile herself to a form of normality enjoyed by others. Nowhere in her *cahiers* and diaries does she record an expression of affection for Brandel, let alone a wish to force herself into desiring him or forming some long-term relationship. She provoked and dismissed his marriage proposals rather than countenancing them as serious possibilities. Similarly, she regarded Lipshutz as farcical and incompetent.

Highsmith was manipulating both of them, not out of aversion, but perhaps because they embodied normality. Brandel was the dashing, esteemed novelist who would be a perfect husband for an aspiring author and Lipshutz would set her on the route to propriety, conformity and the lifestyle that would make her an appropriate partner for Brandel. She was not taking them seriously, but neither did she distance herself from them. By participating in their routines of normality she became the subversive intruder. She wanted to establish a tension, a dynamic between the world of conventional inclinations and morals and a life of perpetual deviancy. Using Brandel and Lipshutz as bastions of the former she could pass between them while experimenting with another spectrum of norms and deviances, levels of proper and murderous behaviour – in her draft of *Strangers on a Train*.

The novel is told in the third person, but the narrator alternates perspectives, chapter by chapter, between Guy and Bruno. As we shift between the two figures, our predisposed moral sympathies are complicated and compromised. When Bruno approaches Guy on the train with the one-for-one murder proposition, it seems clear enough that the former is deranged and evil while Guy is the decent, ambitious architect dragged into his foul embrace. But as the narrative proceeds the mutual affection between the two men becomes evident. Below is the description of Guy when he is on his way to kill Bruno's father:

> He [Guy] was like Bruno. Hadn't he sensed it time and time again, and like a coward never admitted it … why had he liked Bruno? He loved Bruno. Bruno had prepared every inch of the way for him, and everything would go well because everything always went well for Bruno.

If there is any doubt that Guy and Bruno's murderous alliance is founded on homosexual attraction, consider Bruno's account to Anne of his feelings for her fiancé. 'There is nothing I wouldn't do for [Guy]! I feel a tremendous tie with him, like a brother', and later, 'if he could strangle Anne, too, then Guy and he could really be together.' Shortly after Bruno's death Guy falls into despair: 'Where was his friend, his brother?' When the detective Gerard begins to suspect each of them of murder Bruno observes:

> Who else was like them? Who else was their equal? He longed for Guy to be with him now. He would clasp Guy's hand, and to hell with the rest of the world!

The Brandel and Lipshutz episodes were Highsmith's experiment with lying and pretending. She was deliberately creating a real-life equivalent of the relationship between Bruno and Guy. Like her two creations, Highsmith pretended to respect the behavioural and moral ordinances of the conventional world while leading a secret, more sordid life of her own. True, her masquerade involving Brandel and Lipshutz didn't include a homicide plot, but when we consider how frequently the word 'murder' appears in her notebook entries on her lesbian relationships it is evident that sexual deviancy – at least from a socially orthodox perspective – overlapped, for her, with notions of killing.

The novel was published by Harper & Brothers on 15 March 1950, having been placed with this esteemed press by Highsmith's agent Margot Johnson less than a year earlier. The $200 advance was generous enough for a writer who had brought out only a few short stories in magazines, but it disappointed Highsmith. Two days later she hosted a rather overcrowded launch party in her small apartment, attended by her college friend Kate Kingsley Skattebol, her Harper editor Joan Kahn, Margot Johnson and, surprisingly, Virginia Kent Catherwood, with whom she had hardly exchanged a word since their acrimonious break-up in 1948. Journalists from *The New Yorker*, the *New York Herald Tribune* and the *New York Times* were there, mainly because Johnson had also succeeded in securing reviews for the book in each newspaper, all of which turned out to be positive. *The New Yorker* stated that 'there is a warning on the jacket of this book that will make you think twice before you speak to a stranger on a train … unquestionably the understatement of the year … A horrifying picture of an oddly engaging young man [Bruno] … Highly recommended.' Mary and Stanley did not attend and there is no record of whether or not they were invited, nor of their response to Highsmith's new-found fame.

Margot Johnson was working hard to ensure that her celebrity status would endure beyond the impact of her debut novel. Two months before publication she sent review copies to Alfred Hitchcock and several other film-makers. Astutely, she pointed out to Hitchcock the similarities between Highsmith's novel and his recent production, *Rope* (1948), which today is regarded as a classic, but at the time received mixed reviews and was only a moderate box-office success. She hoped that Hitchcock would recognise its potential as a chilling improvement on the *Rope* prototype. Her instinct paid off.

Bidding began within days of the launch party, with MGM offering $4,000. Johnson turned them down, contacted Hitchcock and he replied with an offer that he expected would close down the auction: $6,000 for rights in perpetuity and an additional $1,500 for work, by Highsmith, on the script and screenplay. The film was made with extraordinary speed, at least by today's standards, going from the purchase of rights to completion for box-office release within eight months. In late September 1950 Hitchcock telegraphed Highsmith, asking if she would be willing to help out on set. We do not have a copy of the telegram but it is clear from circumstantial evidence that he wanted her to rewrite her book as a usable screenplay. In July he hired Raymond Chandler, for $2,500 a week, to adapt the novel and this generous amount reflected Hitchcock's view of the production as a worthwhile investment.

Chandler was the most respected crime novelist of the era and the only one with an established reputation as a script and screenplay writer for films. But Chandler was dismayed by the project, mainly because he could not see how a book so bizarre and disturbing could be made acceptable to the US Board of Censors. He saw it as advocating nihilism, moral anarchy and homosexuality, a licence for murderous compulsion, and he incorporated all of these in his screenplay, effectively issuing a challenge to the censors. A day after Hitchcock received it on 25 September he telegraphed Chandler, informing him of his dismissal. It was then that he contacted Highsmith, but she declined to take part in the adaptation. Next, Hitchcock hired Czenzi Ormonde, and she was responsible for turning the film into something very different from the novel. Guy becomes a bastion of decency, the professional tennis player who is Bruno's victim rather than his alter ego, the man who, unlike Highsmith's Guy, refuses to commit murder. The film is disturbing enough, but it is Hitchcock's candy to Highsmith's arsenic.

Shortly after she lunched with her Harper editor in June 1949 she decided to sail on the *Queen Mary* to England to see London, and later went on to continental Europe. Brandel and her mother saw her off at the docks in NewYork and while she had not informed him that their relationship was over, she had made it clear to Ann Clark that she regarded further sexual contact with him as a vile prospect and that, as an individual, she regarded him with contempt. She was playing out another story of deception in her own life.

The savings from comic-book work and her modest advance meant that she had to sail 'cattle class', sharing a cabin with three other women and eating in a cafeteria that seemed stocked with food left over by the wealthier passengers in first class. The night before she boarded the liner she had dined with Marc Brandel and agreed that she would marry him on Christmas Day, 1949. How seriously she took this should be judged in relation to the fact that she had affairs with two women in Europe, and on her return in her diary confessed to a 'completely irresponsible desire to drift about, picking up strangers, especially girls' and referred to Brandel as her 'vile memory'.

Highsmith first met Kathryn Hamill Cohen at a party hosted by Rosalind Constable in NewYork. Kathryn, an ex-Ziegfeld girl, was twenty-four, beautiful and from a moneyed family. Her husband, Dennis, founded the Cresset Press (later an imprint of Bantam Books) which would eventually publish UK editions of *Strangers on a Train*, *The Blunderer* and *The Talented Mr. Ripley*, but Kathryn had an impressive professional life of her own. Following her early years as an actress, she read medicine at Newnham College, Cambridge, and, before being employed as a hospital physician, she worked as a personal assistant to Aneurin Bevan, the British Minister of Health who was instrumental in the formation of the National Health Service. She was more than Nye Bevan's secretary; her self-evident intelligence and experience in medicine brought her to the attention of members of the egalitarian, if not quite feminist, Labour government. By the time Highsmith arrived in London, Kathryn was working as a doctor in St George's Hospital, and lived with

Dennis in an elegant Georgian house in Old Church Street, Chelsea, one of the most prestigious districts of the city. Highsmith stayed there with them after arriving by train from Southampton where the *Queen Mary* docked. The Cohens picked her up from Waterloo Station in their Rolls-Royce saloon, and thereafter Kathryn made use of her contacts in the theatre and the arts to create a daydream for Highsmith. They took lunch with Peggy Ashcroft, one of the most respected classical actresses of the era, and went by train, first class, to Stratford-upon-Avon to see another friend of Kathryn's, Diana Wynyard, play Desdemona. Afterwards the three of them went for dinner, and back in London Kathryn escorted her guest around the National Gallery and the Tate, where she introduced her to the then director, Sir John Rothenstein.

Kathryn knew from her husband that Highsmith's debut novel was in press with Harper but she was certainly not, as yet, even a noviciate literary celebrity. They had only met once before, briefly, and in this respect Kathryn's generosity as a host, which included taking days off work as a full-time clinician, is curious. What occurred soon afterwards indicates that their first encounter in New York involved something more than exchanges on mutual interests in the arts.

At the end of June Highsmith took the ferry for France and spent around ten days in Paris, visiting the openly lesbian club Le Monocle, drinking too much and attempting to fit in with the debauched culture of the Latin Quarter. On 1 July she entered in her diary that 'I want Kathryn, or Ann [Clark],' adding that she had an equal longing for a Chloe, who might well have been the mysterious, ghostly presence from her diaries of several years before. On this one occasion she is awarded a surname, 'Sprague', but this brings us no closer to the proof of her existence given that there are no external records of a person called Chloe Sprague. Ann and Kathryn were certainly real but by recruiting them into the same universe as Chloe, Highsmith felt that they too were becoming her possessions.

After Paris Highsmith took the train to Marseille, where she stayed with her mother's cartoonist friend, Jean David, who attempted (unsuccessfully) to seduce her. From Marseille she telegraphed Brandel informing him that their engagement was, on his part, a fantasy and, on hers, repulsive.

Via Venice, Bologna, Genoa and Florence she arrived in Rome in August and telegraphed Kathryn asking her to join her in Italy. She agreed to do so and arrived around two weeks later, in September. One has to assume that the two women had talked of a romantic, probably sexual liaison long before this. A professional physician does not leave her job, and her husband, to take a journey to Italy just for the sake of it. The two women spent three weeks together, first in Rome, then in the beautiful coastal village of Positano, followed by boat trips to Palermo and Capri. Highsmith's diaries indicate that following nervous prevarication for both, they became lovers within a week. After Highsmith's departure for America from Genoa, they communicated by letter only once, and spoke to no one of their affair. It happened – records show that Kathryn had abandoned her life in London for an encounter with Highsmith in Italy – but her marriage was seemingly unaffected by it.

Its impact on Highsmith is most evident when we read *The Talented Mr. Ripley*. Kathryn is to Highsmith what Dickie Greenleaf is to Ripley, a relationship involving love, envy and fantasy. Positano, the village they visited on the Amalfi coast, would become the primary setting for the novel (reimagined as the fictitious Mongibello), to which Ripley follows Greenleaf and where he eventually murders him. Once more, Highsmith's preoccupation with killing and love as intertwined resurfaces. Nothing like this happened between Highsmith and Kathryn, but the book and the real-life events are linked: Highsmith and Ripley are sexual predators, each manipulates the people in their lives and Highsmith transfers this to the relationships between her fictional creations.

In April 1950, shortly after the publication of *Strangers on a Train*, Highsmith received a letter from Kathryn regretting and ending their involvement. Two days earlier Highsmith had sent a letter to Brandel, affirming finally that their relationship was over – despite having already ended it by telegraph from Italy.

The day after she first came across Kathleen Senn in Bloomingdale's, Highsmith went through the account books of the store and found exact details of her name and address: Murray Avenue, Ridgewood, New Jersey. She took a bus out to the district before leaving for Europe and six months after her return did so again, this time recording her feelings in detail, notably describing her love for Kathleen and a desire to murder her (1 July 1950). On the day of the journey she wrote that 'Today, feeling quite odd – like a murderer in a novel I boarded the train for Ridgewood, New Jersey' (Diary, 30 June 1950). Leaving the train for the bus she asked the driver about how she might find Murray Avenue, only for the other passengers to repeat the name of the street loudly and offer directions. This terrified her, causing her to feel as if she had been discovered in some shameful and illegal act. Finding Murray Avenue, the first thing she saw was an expensive-looking aqua-blue saloon being driven down the road by a woman with blonde hair wearing sunglasses. She hoped this was Kathleen but, feeling terrified again, hid behind a tree while the car disappeared down the road. On her return to the city later that day she felt that strangers were staring at her, as if they sensed in her something guilty and suspicious.

Over the following six months she pressed ahead with and constantly revised the draft of *The Price of Salt*, a mixture of autobiography and fantasy. Highsmith was certainly Therese, a young woman working in a department store in order to launch her career as a theatre set designer. Her mother is a widow, into which we can read Highsmith's belief that her real father was all but dead, and a religious fundamentalist – Mary's affiliation with Christian

Science translates as strict Episcopalianism in the novel. Carol Aird's house was, like Kathleen Senn's, in a respectable district of New Jersey. While Highsmith knew nothing of Kathleen's marriage, she projected onto it her experience with Virginia Kent Catherwood. Carol, like Virginia, was denied access to her daughter after her husband employed a private detective to find evidence of her secret life as a lesbian. The most exhilarating part of the novel involves Carol's dealings with the private detective. She offers to pay him for the tapes that disclose her sexual relationship with Therese, even though he tells her that he has stored copies in New York. To ensure that she still has rights regarding her daughter, Rindy, she finishes her relationship with Therese. However, on her return to New York she capitulates to her husband, Harge, aware that even an accusation of lesbianism would compromise her case in court. She agrees to limited visiting rights to her daughter and accepts she will spend the remainder of her life alone.

This is the point in the draft that Highsmith had reached at the end of 1950. She had incorporated what she knew of Kathleen Senn (which was largely speculative) with thinly disguised versions of her own recent personal history. But now she faced the question of what would happen next. How would the activities and fate of the woman she did not know, but with whom she'd fallen in love, compare with what was happening to her proxy in the novel? At the end of January 1951 Highsmith once more took the train and this time found the exact house on Murray Avenue owned by the Senns. It was quasi-gothic, with turrets and miniature towers, and struck her as a shrunken version of Yaddo. In her diary she wrote 'I am delighted that my Beatrice [from Dante's incarnation of beautiful love] lives in such a house' (21 January 1951) and while she saw nothing of Kathleen, two children were playing on the terrace.

Highsmith revisited her draft and has Therese and Carol meet again, but after this they part once more. It is only after Therese's brief unhappy relationship with an English actress – clearly based on

Kathryn Cohen – that she decides to return to Carol, who greets her eagerly.

From her earliest years as a writer, Highsmith recorded in her notebooks an uncanny perception of her real life and its fictional counterpart as aspects of the same narrative. Sometimes she wrote in her diaries and *cahiers* of people who did not exist and events she'd fabricated, while never admitting she'd made things up. Just as bizarre was her tendency to use her private records as intermediaries between fact and invention; often she seemed to regard her power as a writer as something that would affect the lives of people she knew. She completed the draft of *The Price of Salt* in autumn 1950 and one has to wonder what her career as a writer might have come to had she learned of what occurred roughly three weeks later in Murray Avenue. At midday on 30 October when her children were at school and her husband at work, Kathleen closed the garage door, started the engine in her elegant aqua-blue saloon and waited in the driver's seat for the carbon dioxide from the exhaust to suffocate her. Highsmith never knew of what happened to the woman with whom she fell in love in an instant, and who became the inspiration of her second novel. She had, as we have seen, cultivated an obsession with the relationship between writing and murder and had she learned of the fate of Kathleen, she would surely have been filled with contempt for both herself and her new vocation.

Elsewhere in New York, another writer had been busily remaking fact as fiction. Following their final break-up, Marc Brandel began to learn from mutual friends that Highsmith had been treating their relationship not only as a means of revenging herself against the world of heterosexuals and societal respectability; it became evident that she had also taken particular pleasure in humiliating him as an individual. With remarkable speed he completed and published *The Choice* (1950). It is a grotesque piece of work involving Nat Mason, a cockroach exterminator, who sends poison pen letters to his clients and, if they are women, steals their underwear. Brandel cleverly implies parallels between Mason's mixture of sadism and perversion and his ex-fiancée, or at least these would become evident to those who knew Highsmith best. Her mother vomited after reading it. Brandel also peppers traces of Highsmith throughout the triangular relationship between Ned, a comic-book artist, his girlfriend Jill, who bears a close physical resemblance to Highsmith, and Ann, Jill's lover who is made up of temperamental features of Ann Clark (now Smith) and Highsmith herself. The implication is that Highsmith was capable of infecting those around her with her own essential brand of evil. We might regard Brandel's novel as unduly malicious but when we look at Highsmith's behaviour over the next few years it comes across as prescient.

5

CAROL

In October 1950 Highsmith was introduced to Arthur Koestler, an international literary celebrity. His closest friend, George Orwell, had died earlier that year. The two of them were the most prominent 'liberal' writers brave enough to show that Stalin's Soviet regime was as brutally authoritarian as the recently defeated Nazi Germany. Koestler read parts of the draft of *The Price of Salt*, praised the book, made constructive comments and soon afterwards attempted to seduce its author. She slept with him but was appalled that his apparent pleasure in having sex with her was based on sadomasochism. 'A miserable, joyless episode,' she wrote. 'There is a mood of self-torture in me – when it comes to men … And so, hostility, masochism, self-hatred, self-abasement.' She does not explain why she slept with him, but it is evident that Koestler knew she was gay and was, in a cruel and perverse manner, intent on exploring unknown territory and subjecting her to a form of abasement. Highsmith: 'Koestler, efficient as always, decides to abandon the sexual with me. He did not know homosexuality was so deeply ingrained, he said' (Diary, 14 October 1950). She implies, with 'he said', that both of them knew he was lying.

Within a month she decided to embark on her own rather perverse self-destructive antidote to what Koestler had done to her. From October onwards she began to consume vast amounts of wine and spirits on a daily basis and at the end of the month she wrote of 'taking therapeutic measures against alcoholism. Something must be done.' We should not regard this as her affirmation that she would dry out. Quite the opposite. She continued to drink, and it became evident that alcohol was more a calculated means of emboldening herself for obnoxious behaviour rather than a latent addiction.

Soon after entering this curious mantra in her diary she contacted Elizabeth Lyne, a well-known dress designer and occasional portrait artist whom she'd got to know at the several *à la mode* cultural events she now attended. Accepting Highsmith's invitation, Lyne joined her for an afternoon of drinking at Café Society, a bohemian club that targeted its conspicuously downmarket décor to New Yorkers who aspired to membership of the in-crowd – it was known as 'the wrong place for the right people'. They chatted and eventually Highsmith leaned towards her, described in graphic detail the kind of sexual acts she most enjoyed and asked if Lyne would care to take part. Lyne, amused rather than offended, replied, 'Come on Pat, snap out of it.' She meant that her companion was fully aware that she, Lyne, was a married heterosexual who had never shown the slightest inclination towards gay sexuality. The same night Highsmith recorded that Lyne's response had 'crushed me', which is curious since prior to that day she had not indicated, privately or otherwise, that she regarded Lyne as anything other than a casual acquaintance, and it was not as if she felt deprived of lovers, potential or actual. Perhaps, taking her cue from Koestler, she regarded her own sexual desires as a painful endurance that others should accommodate.

Three weeks later, after Lyne had politely declined her invitation to another soirée, this time at her apartment, Highsmith visited her agent Margot Johnson, ostensibly to discuss a likely publisher for *The Price of Salt*. In the middle of their exchange she informed Margot 'on impulse' that 'I'd seen Kay G [Margot's lover] several times, which being behind M's back, precipitated her breaking with Kay the following morning' (Diary, 8 December 1950). We cannot be certain of why Highsmith told her agent she had stolen her girlfriend; contrition seems unlikely. Margot seems to have been a tolerant individual, indicating no wish to terminate her contract with her client; or perhaps her decision to keep Highsmith was based on professional astuteness.

The day after that, at a drinks party in Margot's apartment, Highsmith propositioned a guest, another literary agent whose name is recorded in the diary as 'Sonja'. We have an account of what happened later that evening in Margot's bed, which she appears to have borrowed for sex with Sonja. 'I had almost forgotten that pleasure beyond all pleasures, the joy beyond all treasures ... the pleasure of pleasing a woman...' (Diary, December 1950). That she had 'forgotten' such a pleasure is doubtful given that at this point she was still secretly seeing Kay. Perhaps Kay, by comparison, was a disappointment. Two days later she obtained the telephone number of Sonja's long-term lesbian partner, phoned her and announced triumphantly that she was, after their extraordinary sexual encounter, 'in love with her [Sonja]'. She was still drinking heavily, but we have no reason to suspect that all of her diary entries were grotesque exaggerations or inventions.

Others later testified to her behaviour as dismaying, to say the least. Carl Hazelwood lived in Ridgewood and after being introduced to Highsmith at a party agreed to drive her to New Jersey for one of her attempts to make visual contact with Kathleen Senn, though she kept from him the true nature of her visit. Shortly before her disclosure to Margot that she had stolen her lover, Highsmith asked Hazelwood if he would like to come with her to see De Sica's *Bicycle Thieves*, a brutally realist account of poverty and desperation in post-war Rome. Neither treated the afternoon as the prelude to a sexual encounter but he remembers that the film depressed her immensely and she wrote in her diary of her horror at 'People ... having to live like dogs'. What stunned Hazelwood most was what happened after they left the cinema and went on to the plush St Regis Hotel, where Highsmith ordered an entire plate of snails, clearing it with the assistance of an expensive bottle of white wine. An insatiable appetite for things, and people, stolen from or denied to others, seemed to have become her *modus operandi*. Later in life she developed a love affair with snails as pets, careful never to harm the colony of them kept in her garden and treating those who ate them as murderers.

The antisemitism of her early years is incontrovertible, notably during her time working for Ben Zion Goldberg, but in America in the 1930s and 1940s treating Jews as different in terms of the presiding notion of WASP superiority was not at all unusual, and largely tolerated by Jews themselves as a feature of centuries-old European mores exported to the multi-ethnic New World. Jews took for granted that, like second-generation Italians, Slavs or Chinese, they were unlikely to become members of, say, the most prestigious New England golf clubs. By the late 1940s, however, the true nature of the Nazi regime's Final Solution was gradually featuring in the American news media. Despite the fact that during the war many US newspapers had played down well-recorded evidence of mass killings, especially in Eastern Europe, the Nuremberg trials of some of the most senior Nazi officers and politicians in 1945–6 along with newsreel footage of the liberated camps soon made it impossible to deny that the regime had implemented a programme which involved the systematic extermination of Jews. As a result, antisemitic prejudices as a social routine gradually became *de trop*.

During the same period Highsmith's references to her friends and lovers as Jews became more frequent. For example, in her description of the 'pleasure beyond all pleasures' obtained during her first experience with Sonja, she adds that 'she is mysterious in a Russian Jewish way, melancholic, devious by nature...' Caroline Besterman (pseudonym), her lover during the early 1960s, recalls that Highsmith became preoccupied with the fact that all of her dentists were Jews. She did not seem particularly displeased by this but at the same time she would, for no apparent reason, pepper her observations on it with words and phrases she seemed to have borrowed apparently at random from German, most obviously *bitte* and *danke*. Sometimes she would launch into passages of poorly constructed syntax and according to Besterman, 'these lapses into German, there wouldn't be an afternoon or a lunch that would pass without a German phrase being included ... She knew nothing about Germany. This enormous race, intelligent, cultured, which produced without turning a hair instantly a race of maniacs' (Schenkar, p. 278).

Her earlier *cahier* of 13 August 1951 suggests otherwise. She discusses the collective aspirations of the Germans before the Second World War, especially their desire to become a purified nation state, a master-race cleansed of the *Keime*, the 'germs', of 'unsuitable and infectious' ethnicities, especially Jews. She writes of herself as being 'German identified' and being 'gassed' by 'Jewish dentists', and of '*Little Keime* – the Element of Dental Gas in the German Nationalism and Psyche'. The experience of being gassed, and brought close to death, had obsessed her since 1949 at around the time that the methods of the Nazi extermination camps were being publicised.

GAS

My sensations under gas are really too compelling for me to ignore any longer ... a recurrent pattern with cosmic suggestions ... I feel all sensations, wisdom, achievements, potentialities, and the stupendous failure of the stupendous experiment of the Human Race. (*Cahier*, 19 December 1949)

She identified with the intellectual greatness of Germany and saw herself as being extinguished, as its representative on her father's side, by Jewish dentists, using gas. Highsmith was not a Holocaust denier. She regretted that the Nazis had not completed the Final Solution and felt that Jews had systematically used the Holocaust to advance their interests at the expense of others.

In October 1950 Highsmith showed Margot Johnson two versions of *The Price of Salt*, or to be more accurate, the same novel with two different endings. In one, Therese and Carol wearily accept that their relationship is doomed, and in the other we are shown Therese walking towards Carol, leaving us in little doubt that they will remain together, and that the married woman has accepted that she will lose access to her daughter as a consequence. Johnson faced a dilemma because at that point fictional representations of lesbianism were made up largely of short stories in 'pulp' magazines, with a few notable full-length versions such as *Pity for Women* (1937) by Helen Anderson and Gale Wilhelm's *Torchlight to Valhalla* (1938). Such works were treated as the literary equivalent of mild under-the-shelf pornography, not sufficiently explicit and too badly written to merit the attention of censors. Highsmith's manuscript would be the first to raise itself above this trashy sub-genre and it was impossible to second-guess the response of publishers, let alone the literary establishment, readers and those appointed by the state to monitor what its literate citizens read.

It would be too easy to neglect the importance of this moment in the history of Western literature, as Highsmith's agent pored over a work that dealt with homosexuality directly rather than through insinuations, and treated gays as individuals possessed of intellectual and emotional gravity rather than as sad compounds of their debauched inclinations. Its only notable predecessor was Radclyffe Hall's *The Well of Loneliness* (1928) which prompted the editor of the *Daily Express* James Douglas to write that 'I would rather give a healthy boy or girl a phial of prussic acid than this novel.' Hall is explicit in her presentation of lesbianism but there is a sense that she sees it as an affliction that should be tolerated. While the lovers in *The Price of Salt* are forced to hide themselves, they are not ashamed of who they are, and nor is their creator. Perplexed, Johnson told her client that the 'happy ending' was the best option, though she was relying on guesswork rather than informed discrimination, and it turned out that she was wrong, at least in terms of securing a major publisher. Harper & Brothers, who had brought out *Strangers on a Train*, rejected it after a first reading. Later, in 1951, it was accepted by Coward-McCann, smaller than Harper but still a respectable press, who published it in May 1952 when Highsmith was in Europe. There were several decent reviews, notably in the *New York Times* who acknowledged it as tackling a 'high voltage subject ... with sincerity and good taste'. Despite the fact that the East Coast literary establishment tolerated it while pretending that it did not exist it sold more than a million copies in paperback during the forty years of its existence under Highsmith's nom de plume, Claire Morgan. Johnson advised her that admitting to being its author would involve professional suicide. Only in 1990, when Bloomsbury reissued it as *Carol*, did the name Patricia Highsmith appear on the jacket. During the first five years of its time in print Coward-McCann received, on average, ten to fifteen letters a week asking for them to be forwarded to Miss Morgan. Most were expressions of gratitude to an author who had created a universe in which they might freely live their undercover existence.

Johnson was shrewd in advising Highsmith to adopt a pseudonym. The year before *The Price of Salt* was published Senator Joseph McCarthy, who would initiate and maintain the purge against all figures sympathetic to liberal-leftist causes, especially in the media, literature and the movies, had declared that homosexuals of both genders were 'contrary to the normal accepted standards of social behaviour' and therefore prone to communist inclinations. By the end of 1950 over 150 men suspected of being homosexual had been sacked from their posts in the State Department. In the same year that *The Price of Salt* was rejected by Harper & Brothers, its closest counterpart went into print, *Women's Barracks* (1950) by Tereska Torrès, which was based on the author's experiences as a member of the Free French Forces in London during the war. McCarthy's House Select Committee denounced it as 'promoting moral degeneracy' and several US states banned it. This served as excellent publicity and during its first five years in print the novel sold four times as many copies as Highsmith's did over the subsequent forty. The House Select Committee ignored Highsmith's book, possibly because it maintained a lower profile within the literary world and the media – but even if any of McCarthy's team had noticed it, they would have found a striking difference between the two novels.

Women's Barracks might best be described as a precursor of the kind of hardcore realism of the later 1950s, representing the lives of ordinary people with tough honesty. Torrès was a secretary to the office of Charles de Gaulle – and she tells of how becoming part of the war effort encouraged women to follow their sexual instincts with few inhibitions. Later in life Torrès refused to have it reissued in French, fearing that some might see it as a presentation of Free French fighters and workers as frivolous hedonists. By contrast, *The Price of Salt* invokes the romance-novel tradition of Austen's *Pride and Prejudice* and Brontë's *Jane Eyre*. In each, circumstance conspires against the coming together of two people whose love for each other is unconditional, except that Therese and Carol are divided by social mores and prejudices rather than temperamental incompatibility. Moreover, in their case lesbianism seems almost incidental to their exemplification of fidelity bordering on virtue. There is no hint that either of them has previously had a relationship with, or been attracted to, another woman; their involvement with men, particularly Carol's husband, is presented as an unfortunate outcome of a society that recognises only heterosexual attachments. The only notion of them as sexual radicals going against socially ordained norms is when Carol's husband employs a private investigator to follow them across America.

Elsewhere, their relationship, particularly when they are in physical contact with each other, is described in a way that was unprecedented. There are echoes of the sensuousness of D. H. Lawrence and of the descriptions of homosexual relationships by Genet and Vidal but no one had dared to offer such an unapologetic portrait of intimacy between two women:

> Then Carol slipped her arm under her neck, and all the length of their bodies touched, fitting as if something had prearranged it. Happiness was like a green vine spreading through her, stretching fine tendrils, bearing flowers through her flesh. She had a vision of a pale white, shimmering as if seen in darkness, or through water. Why did people talk of heaven, she wondered.

Throughout the novel, sex as selfish gratification is crowded out by evocations of their physical relationship as profound and almost metaphysical:

> [...] Therese smiled because the gesture was Carol, and it was Carol she loved and would always love. Oh, in a different way now, because she was a different person, and it was like meeting Carol all over again, but it was still Carol and no one else. It would be Carol in a thousand cities, in a thousand houses, in foreign lands where they would go together, in heaven and hell.

There is a striking similarity between sexuality as presented in the novel, a unique and spiritually uplifting experience between two people at the exclusion of all others, and Highsmith's records of her affairs in her notebooks. Her relationships, or obsessions, with Rosalind Constable and Virginia Kent Catherwood generated notebook entries which echo the unreserved devotion that Therese feels for Carol, hyperbolic exaltations regarding something so sublime that it almost escapes description. With Virginia, for instance, she writes of how she had given her a 'oneness', a 'timelessness', that she was 'the other half of [their] universe ... together we make a whole' (*Cahiers*, 29 April 1947; 1 September 1947). Similarly, Therese thinks of Carol: 'And she did not have to ask if this was right, no one had to tell her, because this could not have been more right or perfect.' The relationship in the novel is incorruptible, strengthened by the apparent determination of those outside it to wreck it, while Highsmith's unrestrained commitment to her lovers seems always linked to a self-destructive codicil, usually involving a fling with someone else. When the ideal of the transcendent lover faded Highsmith sought refuge in drink, self-loathing and promiscuity.

The Price of Salt was a unique enterprise. It is a fantasy novel designed not to feed the escapist appetites of its readers but rather to reinvent and purify in fiction the life of its author.

Before Hitchcock's adaptation of *Strangers on a Train* had appeared in cinemas, Highsmith decided to make use of the payment negotiated by Margot Johnson to fund another trip to Europe, this time by air. The so-called 'Star-Ribbon-Route' from New York to Paris Orly had opened in 1946 with the new transatlantic Lockheed Constitution four-engine aircraft, run by Air France, taking almost twenty-four hours to complete the journey. On average, a one-way ticket cost $600, more than $4,500 (around £3,400) by today's standards, and clearly Highsmith felt that she had become a member of the intercontinental elite.

She left New York on 5 February 1951 and spent just over a week in Paris, mostly in the company of Janet Flanner, *The New Yorker*'s France correspondent, and the publisher Natalia Danesi Murray. It is worth reflecting on the fact that when *The Price of Salt* came out as *Carol* under Highsmith's name, she commented that it had been written during a period when lesbianism involved 'hidden lives' and 'dark doorways'. This was an accurate conception of how lesbians and gays were treated by society as a whole but it was a misrepresentation of Highsmith's world in the arts.

Highsmith's hosts in Paris, Flanner and Murray, were a gay couple who lived in the same apartment. Margot Johnson recommended Highsmith to them as a guest only partly because *Strangers on a Train* had received good reviews and media promotions for the film were beginning to reach Europe; mainly she indicated that her client had become part of a select, protective network. Gay and lesbian writers within the culture of the arts, literature and publishing certainly did not alienate themselves from straight people – in the end making a good living was their primary consideration – but they certainly went out of their way to secure their own from the kind of prejudice that would inhibit their professional aspirations or cause difficulties in their private lives.

In this regard *The Price of Salt* is both truthful and biased. Neither Therese, a shopworker, nor Carol, an affluent housewife, entirely dependent on her husband, could rely on a sympathetic network of similarly inclined figures. Highsmith's feeling that she was part of yet separate from the dilemmas faced by Therese and Carol is what lay behind this otherwise gnomic comment in her diary: 'I worry that Ginnie [Virginia Kent Catherwood] may feel Carol's case too similar to her own' (Diary, 11 October 1950). She was not concerned that Virginia, if she read the book, would feel distraught at being cast as a lesbian – she did not deny this. This cause of Highsmith's 'worry' was that Carol's situation would further remind her that both of them were outsiders without allies. Virginia, like her fictional proxy, had been spied on by a private detective employed by her husband and faced the prospect of losing her social standing and, worse, her child as a consequence. In the novel Carol at least finds true love in Therese as a compensation for suffering at the hands of a ruthlessly homophobic society, but in the world outside it Virginia is an outcast, without a permanent partner and excluded, by circumstances rather than prejudice, from the circles in which lesbians and gays protected each other's interests. Just as she was completing the novel Highsmith wrote in her diary that 'I know her so little, my conception of her is absolute, unchangeable' (28 July 1951). On the surface this reads as nonsensical and self-contradictory: how can one's 'conception' of someone be 'absolute' and 'unchangeable' when one knows them 'so little'? She meant that the version of Virginia she had borrowed for the novel was so different from the original that it had become her property. And she felt guilty that the real woman, to whom she had declared her surpassing love, had been left behind, helpless, by the one she had invented. Therese is Highsmith, and at the close of the novel she walks towards Carol, who welcomes her, and we leave the narrative convinced that whatever difficulties the couple will face in the future their commitment to each other will sustain them.

6

ELLEN

After eight days in Paris Highsmith flew to London, again an expensive method of travel, indicative of Highsmith's sense of being close to celebrity status. This time the Cohens did not collect her in their Rolls-Royce, and Highsmith took a taxi to their Chelsea house where she stayed for almost six weeks. Dennis was aware of his wife's affair with Highsmith and maintained the cool indifference of the liberal aristocrat. Throughout the visit Kathryn seemed distressed, had lost a good deal of weight, and Dennis treated Highsmith with no more than cold courtesy. She showed Kathryn a typescript of *The Price of Salt*, indicating that it might reignite something of what they had experienced, but Kathryn refused to read it.

In Chelsea Highsmith caught chickenpox, which might have encouraged the Cohens to be more charitable regarding the length of their guest's stay, but just as importantly she began two closely related pieces of fiction while she was bedridden. One involves a young man who allows his wife to become the mistress of his friend, and the other a man who watches from a distance as his wife, 'the dearest thing we possess, goes a-whoring'. Highsmith suggested to Kathryn that they might restart their affair, this time with something close to permanence. She wanted Kathryn to come with her to Europe for good and not as an excursion from her marriage. Kathryn told her that the prospect struck her as repulsive and Highsmith departed from the Cohens, for the last time, on 14 April. We will never know of her true feelings for Kathryn but the parallels between the fantasy of Therese/Highsmith in *The Price of Salt* and Highsmith's attempt to make them real in her potential relationship with Kathryn are self-evident.

She followed the exact course of her time in Europe with Kathryn for the next six months, with eerie precision. She spent a week in Paris, and then in Marseille, replicating the episode in which she had been alone but had telegraphed Kathryn asking if she would join her later. She timed her subsequent journeys meticulously as replicas of her travels with Kathryn two years before. Not only did she stay in each of the northern Italian cities for exactly the same number of days, consulting her diaries as a guide, she did her best to book tickets for the same departure times of trains. Arriving in Naples she spent a day at her hotel before taking a taxi to the railway station just as she had in 1949 when Kathryn had arrived there from London by train. She spent four further days in the city, as had the two women who were cautiously making use of its cafés and historical buildings to test their sense of each other. This time she visited the same sights alone. A friend of Kathryn's had driven them to Positano on the Amalfi coast but now Highsmith improvised by using antiquated local railways, the prolonged and rather chaotic journey obliging her to spend only one night in Positano before returning to Naples. She was determined not to disrupt her repeat of the schedule at this stage, because from Naples she and Kathryn had taken a boat to Palermo and there became lovers. When she returned to Naples this time Highsmith made a point of wearing the pink and blue scarf that Kathryn had bought for her in Capri.

Did she love Kathryn? Given that their sexual relationship had lasted little more than a week, in Italy, one has to question whether she meant any more to Highsmith than the many other women with whom she'd had brief encounters. Yet the closer we look at her pre-middle-age affairs the more evident it is that love, for her, had as much to do with fantasised social ambition as emotional commitment. She only truly desired women who came from the kind of social, cultural and intellectual ranking to which she aspired.

More significantly she seemed particularly attracted to women who had been born into privilege, rather than those who had reached beyond their lowly origins and earned themselves esteem.

Highsmith wanted to draw Kathryn into the closed circle of lesbianism not only because she hoped to free her from the confinement of heterosexuality. Her desire was also to recruit a figure from above her in the social hierarchy so that sex would perform the levelling function we usually associate with socialism.

After Capri she said goodbye to the ghost of Kathryn and continued with a European Grand Tour of her own, visiting Venice, where she was invited to cocktails on several occasions by Peggy Guggenheim, one of the wealthiest patrons of the arts in Europe and America. Guggenheim owned a palatial apartment in the city and was busy establishing her collection of paintings and sculptures that would eventually rival St Mark's Basilica as a magnet for tourists. Aside from her interest in the visual arts she had assembled a rolling salon of literary writers, ballet dancers, opera singers and architects that outranked anything in the economically depressed environment of post-war Europe. It invites comparison with Gertrude Stein's assemblies in Paris of the 1920s, except that Guggenheim made her guests feel more like aristocrats than bohemians. At one of Guggenheim's gatherings Highsmith conversed at length with W. Somerset Maugham, who seemed more interested in cocktails than the arts, instructing her in detail on how to assemble the finest gin-based drinks.

We know of this only from Highsmith's notebooks. Schenkar speculates that Buffie Johnson, the New York-based socialite, might have been responsible for introducing Guggenheim and Highsmith to each other, a presumption based only on the fact that Buffie had met Highsmith briefly in New York and had once exhibited her own work at one of Guggenheim's galleries. Tenuous seems a barely adequate description of the link. According to Highsmith's diaries and *cahiers* she received two further invitations to events at the Guggenheim residence and she implies that the two women became sufficiently friendly for them to meet for cocktails at the legendary Harry's Bar in the city. Truman Capote, Charlie Chaplin, Orson Welles, Ernest Hemingway, James Stewart and indeed Peggy Guggenheim are advertised by the bar as customers who made a point of drinking there when in the city, but there are no records of Patricia Highsmith as one of its clients, except in her own notebooks.

Whatever did happen in Venice, Highsmith left the city in the middle of June for Lombardy and then Florence. In July she took the train for Munich, booking into the Pension Olive on Ohmstrasse. Why exactly she chose the capital of Bavaria as her destination remains an unanswered question. Since the 1930s it was known throughout the world as the birthplace and nerve centre of Nazism and by the time Highsmith arrived it was not a particularly charming location. Much of the once magnificent old city had been seriously ruined by British and US carpet bombing in the final year of the war, though compared with Berlin, Hamburg, Cologne and notoriously Dresden it had got off relatively lightly, and many of its ancient buildings were being restored rather than bulldozed and replaced with unattractive concrete structures.

Much of Ohmstrasse had survived but the rest of the city would have seemed to her like a gigantic building site. London, which she'd visited twice, was undergoing very gradual rebuilding, with many bombed buildings left largely untouched since the Blitz, but in Munich there seemed to be a manic collective desire to return the place to its former glory. Also, given its recent history, it had become one of the centres for the Anglo-American programme of denazification, principally the investigation and exposure of supporters of the regime who had retained positions of power in the civic and legal infrastructure. By the time Highsmith arrived the Americans and British were shifting their attention to enemies in the East, and the onset of the Cold War had distracted them from the aftermath of the one against Hitler. If individual West Germans were seen as useful members of the frontline state in the new conflict, their previous affiliations were often overlooked. The grand city was energetically returning to its past, architecturally, and, less agreeably, politically.

She did not know anyone in the region and it was by pure accident that she ran into 'Jo' (surname undisclosed), a near-contemporary from Barnard, with whom she began an affair almost immediately, and soon after that a ménage à trois with Jo's lover, Tessa. Highsmith was also taking driving lessons and had enrolled as a pupil with a typing agency. She hoped to support herself in the city by doing part-time work for occupying American forces as a driver and typist, and being able to type her own work would, she assumed, quicken the drawn-out procedure of scrutiny by her agent and editors. In both endeavours, she failed her examinations regularly, though she managed to scrape together enough money to purchase a battered pre-war BMW saloon which she drove without a licence.

While in Munich she heard from her agent that *The Price of Salt* had been rejected by Harper and, shortly afterwards, accepted by Coward-McCann with an advance of $500, which was reasonably generous given that they thought that this was the debut novel of the unheard-of 'Claire Morgan'. Highsmith would spend the remainder of her time in the city revising the draft for publication. Soon after that she learned that *Strangers on a Train* had not won the prestigious Edgar Allan Poe Prize, for which it had been shortlisted. The winner, *Nightmare in Manhattan* by Thomas Walsh, is a noir-ish story of the kidnap of a child and it survives only as a curiosity-reprint for connoisseurs of the genre. The fact that Hitchcock's film adaptation of Highsmith's book appeared in cinemas so soon after the announcement of the prize ensured that her standing as runner-up became largely irrelevant. The reviews of Hitchcock's production were loaded with insinuations as to the weird, slightly erotic relationship between Bruno and Guy and readers descended on bookshops in their droves to see if the novel might tell them a little more about this exercise in murderous sensuality. Sales rocketed.

In Munich, Highsmith was taking afternoon drinks with Jo one day in an outdoor café-bar. It was August, still a warm summer, and across the bar she noticed that 'a woman was staring at me … I stared because she was the only attractive woman I'd seen in days, and the staring is inevitable in this town' (Diary, 29 August 1951).

Ellen Hill had acquired her surname in 1941 by marrying a kind British gentleman in California and shortly afterwards arranging an amicable divorce. As Ellen Blumenthal, a first-generation German-Jewish immigrant, she feared for her status and the marriage of convenience enabled her to acquire a British passport. At Stanford University, when the US entered the war, she taught 'Area Studies' – a euphemism for an aggregate of courses on European politics and more significantly languages, designed mainly as an apprenticeship for graduate entrants to the Office of Strategic Services (OSS, the forerunner to the CIA) and army intelligence. Soon after the war ended, she was employed by the University of Zurich, looking after students who sought to improve their competence in French and English; her own fluency as a speaker of German was extraordinary in that few, if any, would not regard her as a native of Germany or Austria. When Highsmith met her, she held a senior post in the International Refugee Organisation (IRO), ostensibly charged with dealing with the masses of people, mostly from Eastern Europe, who had lost their homes and were continually crossing borders in an attempt to secure something like stability in a continent that seemed intent on dividing itself into two mutually hostile camps. The IRO was nominally a charity overseen by the United Nations, but 40 per cent of its funding came from America and it functioned as a weather eye for several Western intelligence agencies.

Ellen's earlier and ongoing association with the world of subterfuge was not something that Highsmith learned of for several weeks but it increased her allure intensely. Unlike Virginia Catherwood and Kathryn Cohen, she did not come from money and the gentry, but she outclassed her predecessors as a woman who was able to distance herself from the mundane and the ordinary. Highsmith wrote that Ellen 'blotted out anyone who's been between Ginnie and her' (Diary, 12 September 1951). As yet she had not quite become a figure who would cause Highsmith the kind of masochistic delight that predominated in her affairs – but this was only three weeks after they met.

At their first meeting Jo left the two of them alone and they made small talk. Highsmith remembers being asked if she preferred Baroque to Rococo castles, which she took as Ellen caricaturing people who overvalue their aesthetic discrimination and have little talent for conversation. Rococo and Baroque are variations on the same architectural technique, but the former is thought, by some, to reflect a taste for exuberance, even excess. Ellen wanted to see if Highsmith could decode the question as a prompt to treat art as an index to personal idiosyncrasies rather than a storehouse for erudition. Highsmith failed to pick up Ellen's clue and this moment of mutual misapprehension would continue for the duration of their relationship: four years, Highsmith's longest. Kate Kingsley Skattebol, who met Ellen only twice, later claimed that she 'was like a governess ... they had a love–hate relationship' (Wilson's interview with Skattebol, 1999). All accounts of the affair present Ellen, variously, as an intellectual snob, a bully, and selfishly intolerant of Highsmith's personal traits and habits, and all come from friends and associates of Highsmith. It is difficult to be impartial on what happened between them because Ellen left no record of their relationship, but a combination of circumstantial detail and supposition causes us to question the consensus that Ellen was the primary cause for its demise.

Their first proper date was at Lake Tegernsee, a little outside the city, where Highsmith learned that Ellen was just over ten years older than her, forty-one, despite looking like a 'small, quite chic, good-looking' woman in her early to mid-thirties. Thereafter her notebook entries echo the hyperbole of her earlier obsessive commitments: 'Oh the benevolence! Oh the beautiful world! Oh the generosity of the heart as I go walking down the street ...' (*Cahier*, 9 August 1951). 'Darling, come to me in a silver dress with dragonflies' wings, come to me on a column of smoke ... Come into my room through a keyhole and through the crack of the door and the floor ... I turn like an idiot in quest of you' (Diary, 1 November 1951). A month later she writes 'She [Ellen] loves to dominate me, I feel ... by ordering my life to give me a sense of helplessness and dependence on her,' commenting that Ellen remonstrated against her tendency to drink too much and as a consequence leave her apartment in a state of chaos with the bed unmade, empty bottles left standing on tables, glasses, pots and plates unwashed in the sink.

Most of Highsmith's friends recall that Ellen lived in an orderly manner, and the term 'governess' is used not only by Skattebol, along with 'school mistressy', as we will find from Huber and Lewis, below. But again, this notion of Ellen as the buttoned-up academic and civil servant who could not deal with the emancipated lifestyle of the artist simplifies a more complex clash between personalities. In an undated *cahier* from close to the period when they first met, Ellen told her that 'I hate the common man', which from her Jewish background and her experience of Europe after the war could be taken as a condemnation of populism as the fuel for fascism and other forms of political extremism. In a 1981 interview Highsmith spoke of a 'sociologist friend', Ellen, whose 'opinion is that most people are quite ordinary, that universal education hasn't brought the happiness and beauty that people had hoped' (*The Armchair Detective*, vol. 14, no. 4, 1981).

Ellen felt that the liberal democratic ideal of universal education as a route to collective justice and social equality was a worthy ideal doomed to failure, evidenced in what had occurred in the civilised nations of Europe in the middle of the twentieth century. In her diary of 4 September 1951 Highsmith writes an entry that is by equal degrees gnomic and revealing: 'Ellen and I argue and misunderstand each other in all our conversation,' because she, Ellen, 'was Europe as it is supposed to be, and so few individuals find.' Ellen had lost family members in the Holocaust and was perfectly able to appreciate the bizarre contrast between an aspiration towards high culture and intellectual esteem in Europe and the almost simultaneous cultivation of unsurpassed evil. Many of Highsmith's characters after *The Price of Salt* exhibit a taste for foul behaviour, murder included, while seeming to respect and adhere to the general mantra that intellectual and aesthetic discrimination are correctives to malevolence. Ellen's frightful, despairing sense of something having gone wrong with civilisation played a part in her lover's creation of figures who readers might recognise as versions of themselves and be at once horrified by what their mirror images are capable of doing.

Highsmith eventually came to treat her relationship with Ellen as a form of penance for her various failures and shortcomings. Even after their affair was over – and it ended painfully – she remained in contact with her as if observing some kind of penitential rite. Both knew that they would never again be lovers and the antipathy that had drawn them apart endured and increased. As we shall see, the casual antisemitism she displayed in her early life mutated in late middle age into something more pronounced and visceral. She even preferred to refer to herself as 'Jew-hater' rather than an antisemite, making sure that loathing should not be mistaken for mere prejudice. We have to take seriously the possibility that Ellen's ethnicity played a part in this.

In mid-September they set off on what had become Highsmith's ritual odyssey with new lovers, in Ellen's car, an Opel Kapitän, with Ellen driving (Highsmith had still not passed her test). The episode is striking as a weird replica of the *Thelma and Louise*-style excursion undertaken by Therese and Carol in *The Price of Salt*. No one was chasing them but they seemed intent on pursuing a journey that was untraceable, and that, for as long as they wished, distanced them from their lives and work. They crossed the border into Alsace, went south through the Rhône-Alpes and Provence and turned east into northern Italy, visiting places Highsmith had been to before, remembered from her time with Kathryn, and then to Venice. In her diary Highsmith records having cocktails with Peggy Guggenheim at Harry's Bar, recording that Peggy's son, Sinbad, looked 'sickish' and complaining that Peggy 'barely took in the fact' that the film version of *Strangers on a Train* had received eye-catching reviews in the US.

Once more we must rely on Highsmith's notebook for the authenticity of this and indeed that the individuals mentioned took cocktails together at all. There are no accounts of it from any of the others, in print or interviews. Highsmith also reports that following two days in 'darkish rooms' they took a beautifully lit suite in the Gritti Palace, a sixteenth-century mansion favoured by, amongst others, Hemingway and Somerset Maugham, and one of the most expensive hotels on the Grand Canal. Margot Johnson had recently sold the rights of *Strangers on a Train* to a Swedish publisher for $200, a welcome but not outstanding addition to Highsmith's precarious earnings as a freelance author, much of which would be squandered on the extortionate rates of the Gritti Palace and on her insistence that they dined in the most exclusive restaurants in the city. An indication that the idyll was less than perfect comes from the contrast between two diary entries. On 14 September she writes that 'I feel like a coolie the gods have suddenly snatched up and made a prince, with ring, a halo, and immortality.' Two days later: 'I must watch Ellen from moment to moment to judge her temper. She is *not* easy to get on with.' A week after that she booked them into an equally exclusive place ('swankiest hotel' in her words) on Lake Como: 'I care nothing about money these days, not that I have any … it is the unknown side of me that Ellen finds attractive: impracticality, generosity, imagination, the poet, the dreamer, the child. And I am too inclined to act a part in all of it' (Diary, 20 September 1951).

Highsmith's friends agree that the fantastic nature of the first month of their relationship would soon descend into something more erratic, sometimes horrible. Peter Huber, Highsmith's friend in later life who knew Ellen only from very brief exchanges said that she 'was one of the most unpleasant women I have ever met' (Wilson, p.177), which is a curious estimation given that he only ever 'met' the full Ellen by proxy, from Highsmith's stories of her thirty years after the affair.

Peggy Lewis encountered the two of them at the close of their affair in 1953 and her judgement that Ellen's being 'quite brilliant, very intelligent, but a little snobbish' (Wilson, p.177) was the cause of the break-up should be treated with caution given that she observed them together for only two weeks but heard biased descriptions of the relationship from Highsmith regularly during the subsequent twenty years. They returned to Munich via Switzerland, staying for several days in Zurich, again in an opulent city-centre hotel, and once they were back in Germany Ellen insisted that they spend most of their time at her apartment on Karl Theodorstrasse, not much bigger than Highsmith's but a reflection of its occupant's commitment to hygiene, order and cleanliness. Apparently, 'Ellen ... can be damned unpleasant, especially her voice ... "The minute something goes wrong, you take to the bottle," Ellen accuses me unjustly' (Diary, 22 October 1951). Later in the same entry: 'I've never been so in love with anyone, not even, I think, Ginnie, (At last!).' And she records what Ellen had, allegedly, told her: '"You're the best lover I've ever seen – heard of – read about ... I absolutely adore you. You're exactly what I want."'

In Highsmith's diaries and *cahiers* her feelings towards Ellen often shift abruptly between devotion and loathing. We will never know if the cause of this was her own inability to decide on the kind of woman who would make her happy, or more straightforwardly their temperamental incompatibility. The following passage at once encompasses this sense of uncertainty, without explaining it:

> A strange sensation ran through her at the touch of her fingers. A start of pleasure, of hatred, of a kind of hopeless tenderness that [she] crushed as soon as her mind recognised it. She had a sudden desire to embrace her hand at this last minute, then to fling her away…

These are Highsmith's words, and they could indeed be an extract from a *cahier* during the 1951–2 period – except that I have changed the gender of the principal character from male to female. The person who feels, almost simultaneously, 'hatred' and 'hopeless tenderness' is Walter Stackhouse, mild-mannered lawyer, and the woman towards whom he targets his blend of loathing and affection is his wife, Clara. They are the two central characters in the novel *The Blunderer*, Highsmith's third, which she began to write during the first year of her relationship with Ellen.

In early February 1952, the couple set off again on a rather manic journey through some of the most enchanting regions of Central Europe and the Mediterranean. They went first to Paris, a hurried trip making brief visits to acquaintances such as Janet Flanner and her partner Natalia Danesi Murray, who were appalled by the way in which Highsmith introduced Ellen to them and then seemed to treat her as a regrettable appendage. Then south to Nice, Cannes, Le Perthus, various small resorts on the south-western French coast and then across the border to Barcelona, from where they took the ferry to Mallorca – though despite the improving climate there was no sense of this trip being a relaxed holiday.

The itinerary was anarchic with nothing resembling a schedule of destinations, even less so a plan for how long they might stay at each of them. Once again Ellen was the driver but Highsmith navigated and planned – or to be more accurate, resolutely failed to do either. Kerouac's *On the Road* (1957) is customarily regarded as the archetypal blend of travel book and novel, a chaotic narrative of going everywhere and nowhere across America at great speed and with no particular purpose. Highsmith did it first, and her nomadic reluctance to stay anywhere for long underpinned what would become the novels that grew out of her time with Ellen, *The Blunderer* and *The Talented Mr. Ripley*. Anyone with a hint of sense would have been reluctant to leave the places they visited irrespective of the attractions of their next destination. This was Paris and the Mediterranean at their most enticing. The war had closed down the main resorts to celebrity writers and film stars who had flocked to them in the 1920s and 1930s and the adventurous middle classes of northern Europe were not yet wealthy enough to become their seasonal colonists. The small towns and chic cities retained an antique charm without being crowded, but Highsmith insisted that they race through each without allowing either woman to properly enjoy the experience. *The Blunderer* and *The Talented Mr. Ripley* do not refer directly to the journeys undertaken by the two women, largely at Highsmith's behest, but in each the narrative is driven by a figure with a maniacal energy to keep going while not being clear about their destination or the consequences of their actions.

After spending only a week in Mallorca they sped back through southern France to Italy, to the towns that had become Highsmith's emotional talismans. Venice was visited once more, this time with hysterical brevity, as if Highsmith wished to pay allegiance to the city without unnecessary encounters with other people. During early March, when they had driven from Paris to Nice, Highsmith wrote a short piece of unfinished fiction called 'Hell on Wheels' which lives up to the promise of its title: it tells the story of two people on the road to oblivion, unable to understand the reason for their shared destiny. At a more mundane level the two women quarrelled persistently on everything, from Highsmith's drinking through their tastes for food – Highsmith found local fare in France and Spain repulsive – to Ellen's dog which accompanied them and which Highsmith sometimes plotted to kill. Similarly Stackhouse, in *The Blunderer*, entertains murderous thoughts about his wife Clara's dog.

In Florence, in June 1952, Highsmith writes of a dream in which Kathryn Cohen features. She, Highsmith, sets the naked Kathryn alight but, horrified, her victim emerges from the flames apparently well, apart from slightly singed patches of skin. At the close of the entry Highsmith seems to recognise Kathryn as a version of herself: 'I had two identities: the victim and the murderer' (*Cahier*, 18 June 1952). Kathryn, we should remember, was Ellen's elegant predecessor.

Again, their stay in Florence was brief but their next location seemed to suggest for Highsmith, if not a sense of completion, then an offer of sangfroid. Positano had marked the turning point in Highsmith's brief relationship with Kathryn. Shortly after they left the town they had become lovers and it seems as though she was now experimenting in some manner with the relationship between the past and the present. She recalled it as an idyll, consecrating it on her subsequent solo journey, so perhaps she felt that it might magically rescue her sometimes precarious affair with Ellen. At just over ten days it was by far the longest stay of her trip and the town has since become a legend in the geography of literary history as the model for Mongibello, in which much of *The Talented Mr. Ripley* (1955) takes place. It was not until 1989 that Highsmith wrote in *Granta* of how her stay in the town with Ellen provided the inspiration for Tom Ripley.

According to her recollection she rose early, at around six in the morning, walked to the balcony of their hotel room and 'noticed a solitary young man in shorts and sandals with a towel flung over his shoulder, making his way along the beach ... There was an air of pensiveness about him, maybe unease. And why was he alone? ... Had he quarrelled with someone? What was on his mind?' She adds that she never saw him again and she did not mention him in her *cahier*. This is puzzling given that her *cahiers* and diaries are made up of everything that struck her as even faintly extraordinary. It would not be until the mid-1950s that Positano became a destination for discriminating tourists, prompted by John Steinbeck's *Harper's Bazaar* article of 1953. Steinbeck emphasised the contrast between the beauty of the place – very few of the buildings seemed less than two centuries old – and its desolate state. The old palazzi and bourgeois villas were empty and the population appeared to be made up of poverty-stricken middle-aged fishermen and small traders, with the exception of those who worked in its two hotels. The young man who Highsmith saw on the beach, returning from his swim at dawn, was evidently an outsider, if he existed at all.

In 1989, when Highsmith did the piece for *Granta* ('The Scene of the Crime,' vol. 29, winter 1989), Ripley had become for her the equivalent of Conan Doyle's Holmes, even Shakespeare's Hamlet, the figure who defined her as a writer. By making him real, albeit elusive and mysterious, she was also increasing the saleability of the works in which he appeared as a murderous psychopath. Highsmith had visited Positano twice before she took Ellen. Whether or not we believe her story that the man on the beach appeared to her on this occasion is immaterial when we consider that he did so, according to her, at the time she was sharing a bedroom with a figure who she would also treat as deranged and malicious and who, like Ripley, would be with her in various forms for the remainder of her life.

Highsmith did not tell Ellen that they were repeating in exact detail the journey which she had taken with Kathryn three years before. Had she done so her partner would likely have been mortified. It was a peculiar exercise and it continued in the same manner. Highsmith and Kathryn had left Positano for Sicily, where they'd become lovers, and the relationship had ended in Naples. With Ellen, Highsmith went straight to Naples and Ellen took the train from the city back to Munich. They had not separated but for both it seemed that a brief period apart was the wisest option. To see off

Ellen from the same railway station in Naples where she had said goodbye to Kathryn hints at the ghoulish, particularly since Ellen knew nothing of her involvement in this ritual.

Highsmith then went to Forio, on the island of Ischia, a few miles from the mainland but classified as part of the administrative region of Naples. Panza, Forio's only town, was similar to Positano in that it was made up of exquisite Renaissance manor houses either abandoned or occupied only in the summer by wealthy families from Rome or northern Italy. In 1952 its most distinguished non-Italian resident was W. H. Auden. How Highsmith learned of Auden's address and how he knew anything of her (she had only one novel in print in her own name at the time) remains a mystery but she tells of her encounter with him in a letter to Skattebol in 1967. 'I was prepared to talk of poetry ... and all he spoke of was the cheaper prices of things here' (5 January 1967). Again, one has to ask why she did not enter anything in her notebooks of her meeting with probably the most celebrated poet in the English-speaking world. He was, she told Skattebol, 'barefoot', generally distracted and tended by a 'young Italian pansy'. This account was fifteen years after the alleged meeting, and as with her *Granta* article on the mysterious figure who inspired Ripley, we have to wonder how much of her past she recollected and how much she laundered. There is no firm evidence that she actually visited Auden. All that we have is a letter from him on his appreciation of *Strangers on a Train*, written during the mid-1950s (there is no exact date), praising her characterisation of Bruno, less so of Guy. Nothing in the letter indicates that they had actually met; indeed, he seems to be corresponding with a stranger.

Why would she have distorted facts? Auden was much older than Dickie Greenleaf but they belonged to the same tribe, figures who saw art as their vocation – in Greenleaf's case as a dilettante – and both regarded the villages of the Amalfi coast as their studios. When she visited Auden (*if* she visited Auden) it was as if she were the equivalent of Tom Ripley, the man who wanted to belong to the elite of writers and upper-class triflers who felt that such delightful locations were part of their entitlement. By the time she wrote of the man walking on the beach and of her encounter with Auden, Patricia Highsmith and Tom Ripley were inseparable, both for her devoted readers and in her own mind. The writer and academic Bettina Berch interviewed her in the 1980s and later commented to Wilson that 'she would talk about him [Ripley] like he was a person very close to her ... She'd defend him and think about what he would say about a certain situation. He was very real to her' (Interview between Berch and Wilson, 18 May 1999).

Highsmith returned to Munich in August and in September the couple moved to Paris where Ellen had begun a job with the Tolstoy Foundation, a charitable organisation founded by the Russian writer's daughter. Originally it was politically unaligned, helping displaced persons from all parts of Central and Eastern Europe, but by 1952 it had committed itself to assisting individuals in Russia and the newly established Soviet bloc who wished to move to the liberal democracies of the West. There is no evidence in Highsmith's notebooks or elsewhere of her opinions on her partner's philanthropic inclinations. All that seemed to concern Ellen was her desire to keep their apartment at 83 rue de l'Université clean, the fact that Highsmith's loud typing kept her awake until after midnight, and her dog. According to Highsmith her lover woke her in the early hours of 10 September and attacked her with her fists, and followed this with an interrogation on their future as a couple. 'It is worse than being married,' Highsmith wrote (Diary, 10 September 1952).

In early November there was another violent exchange. Highsmith wrote in her diary that she 'struck at' Ellen 'to ward her off', adding that 'By Christ, I do believe she is insane' (6 November 1952).

Three days later Ellen left for Geneva to offer advice on the establishment of a Tolstoy Foundation office in the city and while she was away Highsmith bought a plane ticket to Florence, date and departure time specified on the document. On Ellen's return they talked again about their future and Highsmith told her partner nothing of the fact that she had already arranged to leave and to effectively terminate the relationship. She flew to Florence but within a few days found that she could not bear to be separated from Ellen, telephoned her and arranged to meet at a hotel in Geneva, equidistant between their locations and convenient for Ellen's continued meetings in the city regarding the Tolstoy Foundation. No entries in Highsmith's notebooks tell of the nature of what occurred but it is evident from the circumstances that they were in some way reconciled. They took a train back to their Paris apartment and within a week Ellen agreed to take an unpaid furlough from her job to see if another bout of travelling might offer some remedy to their problems.

That Highsmith suggested this and Ellen with reluctance agreed is evident from entries in the notebooks. Our knowledge of their sometimes apparently violent exchanges is based on the descriptions of events and feelings and transcriptions of dialogue entered in the diaries and *cahiers*. Ellen never spoke or wrote of these and aside from Highsmith's own records of her all we know of what she was really like comes from observations made much later by the author's friends. We never feel that these figures knew her properly as a person but rather formed an impression of her based on what Highsmith had told them. We can rely on some largely indisputable facts regarding her background and education and her professional life in America and Europe, and from these we can extrapolate a perception of someone of considerable intellectual ability, capable of meeting the rigid demands of an academic community. More importantly, we form an image of a woman disposed to placing her talents at the service of organisations which offered shelter and stability for displaced individuals in a continent fragmented by war, inhumanity and Cold War polarisation.

It is difficult to reconcile what we know of her with the horrid, possessive bully of Highsmith's private records. When making the entries during the early 1950s Highsmith was ambitious enough, but not sufficiently presumptuous to imagine that post mortem fame would turn them into a treasure trove for biographers and scholars. More significant was the almost simultaneous relationship between her private narrative of events and individuals and the one she hoped to sell to a publisher. We will probably never learn the truth about Ellen's character but it is clear from Highsmith's accounts that her lover had become the model for an experiment in mutually destructive uncertainty and disingenuousness. Highsmith seems able to fall in and out of love with Ellen on a daily basis and to perceive her just as regularly as magical and satanic. She also reports that Ellen was something of a chameleon, persistently disclosing and disguising features of her personality. We can only take Highsmith's word for this but more intriguing is the similarity between the two people recorded in the notebooks and two others whose equally troubled relationship, involving attraction and contempt, deception and disclosure, was unfolding simultaneously in another narrative: Tom Ripley and Dickie Greenleaf.

Before Highsmith set off for Florence by plane, she reported that Ellen had pleaded with her to stay, threatening suicide if she left. Nothing came of it but according to Highsmith's account this was a prelude to what would happen next. When they made an attempt at reconciliation, with Ellen taking leave from her job, they again drove through northern Italy but this time decided to go further towards the Balkans, to Trieste, which like Berlin was a region divided between opposed occupying forces. It is, in terms of architectural charm, comparable with Venice, though Highsmith found it dull and depressing. True, they arrived in midwinter, in January, and while the city is not blessed with the temperate climate of the south-western Mediterranean it did not suffer winters comparable with those of Paris, Munich or Switzerland. Some would say it surpasses any other European city in terms of the eclectic style of its buildings and its cultural legacies. Perhaps, in truth, her distaste for the beautiful city was due to the fact that the Tolstoy Foundation was, during their stay, establishing an office there. It was the crossroads of Latin, Slavic and Germanic cultures and had become a magnet for desperate individuals from each.

They stayed there for four months, and while it was possible that Ellen would have continued in employment with the Tolstoy Foundation for longer than that, a variety of factors caused them to leave. Highsmith confessed in her diaries to feeling humiliated because she earned less than Ellen. She had occasional advances, especially as the rights to *Strangers on a Train* sold for translation into various languages, but she did not, like Ellen, have a regular salary. She tried to write some pulp fiction, which was rejected, and applied for a job teaching English, for which she was turned down. She told Ellen that the relationship was over, or so her notebooks record, without offering a reason for its imminent termination. There is no record of which of them persuaded the other that an accord might be possible but events show that they agreed on a stay of execution. They took the train to Genoa, sailed to Gibraltar and, after a while in Spain, boarded a liner to New York, renting a Manhattan apartment for $150 a month for two months.

By June their relationship had once more come close to collapse. Ellen complained that Highsmith was too interested in socialising with people she'd known in the city before she left for Europe. As Wilson puts it, 'Ellen's jealousy reached monstrous proportions – she could not understand why Pat didn't want to spend every evening with her. During one argument about a party – Highsmith wanted to go along, Ellen, as usual, forbade her – Ellen became so angry she ripped her lover's shirt from her back' (p.184). At the beginning of July Highsmith decided she could not take things any more and stated that they must separate. By Highsmith's account Ellen shrieked back at her that she would not allow them to part, drank several very large Martinis, held up a bottle of Veronal (a barbiturate then openly sold as sleeping tablets) and threatened to take all of them, a fatal dose. Before Highsmith left the apartment that evening, Ellen, sitting naked on the bed, told her 'I love you very much' and washed down eight of the tablets with another Martini. Highsmith left, and proceeded to find a pay phone, call Kate Kingsley Skattebol, her friend from college, and her husband, Lars Skattebol, and arrange to meet them at a restaurant for dinner.

Showing admirable concern, she also called Jim Dobrochek, a Czech painter, who Ellen was due to meet for a drink that same evening. Evidently, she informed Dobrochek that Ellen would not be able to make it, though she did not give the reason as her ongoing attempt to commit suicide.

After ending the evening at the apartment of 'Jean P.' (surname not specified in the diaries), where she ate two hamburgers and told Jean of the 'sad story of tonight and Ellen', Highsmith returned to the apartment at around 2 a.m. She was unable to wake Ellen who seemed to be in a coma and she found a note in the typewriter which stated that 'I should have done this twenty years ago' and absolved Highsmith of blame. She telephoned a doctor who was unable to revive her but tried to pump her stomach of the remaining drugs. Ellen was taken to the Bellevue Hospital at 4.30 a.m. and given a less than fifty-fifty chance of survival.

During the weeks before Ellen's suicide attempt, Highsmith had had brief affairs with three other women, notably Jean P., with whom she had flown to Santa Fe for two days in late June, taking Ellen's car to the airport. On the afternoon of 1 July, at three o'clock, four hours before Ellen would take an overdose, she had met up with Ann Smith (previously Clark), her lover from the time she was seeing Marc Brandel, for drinks in a New York cocktail bar. According to her diary, she arranged with Ann for a threesome involving Jean P., at Ann's house on Fire Island, roughly an hour's drive from New York City.

Highsmith does not in her notebooks suggest that Ellen learned of this or therefore that it contributed to her self-destructive state of mind. She does, however, admit that when Ellen first threatened to kill herself, a year earlier, she had looked through Highsmith's diary entries on their relationship.

Highsmith spent the night of 1 July with Jean P., and visited Bellevue the following day where Ellen was unconscious and still, according to the doctors, showing no signs of a likely recovery. Margot Johnson, her agent, offered her a room in her apartment as did Rosalind Constable, now installed with her new lover, Claude. Instead she drove Ellen's car to Ann's Fire Island house and it was only on 4 July, three days after the overdose, that she found out that Ellen had regained consciousness.

Within a few days Highsmith had borrowed an apartment from a friend of Jean P. who was away on a long vacation. Of the events surrounding Ellen's period in hospital the diary tells various stories. In one entry, made on 7 August, Highsmith reports that roughly a month beforehand she had returned to the hospital immediately on learning of Ellen's recovery and held her in her arms – but this is impossible given that she was at Fire Island when she first heard that Ellen had regained consciousness and she did not return to New York City until after Ellen had been discharged.

Much earlier, on 3 July, when Ellen had been in hospital for two days, she wrote of how Ellen's friend Jim Dobrochek, who Ellen was due to meet the night she tried to kill herself, had been the one who had made regular visits to the hospital and reported to Highsmith on the likelihood of her recovery. After learning from Jim, by phone at Fire Island, that Ellen was conscious she makes no further references to her in her diary. It is odd, then, that she tells four weeks later of a kind of tragic reunion at Ellen's bedside in the hospital.

One entry on Jim is intriguing. Before she set off for Fire Island Highsmith remained in regular contact with him.

> Jim had been walking the streets all night. Told me over AM coffee Ellen mistreated him on his arrival here ... buttonholed him at the pier and said: Don't ever tell a soul that I am Jewish!

> I had not known before that she was totally Jewish, from that
> tight, sophisticated, brittle German Jewish set of pre-Hitler
> Berlin. (3 July 1953)

Highsmith had known for some time that her lover was called Ellen
Blumenthal Hill and that, aside from gaining a British passport, the
surname Hill had enabled her to distance herself from her father's
Jewish background. So Highsmith was lying to herself. What is
striking however is her statement that she did not know Ellen was
'totally' Jewish, from the 'tight, sophisticated, brittle German Jewish
set', the integrated, middle-class intellectual Jews of cosmopolitan
Germany that the Nazis took particular satisfaction in persecuting.
The next part of the entry is even more disturbing: '[This] is a major
strike against me, with Ellen's mother … I am escaping from hell.'
Highsmith had not met Ellen's mother and knew little about her
but she did know that the matrilineal line was the guarantee of
Jewishness. It is impossible to believe that one of two intelligent
individuals in a long-term relationship was unaware that the other
was Jewish, but in her notebooks Highsmith confirmed her special,
visceral brand of antisemitism. She could rationalise her sense of
what Judaism meant but now her Jewish lover was seemingly close
to death something much nastier rose to the surface. Dobrochek
confirmed for her what she might only have suspected, that Ellen
was incontrovertibly, 'totally', Jewish – a 'hell' from which she
could now escape.

The plot of *The Blunderer* can be reappraised with the story of
Highsmith's relationship with Ellen at the time she was writing it in
mind. Walter Stackhouse's feelings for his wife Clara are brilliantly
nuanced, in that we sense that he has, prior to the present-day
setting of the novel, developed a gradual hatred for her. The reason
for this is never fully explained but Highsmith drops sufficient clues
for us to assume that she had alienated their friends and in other

ways created for the two of them a world closed off from the rest
of society and dominated by her preoccupation with pettiness and
her paranoid responses to inconsequential issues. So far, we have a
perfect replica of Ellen Hill, or at least the woman represented in
Highsmith's notebook accounts.

In the novel we can never be quite sure if Walter's presentation
of Clara is authentic and unbiased or informed by his prejudices.
She falsely accuses him of infidelity with a pretty, sensuous music
teacher, but, as if prompted by his wife's censure, he later begins
an affair with her. The implication is that Clara has become a
bullying neurotic, forcing him to behave as badly as she alleges of
him. Once more fact filters into fiction. Ellen had read Highsmith's
notebooks and discovered accounts of her liaisons with other
women in Munich, Paris and New York. She knew what Highsmith
was doing but in terms of the practicalities of their life together the
mutual awareness that one partner was betraying the other lingered
uncomfortably without being fully addressed. In the novel Clara
becomes a vituperative, vengeful fictionalisation of Ellen, quite the
opposite of the truth. Ellen knew that her partner was leading a
double life, but she kept her feelings to herself, turned her unease
inwards; all of which contributed to the gradual onset of mental
instability. Highsmith recreates this for Clara, but as a strategy
of aggression. She is intent on ruining Walter's life for sins he has
yet to commit, a complete reversal of the relationship between
Highsmith and Ellen. Ellen suffered largely in silence; Highsmith
cared very little.

Clara's attempt at suicide by overdose is prompted by Walter's
demand that they divorce, and Ellen did the same following
Highsmith's declaration that their relationship was over. There is no
evidence that Highsmith deliberately planned to bring her partner's
life to an end, but it is clear enough that she knew precisely the
levels of stability beyond which Ellen's precarious psychological
state would be ruinously undermined. By the night that her

partner tried to kill herself Highsmith had carefully marshalled and choreographed two related narratives. In the novel Walter fantasises about murdering his wife, while not seriously plotting to take her life. He is a middle-class lawyer who would be fully aware that murderers, particularly domestic murderers, rarely escaped arrest and prosecution. On the other hand, he is minutely alert to Clara's disturbed mental state and how it might affect her behaviour. When Highsmith informed Ellen that they were finished for good and left the apartment, probably not expecting to see her alive again, Walter, in the novel, was wondering what to do next. While Ellen was in a coma Highsmith decided that Clara should attempt to kill herself, but shortly afterwards fact and fiction diverged. Clara's overdose is presented as a form of emotional blackmail; knowing that she is likely to survive she causes Walter to seek reconciliation and, literally, forces him to take her back into his arms when he visits her in hospital. Highsmith did not of course go to see Ellen in hospital but the fact that she entered in her diary four weeks later that she had done so and embraced Ellen is more than sinister, because at this point she drafted the account in the novel of Walter visiting Clara in her hospital bed and reassuring her, untruthfully, that their marriage would endure.

The Blunderer is treated by consensus as Highsmith's most gripping and imperfect novel. It works at several levels, but none seems joined by rationality or plausibility. First, we have Walter's fascination with Melchior J. Kimmel, a middle-aged bookshop manager who everyone, incited by press reports and police bulletins, believes has murdered his wife. Walter visits Kimmel, and shortly afterwards Clara's body is found at the foot of a cliff. We never learn whether she fell or jumped, or if Walter played some part in her death, which occurred during the rest-interval of her bus journey to visit her seriously ill mother. And here we should recall Highsmith's cryptic notebook entry shortly after Ellen's suicide attempt: 'a major strike

against me, with Ellen's mother … I am escaping from hell.' With
Clara's death, on the way to visit her mother, Walter is plunged into
a special level of hell. He is perceived by the thoroughly weird police
lieutenant Corby as Kimmel's acolyte, someone who has taken
lessons from the bookshop manager on how to commit murder. The
Kimmel subplot is incongruous because while we could accept that
Walter might have been guiltily distracted by overblown newspaper
reports on this alleged wife-murderer, his involvement with him
as an uninvited visitor to the shop, who orders a book simply to
allow him to return and talk with Kimmel, is absurd. In his *New
York Times* review of the novel (3 October 1954), Anthony Boucher
observes that once Walter becomes preoccupied with Kimmel the
novel 'passes the point of no return as the author gropes for (and
fails to find) a way out of the intricate situation she has set up'.
Highsmith invented Kimmel when she had failed to unpack the
puzzle of Walter and Clara's marriage. She attempted to answer
the question of who was the most to blame for their ill-suited
relationship, and he becomes a nasty reflection of Walter, beset by
private grotesqueries and quite capable of planning and carrying
out murder without fear or conscience. Walter and Kimmel were
two extremes, two versions of the same problem on how to deal
with a ruined relationship: become a victim of its worst features or
a killer of the person who had perpetrated them. They could have
formed the basis for different novels, and putting them together
in the same one was disastrous. To her credit, Highsmith rescues
the book from utter calamity by bringing in Corby as the maniacal
nemesis who seems determined to bring both Walter and Kimmel
to justice. We look at the two men through Corby's eyes and instead
of seeing two characters who belong in different books we wonder
if the policeman has detected an endemic propensity towards evil
behaviour.

The novel is an extraordinary example of improvisational
composition; it evolves and reshapes itself persistently, with its

author continually attempting to make sense of her original idea, revising and extending it, and then taking a completely different route as if pursued by a narrative demon long released and no longer controlled. In the concluding section Kimmel stalks Walter across Central Park, eventually stabbing him to death. It is a masterly denouement because it combines for the reader a sense of terror with weary resignation. Even before Kimmel catches up with him Walter has lost the will to live, and in this regard, it epitomises Highsmith's struggle with different aspects of herself when she wrote the book. There are few, if any, novels like it and aside from its aesthetic uniqueness we should look at its real-world origins, particularly Highsmith's sense of herself as touched by aspects of Walter and Kimmel. She was unashamedly unfaithful but exchanged anything resembling guilt for resentment at Ellen having found out that she'd had affairs. Ellen's quite reasonable requests that they spend more time in each other's company becomes, in the novel, Clara's campaign to isolate herself and Walter from anything like a normal social life. Highsmith did want Ellen dead, and like Walter she was not a murderer – at least in the sense that she would not fire a shot or deliver a blow – but she knew that her desertion of the drug-filled Ellen on 1 July was murder-by-proxy. Kimmel was her act of confession, if not contrition. Just after Clara's attempt at suicide had been entered in the draft of the novel, she wrote in the diary that 'the suicide and Ellen's character in the book ... I find very disturbing and too personal' (14 August 1953).

7

RIPLEY

Shortly after Ellen's recovery Highsmith began a relationship with the aspiring actress Lynn Roth, a petite blonde twenty-eight-year-old in whose Greenwich Village apartment the two women lived together for almost three months. They broke up in early 1954, prompting Highsmith to enter remarks in her notebooks that veer between self-recrimination, regrets that she had once more chosen a woman, Lynn, who was 'bad for' her, and the fear that she was suffering from some kind of mental illness, probably manic depression. Along with taking instruction from 'how to' books on mental health she listened to news broadcasts which focused on the Korean War Armistice, the mass hysteria regarding America's infiltration by millions of communist sympathisers, prompted mainly by Senator McCarthy, and the controversy that endured following the execution of the Rosenbergs in June 1953 for sending secrets on nuclear weapons to the Soviet Union. With a mixture of relief and guilt she registered a general feeling of unconcern at these reports of national and global crisis.

Convinced that madness was, largely, for others she began to work on her most psychotic invention, as yet unnamed but eventually to become Thomas Ripley. As Highsmith later acknowledged, the plot for the first Ripley novel is borrowed from Henry James's *The Ambassadors* (1903) in which Lambert Strether, a comfortably off, middle-aged Massachusetts man is asked by his fiancée, a wealthy widow, to go to Paris and persuade her son, Chad Newsome, to return to the security of bourgeois New England. According to Chad's mother rumours were circulating that he had become bewitched by the louche decadence of Parisian culture and by one lascivious French woman in particular.

Highsmith had read the novel in 1940 and by the time she began Ripley's version of Strether's darkly comic odyssey she already had a new template for the American Abroad theme, based mainly on her own experiences in Europe during the previous five years. By implication she saw James's book as an honest and prescient account of why well-off Americans were really attracted to Europe, and this had little to do with cultural enrichment. For Highsmith's characters also, Europe is not so much a liberating environment as an excuse for excess and self-indulgence. The incomers who were sufficiently well off – and Dickie Greenleaf, Marge Sherwood and Freddie Miles fall into this category – filled in for the now often penurious gentry of the continent, bringing welcome supplies of dollars to the beautiful villages still suffering from the deprivations of the post-war decade.

Following the breakdown of her relationship with Lynn Roth, Highsmith rented a cottage in the rural community of Lenox, Massachusetts, a means of removing herself from recent events and concentrating on her new book. The cottage was part of the building occupied by the local undertaker who Highsmith befriended in her customarily ghoulish fashion. He had no fridge and she persuaded him to show her how he embalmed and more importantly preserved corpses that might otherwise decay before burial. He told her how he would replace as many internal organs as possible with dry sawdust. From this, she experimented with various plot twists on the novel-in-progress, involving Dickie and Tom fleeing from Trieste in coffins accompanied by an actual corpse stuffed with bags of opium. In one version Dickie's father arrives unexpectedly, is killed, and is used as a container for the export of opium.

The novel was going everywhere and nowhere in particular, and it only found proper direction in September 1954 when

Highsmith moved from Massachusetts to Santa Fe, New Mexico. She rented a Spanish-style villa and in less than a week was joined on this new journey south by an unlikely companion, Ellen Hill. No correspondence survives from the year they spent apart, and Highsmith entered nothing of her feelings about Ellen in her notebooks during this same period. Clearly they had been in contact and agreed to make another attempt at reviving their relationship. After Santa Fe they spent a few days in the border town of El Paso and went on through Mexico, Ellen driving, and stayed at several towns, including Hidalgo del Parral, which looked towards snow-covered mountains and reminded them of their time in Switzerland. Peggy Lewis, who knew both Ellen and Patricia, later told of how in Mexico City, where they headed after Hidalgo, they argued ceaselessly on largely inconsequential matters.

By spring 1955 they had broken up for good. Given that Highsmith ceased to keep journals during 1954 we know little of what actually happened between them during their final year together. But circumstances are tantalisingly suggestive. In the period between their first break-up and the Mexico reunion *The Blunderer* went to press, and it is evident that Highsmith did not envisage a re-run of their first disastrous relationship. She dedicated the novel 'To L', her lover Lynn Roth with whom she had lived in Greenwich Village when she completed it and who she regarded, optimistically, as a happier prospect for her future. Complimentary copies reached Highsmith in Mexico City where she was renting an apartment with Ellen, and she could hardly pretend that the new book did not exist. We have no exact record of Ellen's impression of it, but we can surmise a great deal. The principal reason for Highsmith's cessation of her notebook entries was the fact that Ellen had begun to read them. She was understandably disturbed to discover the enormous difference between her lover's declarations to her and her private reflections on her character, especially her alleged deficiencies. How would she react to reading a version of this in the story of

Walter and Clara? It was her first reading of the novel in which she found herself presented as a maliciously neurotic individual seemingly intent on ruining the life of a partner who had dedicated themselves to her. We might assume from their reconciliation that Ellen was not entirely aware of how Highsmith had behaved during the evening of her suicide attempt and subsequent comatose days in hospital. Insouciance would be a generous description, especially given that aside from showing no concern for the likelihood of Ellen's recovery Highsmith indulged herself with a brief affair while she was unconscious. In the novel, the scenario is reversed, with Walter being turned into the victim of Clara's threats to kill herself and her eventual success in doing so.

It was, for Ellen, bad enough to have lived with the memory of what actually happened when they were together during the first three-year period of their relationship, when Highsmith emerged as a liar and a sadist. Even worse was the discovery that she had rewritten all this with herself as the tormented sufferer and Ellen the perpetrator of her ills. It is hardly surprising that their second attempt at a relationship lasted only a year.

Emotionally, 1954–5 was a failure for both women but for Highsmith it forged the basis for her long-term reputation as a writer. *The Talented Mr. Ripley*, in its readable coherent form, without stuffed corpses, was completed during the first five months of Highsmith's time with Ellen in Mexico.

Tom Ripley is one of the most fascinating exercises in autobiographical fiction ever produced. In all obvious respects he bears no resemblance to his creator, yet when we look closer at the two of them the parallels are extraordinary and bizarre. In New York Ripley is a confidence trickster, a man who makes a living by pretending to be someone he is not and extracting money from those who are credulous enough to believe his lies. Highsmith too had to lead a life of deceit, conducting relationships which, officially, would not be tolerated or spoken of, and producing books that were about stealth and concealment. In Europe, especially with Kathryn and Ellen, she could emerge from behind the curtained environments of America. It was not that the provinces of Germany, France, Italy and Spain were liberal, quite the opposite – most of the places she visited were still controlled by Roman Catholic orthodoxy. However, generally speaking the people who lived there were too preoccupied with making enough to keep themselves and their communities alive to concern themselves with what a pair of American women booked into the same apartment or hotel might get up to.

From all of this came Ripley. He is approached by the shipping magnate Herbert Greenleaf to go out to Europe and bring back his son, Dickie, who seems determined to exist on family money as a harmless, dissolute bohemian in the village of Mongibello, a thinly disguised version of Positano, where Highsmith later claimed to have first seen the young man in swimming trunks strolling along the beach at dawn.

Throughout her time in Europe Highsmith felt uncomfortable, as if she had gate-crashed a party held by and for the elite. Similarly, Tom Ripley makes his way into Dickie and Marge's life in Mongibello by aping the mannerisms of their class, the wealthy Ivy League-educated generation for whom Europe offered hedonism disguised as cultural revelation. The most striking episode in the novel follows the trip that Tom and Dickie make to Rome, in which the former feels that he has almost become a version of his new friend. They seem on effortlessly intimate terms, significant only to each other and insulated against the attentions and demands of the world at large. Tom even suggests that they treat this as a rehearsal for excursions across Europe, destinations and timeline unspecified. They will leave their previous existences behind and dedicate their time to the appreciation of the continent and each other.

The homoerotic overtones are at once self-evident and one-sided in that Tom has misread the nature of their friendship and succumbed to his own fantasy. This hits him suddenly and painfully once they return to Mongibello, and he follows Dickie when he visits Marge at her house. Marge and Dickie are close friends, and Tom assumes that their relationship involves nothing more than that, but when he sees Dickie kissing her passionately he is filled with 'disgust'. After returning to Dickie's place he throws some of Dickie's art supplies into the yard, goes to the bedroom and tries on his clothes, attempts to imitate his voice and physical habits and enacts a scene which is a twisted fantasy of the one he has just witnessed. This time, he, as Dickie, kisses and embraces Marge and then strangles her to death. 'You were interfering between Tom and me,' he informs her imagined corpse. 'But there is a bond between us!' At that point Dickie enters the room, tells him to 'get out' of his outfit and thereafter Tom's idyll descends gradually into a nightmare. Marge already resents Tom's closeness to Dickie – one of the insinuations that he might be homosexual – and begins to accuse him of having made up things about his past, notably his class and standing in East Coast society. Tom and Dickie take time away from the village to travel and socialise in various fashionable parts of Italy and while Ripley gradually becomes closer to his friend, even emulating his mannerisms and speech habits, Dickie grows uncomfortable with this, and urges that they should spend time apart. Ripley responds by murdering the man he mythologises and secretly adores. Once more, Highsmith's diary entries which equate failed relationships with death and murder manifest themselves in her fiction. Back in Rome Tom assumes Dickie's life full-time, a twenty-four-hours-a-day version of the moment in his bedroom when he had tried on his clothes and imitated his voice.

A friend of Dickie's, Freddie Miles, comes close to exposing Tom as a fraud and murderer, only to also be killed by him. Miles visits the elegant apartment Tom claims to be 'keeping' for Dickie, learns from the concierge that Signor Greenleaf is the only resident, returns to the flat and has his skull smashed in by Ripley with a heavy glass ashtray.

It is a superb novel, eroding the boundaries between the popular genre of crime writing and the as yet unestablished field of gothic realism to be pioneered by Iris Murdoch. Most significantly it is morally unhinged, causing us to feel all manner of things about Ripley, depending on our inclinations. He is by far the most charismatic individual in the novel. Indeed, he is so well crafted that we begin to feel that the detached, entitled figures upon whom he revenges himself deserve what comes to them.

That Highsmith completed it at such speed – less than five months – when she was with Ellen in Mexico is not entirely surprising. Ellen enabled her to draw together what had previously been disparate threads of potential and conflicting stories. She was, for Highsmith, what Dickie is for Tom. Certainly, Ellen was an unapologetic lesbian, rather than a heterosexual who Tom believed might confirm his own repressed inclinations, but at the same time there was for Highsmith something about her that was unattainable. As many of Highsmith's friends stated it was a 'love–hate' relationship – a mutable term – but in this case meaning that Highsmith loved the prospect of being with a woman who in truth she neither properly knew nor appreciated. When she wrote the book the muted antagonism between them drove the narrative forward, as did Highsmith's memories from the country, the continent, in which the novel is set.

The French and Italian cities and villages she visited with her lovers, notably Kathryn and Ellen, made up the wonderful, unintendedly liberal environment that Tom saw as the future for himself and Dickie Greenleaf, and the idyll dates back to Highsmith's diary entry the day after her plane landed in Paris in 1951 when she began her first year with Ellen. 'This is the kind of evening (and life) of which I dreamed in college – in a very

Scott Fitzgerald way: Europe, a girl, money, leisure, a car. Now I've had *one* night of it, after twelve years' (23 August 1951). The Gatsby-style fantasy resurfaces for Tom Ripley who crosses the Atlantic first class, at the expense of Dickie's father. He does not, cannot, predict that the price he must pay to share Dickie's lifestyle involves murdering him.

But some time before she invented Ripley, Highsmith had a clear perception of something that would be central both to her state of mind and her fiction. 'Frustration as a theme. One person, in love with another whom he cannot attain or be with' (26 September 1949). At the time she began the draft of *The Talented Mr. Ripley*, Highsmith's four most significant lovers had been Rosalind Constable, Ginnie Catherwood, Kathryn Cohen and Lynn Roth. Each of these women, by virtue of their beauty, cosmopolitanism, wealth or social standing, was what she was not. Her longest relationship had been with Ellen, but Ellen was different from the others. In some respects, she outranked and overstretched Highsmith intellectually – often the cause of their seemingly incessant arguments – and like Dickie she had moved seamlessly into the social and cultural fabric of Europe. Her multilingual abilities are due in part to her family legacy, her parents' origins in Europe; she does not sound like a foreigner. Highsmith and Ripley are embarrassed by their competent but unsophisticated grasp of French and Italian and work hard at becoming more accomplished as natural speakers. In July 1954, shortly before she contacted Ellen to suggest they try again, she wrote, while at her cabin in Massachusetts, 'I am always in love with the worthy and unworthy ... and I wonder now if it is a giving or a taking' (3 July 1954). She seemed to be weighing up her lovers in terms of their social standing, and assessing her collateral debt to them, or theirs to her. Wondering, perhaps, if she was once again to begin an affair with someone all too like herself.

In Peggy Lewis's recollections of the arguments between Highsmith and Ellen in Mexico City they come across as versions of the same person, figures with so much in common that persistent close proximity will inevitably result in acrimony (Interview with Wilson, 14 December 1999). At this point Highsmith had got to the climactic chapters of the narrative, after Tom has murdered Ripley and adopted his identity in Rome. Tom, playing Dickie, does not argue with himself but a residual sense of guilt at what he has done and fear that he will be caught causes him to become disturbed. On one hand, he enjoys the fantasy made real; he has not only become part of Dickie's set, he has replaced him. At the same time, he can never stop being Tom Ripley. At some point the dream must come to an end, either through his arrest or by his voluntary departure from it. And in this respect Highsmith's relationship with Ellen played a crucial role in enabling her to complete the novel. She was drawing energy from a partnership which she knew was destined for disaster.

Tom neither plans nor takes pleasure in despatching Dickie but it gradually becomes clear to him that the act incorporates a blend of natural justice and destiny. What Dickie denied him in life – a form of unique togetherness – would be replaced in death by a sharing of their personalities. Highsmith had not clattered Ellen over the head with an oar but her callous disregard for her fate when she left the apartment on the evening of her suicide attempt came close to wishing her dead. For three days in 1953 Highsmith believed that Ellen had died from an overdose and even when she learned that she had survived she showed no sympathy for her condition or, more importantly, her state of mind. When she almost magically rekindled their relationship, it was as though she had, like Tom, brought her victim back to life. For Tom the dead Dickie, for whom in life he felt little genuine affection, enabled him to sustain a delusion; and for Highsmith the stomach-pumped, revived Ellen provided energy for a gruesome fictionalised projection of their relationship. If *The Price of Salt* was a transference of private fantasy into literature, *The Talented Mr. Ripley* put a ghastly twist on this exercise.

Ellen made no public comments on all of this, but we know that she read the manuscript and that their attempt at reconciliation collapsed shortly afterwards. She would have been appalled to find that following the reworking of her death in *The Blunderer*, Highsmith had repeated the exercise in her new novel. Ellen should be commended for her tolerance and indulgence in that she remained in regular contact with Highsmith until the author's death, though there is no hint that they would ever be more than cautiously respected associates. One feels that, had he survived, Dickie Greenleaf would have been far less forgiving.

There is a story – and story it is, because no one but Highsmith can authenticate it – that once she had completed the manuscript, shortly before the break-up with Ellen, she posted it to Willie Mae Coates in Fort Worth, who died shortly afterwards, apparently of a stroke, on 5 February 1955. Why exactly she assumed her eighty-eight-year-old piously Christian grandmother would be entertained by an exercise in Grand Guignol homoeroticism remains a mystery but apparently the manuscript was lost at some point between its arrival and Willie Mae's burial. Highsmith did not attend the funeral and later blamed her mother, who did, for conspiring with the 'negroes' to destroy the draft. 'Inexcusable. Inexcusable. I said to my mother, "How could this happen?" She replied that "Well, the negroes were sorting it out,"' and Highsmith replied, rather cryptically, 'The negroes were sorting out the … what are you *talking* about?' (*The Times*, Saturday Review, 28 September 1991). In all of the accounts I have seen there is an uncertainty about whether she sent 'the manuscript', 'a manuscript' or 'a copy of the manuscript' to Fort Worth and it is puzzling that no one has drawn attention to these potential anomalies. It would have been impossible for her to rewrite, from memory, another version of the novel in time for publication; it came out in December 1955. But the story that the single manuscript sent to Fort Worth disappeared persists. The mysteries surrounding this lost draft emerged when Highsmith gave interviews decades later on her most famous book. Once more we have to suspect that fiction was for her some kind of magical potion, not simply a form of entertainment for others but a means of manipulating those aspects of her life that bored her or which she distrusted.

8

MARIJANE

The Talented Mr. Ripley won the Edgar Allan Poe Award for Best Novel, one of the most prestigious prizes for crime-mystery novels, in early 1956. During December of the previous year the reviews in the mainstream American newspapers were excellent. Anthony Boucher in the *New York Times Book Review* praised Highsmith for her 'three-dimensional portrait of what a criminal psychologist would call a "congenital psychopathic inferior"'. He was impressed that Tom Ripley could transform character traits that would normally sideline him as an undistinguished failure into calculatingly evil tendencies, without seeming a contradiction in terms. The anonymous reviewer in *The New Yorker* agreed, finding Ripley 'one of the most repellent and fascinating characters' in literature, who comes across 'very engagingly indeed'. There was a general consensus that while the main character was vile and immoral Highsmith had somehow insulated him from the reader's inclination to judge. He seemed to exist in a world of his own, cut off from the emotional and legal environment shared by everyone else, inside and outside the novel.

By March 1956 she had reactivated her *cahiers*, prompted by a new relationship. As usual she begins her account of things with bouts of unadulterated hyperbole. 'The trust in the eyes of the girl who loves you. It is the most beautiful thing in the world' (8 June 1956). Doris was an illustrator and copywriter for a prestigious advertising company on Madison Avenue. She was from decent middle-class stock in the Midwest, had a degree from Ohio State University and held a position with the McCann Erickson Agency, typically staffed only by men. In Manhattan advertising agencies, most female employees were secretaries or administrative workers – the TV series *Mad Men* provides a reasonably accurate account of sexism in such environments – and Doris had clearly proved herself through her ability to make money and win contracts. Wilson refers to her as someone who 'cannot be named' while Schenkar uses only her forename. Doris certainly existed. There were too many documented tracks between her and known figures and circumstances for us to doubt her presence. She lived with Lynn Roth, as an occasional lover, when Highsmith first met Lynn, and Ann Smith refers to her on record as an ex-girlfriend of hers. It is curious that Highsmith's previous biographers treat her as a mystery given that her personal history is identical to that of Doris Sanders, with whom Highsmith produced the children's book *Miranda the Panda is on the Veranda*, published in 1958 and written during the second year of their relationship. There is a photograph of Doris in the SLA archive, cigarette in hand, seated on a raised stool, sketching. She looks exquisitely composed, slim and almost beautiful and once more we find that Highsmith is mixing up sexual attraction with social advancement. Doris was Rosalind, Ginnie and Kathryn, revisited.

After she left Ellen, Highsmith returned to the modest apartment on East 56th Street in Manhattan she'd first occupied in 1942 when she came to the city fourteen years earlier. It seemed an act of contrition, given that the location had certainly not improved. She was pestered for days on end by gangs of teenagers who took control of the outdoor staircases, vandalising or stealing anything that was left unguarded.

Highsmith once left her largest suitcase on the landing but rather than steal it the vindictive youngsters daubed it with paint, as if they were telling her that while they did not want it she would never use it again. They played baseball in the street below her window, with a loud and raucous soundtrack just to ensure residents knew they were there. Highsmith was so affected that she wrote a short story called 'The Barbarians', later published in *Eleven* (1970), in which the tormented tenant drops a gigantic rock onto the head of one of the teenagers and kills him.

Highsmith relieved herself of this self-imposed purgatory by moving with Doris into a small house in the hamlet of Snedens Landing, part of Palisades, New York State, on the Hudson River and one of the most exclusive commuter enclaves for those who spent their working lives in the city. It was expensive and Doris, on a salary that went far beyond Highsmith's irregular royalties and other incomings, covered the bulk of the rent. Once more the idyll became, for no evident reason, something else. 'My dear God … teach me forbearance, patience, courage in the face of pain and disappointment … one day I shall take you by the throat and tear the windpipe and arteries out, though I go to hell for it,' she wrote (29 June 1956).

She was commendably honest about the cause of her dissatisfaction. Things were too good. They had bought a new Ford convertible, again with the assistance of Doris's salary, and during the spring and early summer Highsmith divided her time between writing and planting radishes, beans, peas and tomatoes in the spacious garden while Doris was working in the McCann Erickson offices. She wrote of 'the danger of living without one's normal diet of passion'. As usual she had become bored with monogamy, but 'passion' for Highsmith also involved the attraction of anything else that might disrupt domestic contentment, mostly the onset of mutual antagonism and arguments over inconsequential matters. 'Things are so readily equalised, soothed, forgotten with a laugh' (*Cahier*, 31 July 1956). Later that year she observed that happiness was not conducive to her particular brand of creativity. 'My continuing troubles about my work. My writing, the themes I write on, do not permit me to express love…' (21 October 1956).

She meant that in order to create the loveless, inherently evil figures who were now her speciality, she must exist in a collateral state of bitterness, anger and deception in the real world. She loved Doris, as much as she could love anyone, but their life of tranquil equanimity stifled her as a novelist. Shortly after she met Doris, she had begun *A Game for the Living* which would be published in 1958. It took her more than two years to complete because she was never happy with what she had undertaken. It is routinely referred to as her Mexican novel, set in the country she had visited several times, and involves the unsteady friendship between the Mexican furniture repairman Ramon and Theo, a German expatriate intellectual, each of whom might be responsible for the rape, murder and mutilation of Leila; both have slept with her. Highsmith herself regarded it as her worst piece of fiction, with some justification. Eventually we do learn of the identity of the murderer but rather than being the shocking conclusion of the classic 'whodunnit' it strikes us more as the tapering-out off of a work that should be more accurately described as a 'who cares'. We leave the narrative relieved of boredom but not particularly concerned with what has happened. Joan Kahn, her editor at Harper, returned the draft to her several times, on each occasion stating that the ending was disappointing and unconvincing.

Highsmith dutifully rewrote the conclusion four times and found herself also obliged to alter key parts of the preceding story to ensure that what occurred at the end was consistent with earlier insinuations and nuances. She was revising it backwards and becoming more and more contemptuous of the whole enterprise.

In spring 1957 she and Doris had driven south in their Ford convertible for three weeks in Mexico, principally in Acapulco and Mexico City. This was a reprise of her earlier inspirational protocols: travel with her current lover – perhaps in the expectation that the pressures of elsewhere would initiate friction – and visit locations that recalled previous private and emotional catastrophes. On this occasion Doris seemed oblivious to her provocations and an atmosphere of amiability prevailed. Highsmith wrote in her *cahier*, 'Don't know where I'm going ... resulting in static effect' (1 May 1957). She was referring both to her attempts to inject fractiousness into their relationship – Doris was able to outwit her with an abundance of patience and imperturbability – and to her consequential inability to energise her narrative with thorough nastiness. She returned from Mexico horribly disappointed in what she had hoped to achieve from the visit: they'd had a lovely time.

Another problem with *A Game for the Living* was that she had begun to write it when she was having enormous difficulties completing an earlier novel. *Deep Water* (1957) is a particularly horrible and addictive piece of work. It tells of the sexless marriage between Vic and Melinda Van Allen, residents of the small, respectable Massachusetts town of Little Wesley, and was inspired, like its two predecessors, by Highsmith's relationship with Ellen Hill. She was more than seventy pages into it when she and Hill broke up and once she had moved in with Doris at Snedens Landing she began to lose the energy to continue. Vic cares little about whether or not he continues his hopeless, loveless marriage, but he is too cowardly and conventional to seek a divorce. Instead he allows his wife to take as many lovers as she wishes. He takes credit for killing Malcolm McRae, one of her former lovers, only to present himself as a comic grotesque when the true killer is apprehended soon afterwards. Vic goes on to make use of his role as falsely accused murderer and assumes he'll get away with drowning Melinda's current lover in the pool of a neighbour's house following a party. He does.

Vic is Ellen. Even his physical attributes correspond with Highsmith's notebook descriptions of her: deep-blue eyes, thick brown eyebrows, a firm 'lopsided' mouth indicative of wry unvoiced opinions on life in general, but with a facial expression giving no clue as to 'what he was thinking or feeling'. More significantly Highsmith reverses the roles between herself and Ellen, and Vic and Melinda to suit her rather biased view of their relationship.

Melinda is guilty of numerous infidelities, and in this respect she is a replica of her author, but in the novel Vic/Ellen forces her to become promiscuous. Highsmith saw her infidelities as a justifiable response to an unbearable relationship from which Ellen would not free her.

The novel is much better than *A Game for the Living* but, similarly, its progress was stifled by the apparent stability of her relationship with Doris. When she was due to send the final draft to Kahn at Harper in late 1956 she found herself persistently revising key passages and finding herself unclear about how to proceed. She resolved things by taking the train to Manhattan and arriving unannounced at Ellen's apartment. With indulgent courtesy, Ellen invited her in, they drank wine and Highsmith made a sexual advance, which Ellen resisted, asking her erstwhile partner to leave. She refused and insisted that despite what had previously occurred they could restart their relationship. Ellen was mortified, threatened to call the police and this time Highsmith left for good, fully aware of how Ellen would respond and behave. The whole episode had been choreographed in advance by Highsmith as an exercise in provocation and humiliation, based on recollections of the many occasions when the two of them seemed set on mutually destructive trajectories.

The following day, back in Snedens Landing, Highsmith began a rewrite of the closing chapters which she completed in little more than a week. Melinda breaks with Vic, moves to New York and appears to find happiness with a surveyor named Tony Cameron. Vic agrees to a divorce but pursues Tony through town, murders him and throws his weighted-down body into a flooded quarry.

Melinda suspects that her deranged husband has killed her lover and seeks the assistance of a neighbour from Little Wesley, Don Wilson, who recovers Tony's body and reports Vic to the police. Prior to his arrest – and inevitably his being found guilty of a capital offence – Vic returns to Melinda's apartment and strangles her to death. Don's profession? He writes pulp crime fiction. It is not too difficult to unpick the parallels between this new conclusion and Highsmith's rather sadistic experiment in her visit to Ellen. The visit did not involve murder but it provided the energy for Highsmith to bring her stalled novel to a murderous conclusion. Their lives, as Vic and Melinda, are brought to a close in a particularly violent piece of writing, witnessed by a pulp fiction writer who appears in the novel as a kind of talisman for its satisfactory completion.

Highsmith's encounter with Ellen lasted only a few hours but this was enough to rekindle those feelings of antipathy and masochism that galvanised her fiction and had been drained from it by virtue of a relationship, with Doris, involving nothing resembling aggression, deception or mutual contempt.

Shortly after meeting Doris, Highsmith wrote a poem addressed not so much to a particular woman as to the difference between women who most would treat as the source of happiness and contentment – such as Doris – and a very different type to whom she is masochistically addicted.

> She would love me all my life
> She would always be my wife.
> Oh! Oh! Oh! Oh!
> I want stronger arms around me
> Insane arms and devils' kisses,
> Teeth that bite my lips and wound me,
> Girls whose love will never last.

Three months after *Deep Water* was published Highsmith entered in her *cahier* her feelings about the relationship between her emotional condition and domestic arrangement and her sense of herself as a writer.

> My present house is not big enough for two people, especially if one is a writer ... The interesting thing is why I endure it ... Perhaps what it comes down to is that I have had about enough, perhaps spoilt my last book effort. I am trying to save myself! ... I can exist, and of course grow, only by change, a challenge to which I have to make an adjustment. (3 January 1958)

The challenge with which she had confronted herself was double edged. In her routinely sanguine, unobstructive manner Doris had listened to her partner's complaints about their house as a form of 'confinement'. It was not tiny; rather a modestly sized converted barn with two bedrooms, one of which Highsmith had taken as her private study for writing. Another much larger, colonial-style house was offered for rent in the nearby village of Sparkill and the couple arranged to move there in September 1958. With astute timing Highsmith had to make regular visits to New York City during the previous month, ostensibly to meet with her agent and editor regarding the direction of her work but actually to take drinks in cocktail bars with Mary Ronin, a commercial artist ten years her senior.

It is not clear how exactly they first met but it is likely that Mary was part of the casual social network of women in New York who visited lesbian bars, some in Greenwich Village and others scattered across the rest of the inner city. The majority of these were owned and run by the Mafia, an offshoot of the mob's moneymaking enterprises from the 1920s and 1930s onwards – gambling, drink during prohibition, prostitution and, after the war, drugs – which fed an appetite for produce and activities frowned upon or criminalised by the authorities. The most famous monument to gay bars in New York is the Stonewall Inn, where a riot was prompted by a police raid in 1969, though we should note that it attracted predominantly homosexual and lesbian customers only after the Mafia took it over in the mid-1960s, following a trend established during the previous decades.

In the 1950s lesbianism was not a criminal offence but establishments which openly promoted themselves as meeting points for gay women would, the mob was aware, soon be subjected to all manner of spurious allegations from authorities who would not openly tolerate manifestations of 'debauched' sexuality. Consequently, the Mafia cleverly contrived to undermine threats to lesbian bars before these existed. Such clubs and bars had an air of protective menace about them, with smartly suited mobsters monitoring the entrances to exclude those who seemed not to belong, men obviously, and politely issuing time-stamped tickets to women entering and leaving the toilets; sex on the premises was not permitted. Men served the bar too and the prices on drinks were grossly inflated.

According to Marijane Meaker (Highsmith's next significant other), in a conversation with Schenkar, Highsmith loved the atmosphere of these low-life clandestine clubs and hated herself for enjoying them. Mary Ronin too enjoyed such spaces. She was good at her job, but able to treat it more as an artistic vocation than a means of keeping herself. She was in a permanent long-term relationship with a very wealthy woman who owned a brownstone in New York's Upper East Side and who enabled her to keep her own impressive apartment in Manhattan. Like Highsmith she revelled in the lesbian bar scene as an escape, not only from heterosexual conformity but also from its settled monogamous gay counterpart. Mary suited Highsmith's temperament because she was careless of the impression she left on others. Two years after they broke up, Mary sent her a birthday card depicting a meticulously crafted sketch of herself, naked and smiling lasciviously on a bed. By November 1958 Highsmith and Mary had begun a sexual relationship and within weeks Highsmith left Doris.

In December Highsmith moved back to New York, to a small apartment in 76 Irving Place where she would meet Mary regularly. The affair was brief and by October 1959 it was over for good. But, like her attempt to seduce Ellen two years before, it injected something sufficiently nasty into the mind of Highsmith the writer. While she was with Mary, Highsmith wrote *This Sweet Sickness* (1960) in which the scientist David Kelsey becomes infatuated with Annabella, who marries another man, Gerald. Thereafter David assumes a separate identity as William Neumeister, a freelance journalist, and buys a house in the country which he imagines will be his home with Annabella. David/Neumeister decides to murder Gerald and the rest of the novel is distilled into a Nietzschean blend of fantasy and hopelessness. At the close David/Neumeister imagines that he and Annabella will be able to sightsee in New York, shop together as partners and dine in fashionable restaurants. Highsmith is projecting the relationships she is having and has had into the world of incautious heterosexuality. David has to hide because he has committed murder but there is a clear implication that lesbianism and homosexuality involve a similar fate of concealment and fear of being pursued by the forces of orthodoxy.

Highsmith's affair with Marijane Meaker was significant; though brief, it marked a crossroads in her life. They met in spring 1959 before Highsmith had separated from Mary – adultery, disclosure and conflict was Highsmith's customary route towards the finishing of a relationship. Meaker was a successful writer, publishing under several pseudonyms. As M.E. Kerr and Ann Aldrich she produced fiction for children and young adults, and as Vin Packer she shifted from hardcore Mickey Spillane-style crime to novels that offered realistic accounts of lesbian life, mainly in New York. *Spring Fire* (1952) is regarded as a ground-breaking classic in this respect.

A bar in MacDougal Street in Greenwich Village called Eve's Hangout was one of the few that was run by a lesbian woman and remained independent of the Mafia. A notice at the entrance

announced that 'Men Are Admitted But Not Welcome'. Highsmith
frequented it regularly, mainly because among the clientele she had
become something of a legend. For most who bought and read
The Price of Salt its author remained a mysterious figure whose
career had begun and ended with this remarkable novel. Within the
lesbian clubs of New York, however, a particular face and name had
become the subject of gossip. Marijane later disclosed that when
Highsmith arrived in a bar and ordered a drink whispers would pass
through the room: 'Claire Morgan is here.' 'Starstruck', Marijane
introduced herself to Morgan/Highsmith and their affair began
within days. We should not assume that Highsmith was simply
transferring her affections from Mary Ronin – or indeed Doris,
whom she still sometimes visited – to her new, reverent partner.
A month before they met Highsmith recorded that her libido had
peaked, that she was having sex ten times a day with women she'd
met in bars and that 'it is surprising how the girls come' (*Cahier*,
15 February 1959). She was, as Marijane disclosed, something of
an underworld star.

It was a bizarre relationship. At first Highsmith was so transfixed
with Marijane that she postponed her trip to Europe, with whom
she would be accompanied by her mother, Mary, and for which she
had, astonishingly, persuaded Mary Ronin to join her once she left
Paris for the Mediterranean. Mary had agreed to fly to Italy and then
to meet up with her in the Greek islands. Eventually Highsmith
cancelled her visit to Greece and met up instead with Doris, in
Milan. We do not have the exact details of these arrangements,
but it seems fair to assume that before she left America Highsmith
must have persuaded Doris to fly to Italy. It is striking that even
someone as promiscuous as Highsmith would have planned two
consecutive holidays with two different women in neighbouring
regions of the Mediterranean and her plan came to nothing only
when Mary Ronin decided against joining her. Doris filled the
gap and was subjected to the full tour of locations and cities that

Highsmith had established as her ritual of sexual tourism almost a decade earlier.

To add a bizarre twist to the excursion, her mother Mary presented herself to the press in the lobby of their Paris hotel once Highsmith had gone south. But rather than speak on behalf of her now acclaimed crime-writing daughter she claimed to *be* her. Confused journalists checked their notes on Highsmith's background, notably her date of birth, but hid their perplexity as Mary, evidently a woman in her late fifties at least, pretended to be her daughter and offered gnomic observations on what had inspired her novels.

When she returned to America, Highsmith suggested to Marijane that they should move out of New York and to a place immune from the prejudices and secrecies of the city and its collateral urge towards promiscuity. They went to Pennsylvania, to a small farmhouse, a few miles from the bohemian community of New Hope. Bucks County, the region encompassing New Hope, had since the 1930s been a popular location for bohemian eccentrics of various types, notably Dorothy Parker and her husband Alan Campbell, as well as S. J. Perelman, George S. Kaufman, and to Highsmith's dismay, Arthur Koestler, who was still an occasional visitor when she arrived.

Although Meaker's memoir, *Highsmith: A Romance of the 1950s* (2003), did not appear until after Highsmith's death we have no reason to suspect that she offered a distorted or biased portrait of her partner. Not once did she speak of Highsmith with bitterness, either in the book or in interviews. She did, however, indicate puzzlement. At New Hope Highsmith seemed to have turned herself into an impoverished version of Jay Gatsby. She made a point of dressing formally for dinner, even when only the two of them were eating together, ironing her meticulously washed white shirts and trousers and cleaning her shoes so that they reflected sunshine. Meaker noticed also that Highsmith exhibited an alarming obsession with dangerous implements, mainly knives. She kept a penknife and switchblade in her jacket, which was curious given that there was nothing, human or animal, against which she would have needed to defend herself in the lanes of New Hope. The population was made up entirely of locals – generally polite, church-going farmers – and artists of various sorts who disliked the pressures of city life. Sometimes she also prowled around the house with a hammer in her hand, with no explanation or apparent inclination to use this instrument for its conventional purpose.

Marijane's sense of her partner as slightly odd is illuminated and clarified when we read Highsmith's notebook accounts of their time in New Hope. Evidently Marijane was unaware of the fact that for most of their days together, from breakfast to nightfall, Highsmith was drunk. She only learned of this later from a conversation with Highsmith's friend Polly Cameron, according to whom she named her drinks not according to their main alcoholic content – practically all were gin – but in terms of the activities and times of the day during which she took sustenance from them: 'Breakfast Drinks', 'Walking Drinks', 'Talking Drinks', 'Cooking Drinks', 'Dressing Drinks', 'Sleepless Night Drinks', 'Planting Drinks' and of course 'Writing Drinks'. Both women enjoyed alcohol but Marijane is astounded by how, in retrospect, she had remained ignorant of her partner's ability to conceal and minimise the effects of such an extraordinary quantity of gin.

What, we must wonder, would she have made of Highsmith's opinions on her and on their relationship which she confined largely to her journals? She described herself as being 'terrified of [Marijane's] temper', a comment that should be considered in the context of later accounts of Marijane's disposition and personal characteristics by those who knew her, who present her as, variously, reserved, considerate and amiable. But according to Highsmith, 'The morning was the worst. The worst of any verbal conflict to date. M.J. keeps me on the defensive, by wild attacks ... e.g. accusing me the night before of having whined, of having said that I have the worst of it...' (*Cahier*, 22 March 1961). Regularly she describes herself as the 'victim' of their exchanges, that 'her insults towards me have gone beyond bounds'. After six months of living together permanently Highsmith moved out and rented another house, in South Sugan Road, on the other side of the village. Thereafter, for several more months, they existed in a semi-detached relationship, communicating by telephone to discuss meals together which might sometimes lead to overnight stays. We should be aware that all of Highsmith's accounts of the state of things between them were entered in *cahiers* kept when she was in South Sugan Road and that each entry was a retrospective record of what had happened when they had spent virtually twenty-four hours a day together. Did she feel that she needed to guard herself against the exposure of her diaries and *cahiers* to her lover as had occurred, with disastrous consequences, with Ellen? In a different house it would be easier to hide them. This is possible but it is just as likely that Highsmith made use of their separation to enable inventive distortions to replace day-to-day documentary reports of what actually occurred. For example, we frequently come across passages in which the narrative of what took place is interspersed with dialogue. 'You're trying to defend yourself with what's left of your logical mind, because gin has got it. You can't make it with Marijane Meaker. I threw you out, Pat, because you're a common drunk'. This, allegedly, is what Marijane said to her shortly after she left for South Sugan Road, and Highsmith reports her own reply: 'I said, "Hang on to it [the house]. It's all you've got"' (*Cahier*, 22 March 1961). This is utterly at odds with Marijane's memoir where she states she knew only of Highsmith's heavy drinking long after they parted and in which she gives the overall impression of their relationship as sometimes difficult but certainly not beset with regular and vindictive quarrels led mostly by Marijane.

In the end it is impossible for us to decide finally on which of them we should believe, but the contexts of their reports should be given consideration. When Marijane wrote her memoir, she had no reason to assume that she was presenting an alternative to Highsmith's version, let alone defending herself against it. She knew nothing at all of the *cahier* of 1961. She was probably aware that the Highsmith estate had been deposited in the Bern archive five years earlier, but it was uncatalogued and neither she nor anyone else knew anything of the private notebooks and diaries. Highsmith's *cahier* on the two of them seems like the rough draft of a novel; this is significant because the novel that did evolve out of their brief, precarious relationship, *The Cry of the Owl* (1962), confirms that Highsmith treated the ruining of real lives as the principal stimulation for her particular brand of fiction.

Brigid Brophy famously wrote of the novel as one of two which created the subgenre of 'the psychology of the self-selected victim'. The other was Nabokov's *Lolita*. The plot of *The Cry of the Owl* is difficult, one might even say impossible, to summarise because it is made up of at least three overlapping versions of the same theme, all of which involve a stalker and a victim. It begins with Robert Forester, recently divorced, leaving New York for the village of Langley, Pennsylvania, which is an almost exact replica of New Hope. There he becomes obsessed with a neighbour, twenty-three-year-old Jenny Thierolf; roughly six years younger than him, the same age difference as between Highsmith and Marijane. Jenny, once she has met Robert, breaks off her engagement with Greg Wyncoop, who begins spying on the pair. Greg contacts Nickie, Robert's ex-wife, who encourages him to gather incriminating information as a means of punishing her ex-husband. Next, Jenny herself follows Robert, doubting his stories about his job and eventually coming to suspect that he has murdered her former fiancé, and she commits suicide.

In fact Robert had, following a fight, left Greg unconscious, but when a badly decomposed body is found close by the police become suspicious and when Nickie informs them that he once threatened her with a weapon, are convinced of his guilt. Eventually Robert is informed by Ralph, Nickie's new husband, that Greg is alive and has been working with Nickie to frame him for the killing. Robert then becomes the victim of a stalker, Greg, who spies on him at his home and takes shots at him with a handgun, eventually wounding him. Greg is arrested but released on bail and in a bizarre denouement he and Nickie go together to Robert's home where Greg tries to knife him but instead kills Nickie. The conclusion is open-ended, with both Greg and Robert still alive but the latter once more being the police's chief suspect. The predominant theme is that Robert – despite seeming a decent man – has in some way infected all others in the novel with a version of his temperamental peculiarities and condemned them to a fate similar to his.

The opening chapters are superbly disturbing. Once or twice a week Robert visits the garden of Jenny's house and, without speaking to her, appears as though he wishes to possess her: 'The girl had light-brown hair and was rather tall. That was about all he had been able to tell about her from a distance of sixty feet or so.'

Gradually, visit by visit, he moves closer, desperate to turn his distant impression into something almost intimate.

> She was about five feet seven, with largish bones, good-sized feet and hands, and she might have been anything from twenty to twenty-five. Her face was smooth and clear, she never seemed to frown, and her light-brown hair hung down to her shoulders and was softly waved … Her mouth was wide and thin and usually had an expression of childlike seriousness about it, like her grey eyes. Her eyes were rather small. To Robert she was all of a piece, like a properly made statue. If her eyes were too small, they went with the rest of her, and the overall effect he thought beautiful.

Moving from sixty feet to ten he seems to delight in the amount of detail he can secure regarding her posture, her bone structure, the colour of her eyes and so on, and the most disturbing phrase involves him envisioning her as a 'statue', an object of aesthetic wonder, something that he could make his own, rather than a human being.

She does eventually invite him in but is divided between fascination and fear. The mantra for the book is Robert's explanation to his therapist, 'I have the definite feeling if everybody in the world didn't keep watching to see what everybody else did, we'd all go berserk. Left on their own, people wouldn't know how to live.' In the novel, hardly anyone is left on their own – they are spied on by someone else – and most of them die.

The opening chapters, when Robert stalks Jenny, are eerily autobiographical. Highsmith, like Robert, would go back to the house she had shared with Marijane and, before knocking on the door, watch her from the garden or through the window in the kitchen. Just as significantly, she would reinvent their past in her own house on the other side of the village in her *cahiers*, not as the real Marijane but as someone she had invented. In just the same way, Robert was projecting his imagined sense of the actual Jenny onto his private fantasy world, based only on an image glimpsed through a window.

Highsmith did not leave New Hope until March 1962, though she had spent intermittent periods in New York during the previous year. While continuing with her occasional visits to Marijane on the other side of the village she began a relationship with Daisy Winston, who served in one local bar and sang in others, versions of Ella Logan and Marlene Dietrich being amongst her repertoire. Daisy was less than four feet six tall and suffered from nystagmus, which caused persistent involuntary eye movements. She did not have a history as a lesbian but seemed flattered by Highsmith's attention. Highsmith had become known as one of the sophisticated group of writers and artists who had come to the area from New York City. Peggy Lewis, part of the same set, later confessed to puzzlement at what Highsmith 'saw in' Daisy, a euphemistic reference to the fact that she was not particularly attractive and, more importantly, was working class and had no evident interest in the arts. Notably, when Highsmith visited the houses of the local intellectual gentry, such as Glenway Wescott and his brother, Lloyd, she was accompanied by figures such as Peggy Lewis and, when they were on speaking terms, Marijane. She never brought Daisy with her.

Their affair was, however, more than a fling. During the next decade Highsmith would make use of Daisy as a general assistant when dealing with the practicalities of her life – in 1970 flying her out to England so that she could clean a house that she was about to put on the market. This was a curious thing to do given that local house-cleaners would have been cheaper than a return air ticket across the Atlantic. Perhaps she had asked Daisy to do the job for other reasons. In 1965 she had flown her over to Paris to do menial secretarial work, where, as Highsmith knew, she would feel completely out of her depth. Highsmith seems to be reminding her one-time lover, at some expense, that while she felt that Europe was her entitled domain, Daisy belonged in New Hope.

We can never be certain of Highsmith's true feelings for Daisy, but the timing of their relatively brief encounter – Daisy's only known lesbian affair – is intriguing. By 1961 Highsmith had already decided that her intermittent flirtations with Europe would become a full-time commitment. She was planning to move permanently to the region she felt was her true home and destiny, at least in terms of its standing as the birthplace of Western civilisation and its literary offshoots. Daisy was, perhaps, her goodbye note to ordinary America, the one into which she had been born.

9

'SO MUCH IN LOVE'

When she took the flight to London in 1962 Highsmith was still revising a novel she had been working on for more than three years, *The Two Faces of January* (1964). Chester MacFarland, an alcoholic fraudster, is travelling with his young wife Colette in Greece, and wondering if his history of stock manipulation has been discovered by the US authorities. In Athens, a Greek policeman questions him in his hotel room and MacFarland accidentally kills his interrogator. Rydal Keener, a young American law graduate, slides into the plot and offers to help MacFarland and Colette by obtaining false passports for them and disposing of the policeman's body. Colette and Keener, close in age and mutually attracted, infuriate MacFarland, who tries to kill his rival by dropping an ancient stone container on his head but misses and kills his wife instead. When interviewed by the police MacFarland accuses Keener of killing Colette and then hires a hitman to kill him, not realising that Keener has already paid the same man to dispose of MacFarland. MacFarland purchases another fake passport and heads for Paris, hoping eventually to return to America in disguise, but Keener reappears and blackmails him. MacFarland panics, takes the train for Lyon and then Marseille and, after his eventual arrest, is shot dead while trying to escape.

Highsmith's editor, Joan Kahn, saw the first draft in 1961 and wrote to her new agent, Patricia Schartle, that while her client was still writing 'fine' books, this one 'escapes us'. She continued, 'we cannot like any of the characters, but more difficult, we cannot believe in them … it's all so far in a dream now it makes no sense … we cannot publish it as it stands' (Letter to Schartle, 21 February 1961). Highsmith rewrote it three times before Schartle could persuade Kahn to accept it, all during the period when she lived with Marijane, had an affair with Daisy and left America for Europe, but one should commend her agent's skills as an advocate for this piece of fiction because, even when Highsmith had repaired its worst faults, it went into print more as a disturbing reflection of its author's state of mind than as something even a fairly indulgent reader might appreciate.

Many of Highsmith's characters continually mutate into versions of themselves that at first seem unlikely and implausible, but in *The Two Faces of January* disguise and obfuscation are afflictions rather than literary strategies. As a professional conman MacFarland can be expected to take on a variety of personae but rather than turning himself into someone else as a matter of expediency, he becomes addicted to the arbitrary swapping of one name and personal history for another, just for the sake of it. The names and backgrounds of Howard Cheever, Louis Ferguson, Philip Jeffries Wedekind, William Chamberlain, Richard Donlevy and Oliver Donaldson all appear on his faked documents but MacFarland – if this is indeed his original surname – takes a particular interest in making up a fictional past not simply as a disguise but as if it had actually happened. Colette's original name is Elizabeth, but she changed it at the age of fourteen: how and why? Don't ask. Keener is from a solidly middle-class background, the son of an Ivy League academic, but he enjoys switching roles between the quasi-beatnik Joey, Enrico Perassi, an Italian with impeccable English, and the similarly bilingual Frenchman Pierre Winckel. Had the three of them had prior knowledge of their obsession with becoming other people then this might stand as some explanation for their unhealthy mutual attraction, but this is not even hinted at. Keener at

one point confesses that MacFarland reminds him of his father, but
it is left unclear as to whether he wishes to recreate, masochistically,
his unsatisfactory past or improve upon it through MacFarland's
inclination to be different people in different circumstances.

The book received a good review in the *New York Times* as 'an offbeat,
provocative and absorbing suspense novel' and the UK Crime
Writers' Association awarded it the prize for the best foreign crime
novel of the year, 1964. Julian Symons in the *Sunday Times* praised it
for showing 'a doom-laden world where human beings, all of them
emotionally lame, deficient or perverse, are destroyed not by events
but by each other'. During this period practitioners and advocates
of crime fiction were intent upon rescuing the genre from its status
as a niche of popular low culture, easy to read and easy to write,
feeding the appetites of the uneducated. Highsmith, particularly
with novels such as *The Two Faces of January*, suited their cause, in the
sense that she appeared willing to exchange the whodunnit formula
for something more akin to Dostoevsky's employment of acts
such as killing, vengeance and judicial retribution as philosophical
enigmas rather than forms of lurid entertainment.

But Highsmith confessed in her *cahier* that she had abandoned
any interest in its effect on the reader. The novel was a private,
introverted exercise, about 'the ultra-neurotic, which is myself',
and she dismissed the considerations that are generally thought to
inform the activity of writing: 'to hell with [the] reader ... or a
sympathetic character' (3 March 1961).

The parallels between what happens in the book and Highsmith's
life when she was writing and rewriting it are clear enough. Like its
triumvirate of characters she was an inveterate deceiver, becoming
for each of her lovers a convenient modification of the actual Patricia
Highsmith, if such a person could be found. Looking back on her
eighteen years of relationships we are reminded of MacFarland, a
person known uncomfortably to himself but for others perpetually
changeable. MacFarland's various identities always overlap, never

Barnard College
prom, early 1940s
when Highsmith
was a student

Still from Hitchcock's 1951 film adaptation of *Strangers on a Train*, with Farley
Granger as Guy and Robert Walker as Bruno

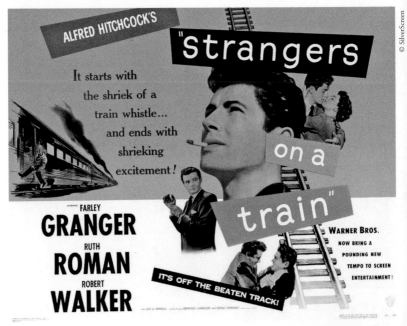

© SilverScreen

Film poster for
Strangers on a Train

© colaimages

Positano, Italy, in the
1950s – the setting for
The Talented Mr Ripley,
renamed as Mongibello
for the novel

Still from 1999 film adaptation of *The Talented Mr Ripley* with Gwyneth Paltrow as Marge Sherwood, Matt Damon as Ripley and Jude Law as Dickie Greenleaf

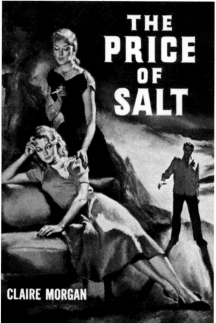

Cover for the first paperback edition of *The Price of Salt*

Still from the 2015 film adaptation of *Carol*, with Cate Blanchett as Carol and Mara Rooney as Therese Belivet

Present-day photograph of the house owned by Highsmith in Earl Soham in the 1960s, then known as Bridge Cottage

Highsmith's friend
Ronald Blythe

Highsmith seated next
to a fountain in New
York City, *circa* 1970

Highsmith with her cat at the
window of Bridge Cottage in
Earl Soham in the mid-1960s

Highsmith behind
a gate outside her
Montcourt house in
France, 1978

Highsmith at the front
door of her first house
in France, 1971

Highsmith on a train
from Locarno to
Zurich, 1987

Highsmith at her desk in her Aurigeno house, Switzerland, *circa* 1987

Posed portrait of Highsmith, 1979

quite allowing a clean break from one to another. Similarly, Highsmith never broke off with one of her partners before ensuring that she had begun a relationship with the next. Whether she wished pain on them or on herself will remain a mystery but in the book MacFarland seems confused by his incapacity to stop hurting people.

Just as striking are the novel's manic shifts in location, mainly between Greece, Italy and France. Highsmith was dividing up her personality and sending it on trips across the locations in Europe to which during the previous decade she had become addicted and, given what happened next, we should treat MacFarland as an alarming prophecy.

In March 1962 Highsmith advertised the New Hope house as a sublet; she was not as yet certain of whether she might need it again if Europe was a disappointment. She arrived in Paris via London in mid-May, stayed with acquaintances from her earlier visits and then flew to Rome where Ellen Hill was waiting for her at the airport. There is no record of which of them suggested this, but subsequent events make it clear that they had made plans for something more than a brief encounter. First, they took a train south and then boarded a ferry for Cagliari, Sardinia, staying for two weeks and then travelling back to the Italian mainland, to Naples, where they boarded a local train for Positano. The village, beautiful as ever and still unmolested by tourists, was for Highsmith a blend of Carroll's *Alice in Wonderland* and Dante's *Inferno*: both a fantasy and the horrid punishment for making the fantasy real. And so it was that she and Ellen spent most of their waking hours howling abuse at each other, claiming to find reasons for why one was to blame for their state of mutual distress. In early July they were still together, travelling first to Rome, then Venice and next back to Paris, where Highsmith visited Oscar Wilde's grave and recited parts of 'The Ballad of Reading Gaol'. Ellen was nauseated and left for Germany. It is worth noting that shortly before she left New Hope for Europe Highsmith entered in her *cahier* an account of how she had dreamed of cleaving open the head of a lover with an axe. The victim is someone she has loved and now hates and is ten years older than her (22 December 1961).

No one seems clear about where she met the woman without a name – given the pseudonym 'Caroline Besterman' by Schenkar and referred to by Wilson as 'X' – but she is certainly real, despite the fact that she will for the foreseeable future remain anonymous. Others involved with Highsmith testify to her existence and Highsmith's own travels, notebooks, and decisions on where to live during the next four years are determined largely by their relationship. Despite not knowing what she was called we have ample information on who she was and what she did. Apart from the second-hand circumstantial testimony Schenkar quotes directly from conversations with her, with her permission. Caroline (which is, I think, preferable to the Ian Fleming-style 'X') was, or perhaps still is, married to a wealthy businessman, and Highsmith likely met her in London shortly after Ellen had absented herself from their nightmarish tour of southern Europe. Caroline would be Highsmith's final excursion into high-society affection and sexuality, a routine which began with Virginia Kent Catherwood. She was (similarly to Ellen) at least twelve years older than Highsmith, had a child and was a member of the English upper classes, living with her husband in a restored Georgian house in Kensington. Subsequent correspondence and entries in Highsmith's notebooks indicate that while their first encounters in Europe were brief, they involved sex and had a long-term effect on both.

Highsmith returned to New Hope in September, as she had planned before setting out for Europe, but found herself unable even to attempt any work. The house had not been sublet, but she was now determined that it was part of her past and the two women exchanged letters daily, despite Highsmith's fear that Caroline's husband might see what they had written, which was unusual on her part. In the past she had gone out of her way to create shock and antipathy by various means: having brief affairs during her alleged commitments, making her presence known to the lovers, even the husbands of her partners, simply as a means of unsettling the emotional equilibrium of others.

Now, however, she seemed happy to defer to Caroline's suggestions. Caroline wrote to her saying that she had made preliminary arrangements to spend time away from the family home in late September and October. We do not know if she offered her husband some spurious explanation for her absence but she was concerned about his discovery of Highsmith's letters. He would eventually adopt a tolerant, liberal attitude towards the affair but the fact that the first few periods the women spent together were shrouded in subterfuge increased the sense of excitement for both of them.

They met in Paris and stayed together in a spacious suite in the luxurious Hotel Lutetia in the 6th arrondissement, an ornate fin de siècle building dating from 1910. It was a magnet for those who might have nothing more in common than their love for it. De Gaulle, when a young officer, spent his honeymoon there, on the recommendation of his army seniors. Gide, Joyce, Hemingway, Picasso and Matisse treated it as the place to drink, dine and stay when income allowed, and Highsmith recorded her feelings about their week there together after she returned to New Hope in November. Over the previous two decades her notebook entries on new lovers – particularly those who embodied her fantasies of immediate social advancement – were often grandiloquent, but her comments on her honeymoon with Caroline achieved new levels of hyperbole. She writes of how at one point in the street, the two of them felt it impossible to wait until reaching the hotel before embracing and kissing so fiercely that one of Highsmith's earrings was dislodged. It rolled down along the pavement but neither could be bothered to retrieve it and she describes what then occurred in the hotel as Caroline being 'smelted by Vulcan'. Vulcan being, of course, the Roman god of fire and metalworking. Caroline 'melts into my arms ... smelted by Vulcan expressly for that purpose.' 'I am', Highsmith adds, 'so much in love – obviously ... that I cannot see anything else ... I am nearly sick ... and must get hold of myself or crack up.' Unlike all of her previous accounts of the beginning of passionate affairs she does not date entries. All we know is that they were made during approximately ten days in New Hope following her return from Paris.

During December 1962 Highsmith decided on two projects, whose connection is so obvious as to hardly merit explanation. She continued to write to Caroline and made it clear that, at least in her opinion, in order to last their relationship had to involve something more than fragmented, often random transatlantic encounters. She did not go so far as to ask her to leave her husband and son, but she offered to move to Europe permanently so that even though their periods together might involve stealth and concealment the two of them would at least become a regular feature of each other's lives. Caroline agreed in principle, or at least offered no outright objection. Highsmith's base would, once more, be Positano, where she had regularly rented a villa for almost twelve years, and in this respect her affirmation that she would detach herself from her past should be questioned. Southern Italy was closer to London than the US East Coast but in the early 1960s, even with the burgeoning opportunities of air travel, 1,300 miles was still a long way. For Highsmith, Positano was not quite somewhere else, but rather the unspoiled village on the Mediterranean to which she had exported her American past, in life and in fiction – particularly in *The Talented Mr. Ripley*. She was getting out, but not quite leaving.

At precisely the time she made the decision to decamp to Europe Highsmith wrote to a New York-based criminal defence lawyer who was mentioned in John Bartlow Martin's *Break Down the Walls*

(1955). Martin was an outspoken campaigner for the reform of the criminal justice system of America which he saw as involving arbitrarily lengthy sentences handed out to those too poor to afford competent defence attorneys, ensuring that indigent whites were not too far behind African and Latin Americans as those likeliest to receive life imprisonment and the death penalty. Following advice from the lawyer she engineered a visit to Bucks County Jail in Doylestown near New Hope, and while she was not allowed to speak to convicts, she spent more than an hour viewing, from a distance, cell blocks and enclosed yards in which inmates were allowed limited opportunities for exercise and fresh air. Shortly afterwards she began work on *The Glass Cell*, involving Philip Carter, falsely accused and convicted of fraud and sentenced to ten years in prison. The novel is informed by her impressions of Bucks County Jail, Martin's book, which focuses on the 1952 Michigan State Prison riots, and most significantly letters she exchanged with a prison inmate, location unknown, who had begun writing to her via her publisher in 1961 and offering vivid and detailed coverage of the day-to-day life of imprisonment, notably solitary confinement. Less conspicuously it was also influenced by the three most tumultuous years of Highsmith's relationship with Caroline.

When she sailed for Europe in early February 1963, she had completed forty pages, mostly describing the soul-destroying boredom of Carter's life. During a month at 15 via Monte, her regular rental in Positano, the manuscript progressed gradually in length but the narrative was going nowhere. Highsmith later admitted to some relief at further progress being postponed by a telegram from London. Caroline asked Highsmith to telephone her and during the call explained that her husband had guessed of their affair since its inception, kept quiet about it but had during the previous few days spoken to her directly of it. He had not, to his credit, demanded details of the relationship and had made it clear that he entirely respected Caroline's decision regarding what would happen next. At no point did he make demands or suggest that, even if she continued to see Highsmith, the future of their marriage would be jeopardised, unless Caroline herself preferred a formal alteration in their circumstances. Even by the standards of the more laissez-faire members of the English gentry he seemed a paragon of tolerance, and there is no evidence that he had extra-marital affairs. Yet his forbearance created more problems than it solved, particularly for Highsmith.

Following the telephone conversation she took a train from Naples to Rome and from there flew to London. On the day she left she wrote that 'the prison book is in my head, but however to get it on paper?' When she arrived in London, she stayed in a hotel close to the Bestermans' home in the West End and immediately found herself part of an impeccably dignified, almost genteel, ménage à trois. The Bestermans accompanied each other to dinner parties, art galleries, book launches and other events that formed the routine of the cultivated upper classes of the city. Caroline's husband reassured her that so long as she did not make an exhibition of their affair – kissing Highsmith when they were with friends for example – he regarded her girlfriend as part of their world and imposed no restrictions on when, where and how long they spent in each other's company. Sometimes the three of them met for cocktails and supper in the Besterman house.

This went against Highsmith's predilection for subterfuge, deception and acrimony and as a distraction she asked her American agent to arrange promotional and media events. One took place in London's most famous bookshop, Foyles, in Charing Cross Road, displaying copies of *Strangers on a Train* – then better known in Britain as Hitchcock's film than as a book – and *The Talented Mr. Ripley*. She also promoted *The Cry of the Owl*, recently released in the UK. Francis Wyndham was a member of the London literary establishment. His maternal grandmother was a close friend of Oscar Wilde, his father a diplomat and scion of the aristocracy; educated at Oxford and a prize-winning novelist, Wyndham regularly contributed pieces to the country's most exalted weeklies and broadsheets. He knew that Highsmith was a newsworthy figure and interviewed her for the BBC Home Service, following this with a lengthy piece on her for England's most prestigious left-liberal weekly magazine, the *New Statesman*.

Within a few weeks Highsmith had made her presence felt in Britain as a writer, but this begs comparison with her other rather ambiguous role as a regular and welcome guest in the Besterman household who would often go for drinks or meals just with Caroline. In her notebooks she records feelings of melancholy and ennui that echo those of Carter in *The Glass Cell*. She only came up with the title for the novel after she'd completed it, and the notion of being both locked into something while seemingly able to free oneself from its restraints seems just as appropriate to her arrangement with the Bestermans.

Unable to continue further with the situation in London Highsmith persuaded Caroline to accompany her to Positano. Caroline's husband, in his customarily insouciant manner, expressed no objections and the two women went south through France and Italy by train. In Positano Highsmith fell ill with a stomach infection which lasted only a few days but within a week Besterman was expressing her regrets at leaving London and less than a month after their departure she returned to her family home.

Alone in the villa Highsmith wrote that she frequently thought of killing herself. Her only distraction was the 'prison book', largely untouched since she had gone to London. She continued with it but while she reached more than a hundred pages quite easily nothing new seemed to have happened to Carter. His day-to-day existence was pointless and undeservedly grim and, in many ways, so was his creator's.

Once more, in June, a telegram from Caroline arrived and following a telephone conversation Highsmith packed her bags and travelled by train for England. This time Caroline suggested that they spend time together outside London, in the Suffolk coastal village of Aldeburgh. The Aldeburgh Festival of Music and the Arts had been founded in 1948 by the composer Benjamin Britten and mainly involved operatic performances but also included a more eclectic range of classical concerts with music by Bach, Haydn, Mozart, Beethoven and others. There were, by 1963, poetry readings and short plays. It was the holiday season for cultivated, wealthy Londoners who hoped that the coast of East Anglia would allow them to enjoy fine wine and food, feel proud as the sponsors of high art and avoid the increasingly vulgar tourist-driven atmosphere of the capital in early summer.

Highsmith and Caroline were, during the Festival, reassured that the region had become a minor province of good taste whose residents, permanent and occasional, remained largely indifferent to what each other got up to. And based on this Highsmith made one of the most important decisions of her life. She returned to Positano and a week later arranged to rent an apartment in Rome, at 38 via dei Vecchiarelli, apparently because she could no longer tolerate the atmosphere of the Positano villa which she now saw as the talisman for the failure of her relationships. Ellen was living in Rome and though Highsmith might have considered making contact she chose instead to stay in the apartment or visited well-heated cafés and bars. Autumn was becoming colder than usual, even in the centre of Italy, and it seems likely that she chose the city as a physical and emotional staging post for a choice she had made but had not yet acted upon. She made contacts with letting agents whose details she had gathered when staying with Caroline in Suffolk, and in November 1963 became the tenant of a modestly attractive eighteenth-century house in King Street, Aldeburgh.

Three days before she moved in she received a letter from her editor at Harpers, Joan Kahn, on why they could not publish the novel in its present form. 'Carter before prison we know too little.

Carter after prison is certainly a man in a mess [which] ... probably existed before ... and not enough to make us care' (13 November 1963). Highsmith was suddenly alert to the similarities between the London arrangement and Kahn's presentation of Carter as a figure without a discernible past or future. When she met Caroline it seemed to be a moment of liberating transformation but soon, not least because of her husband's indulgence, trapped her in a louche social drama. Now, even if only at weekends, she could have Caroline to herself, and it was at this point that she began a radical rewrite of the second part of the novel after Carter is freed. Unfortunately he, like his author, treated release as a licence for irresponsibility.

Aside from the lively weeks of the Festival the region was growing more and more attractive for Londoners who wished for an affordable retreat from the capital. In 1963 the nearby Sizewell B atomic power station was still at an early stage of construction, causing property prices to fall but not, as yet, imposing its daunting ugliness on the landscape. Nuclear power was, despite itself, creating an affordable idyll for bohemians just a two-hour drive from the West End.

Caroline drove herself to the King Street house every weekend and at the end of April 1964 Highsmith seemed to think that their new arrangement, in which her lover had become a regular commuter, offered an indication of permanence. She bought a house in Earl Soham, a quaint village around twenty miles inland from the coast. Bridge Cottage was originally two seventeenth-century workers' cottages, now knocked together with garden space at the front and rear and a small stream in the back garden. Caroline loved the setting, continuing to visit at weekends but refusing to agree to anything more permanent. Highsmith felt she had given up her past for a perfunctory, irregular arrangement designed to suit Caroline's conventional family life and soon afterwards she began to exhibit aspects of her temperament that ranged from outlandishness to derangement.

ECCENTRICITY

Highsmith lived in Earl Soham for a little over three years before moving to France in 1967. By that time, her sexual relationship with Caroline was over for good, though the two of them would meet up intermittently over the subsequent three decades, replicating the peculiar arrangement she would continue to have with Ellen Hill. Both of her ex-lovers responded amicably to prompts and invitations from Highsmith, usually to find that they had involved themselves in her exercises in masochism. Highsmith was never entirely offensive to Ellen or Caroline, but she seemed to take some pleasure in offering them a glimpse into aspects of her abundantly strange condition perhaps to indicate the part they had played in its formation. But she did not reserve such displays of peculiarity for just the two of them.

From the beginning of their affair, Caroline and Highsmith seemed to exist in different universes. In the interviews that she did with Schenkar, Caroline comes across as wearily insouciant, resigned to never having understood her erstwhile lover. All she seems able to recall are her outward mannerisms and idiosyncrasies, her habits in company and her style of dress. Typically:

> [She was] very exotic, the kind of person to whom you would immediately be drawn in a room. And she was still very much in control of her look [in the 1970s], always well dressed, her hair was well cut ... Pat always had a certain style, *comme les*

garçons ... The first time I met her, she was in a yellow sailcloth skirt and tight top and she did rather look like a sailor, there was a dash to her ... She always liked to change her clothes and get nicely ready for supper. She always had beads and a bracelet, her things were well cut and elegant. (Interview with Schenkar, 6 Nov 2003)

Her account is made up almost exclusively of detail that might have been picked up from a secure distance, as if Highsmith was someone to whom she'd been briefly introduced and thereafter observed with interest from the other side of the room. She seems to have decided to preserve Highsmith as a sketch, leaving out any disclosure of what might be behind her taste in clothes and singular habits. She was, observes Caroline, 'awkward in company [and] handled cigarettes very badly – she looked as though she were mending roads with them, stubbing out her Gauloises ungracefully...' Privately, Caroline knew what lay beneath the surface but she had chosen to say nothing of it which, when we become better acquainted with Highsmith, is understandable. Compare Caroline's comments with Highsmith's entry in her *cahier* following her return to New Hope after their first passionate fling in London:

Beauty, perfection, completion – all achieved and seen. Death is the next territory, one step to the left. I don't want to see [her] anymore, to feel or experience anymore ... Pleasure has already killed me ... I am the drunken bee wandered into your household [where they had kissed]. You may with courage eject me through the window; or by accident step on me. Be assured, I'll feel no pain. (5 December 1962)

Evidently, she saw the relationship as disastrous before it had properly begun but she would, within a month, alter everything about her life for it. She would emigrate for the sake of an affair that she already equated with 'Death ... the next territory'. Five months later, while still captivated by Caroline and the prospect of a serious relationship, she wrote that 'I have imagined killing myself, strangely, more strongly now than with anyone else I have ever known' (Diary, 3 May 1963).

What occurred soon after this extraordinary entry was both its continuation and explanation. The privately maniacal Highsmith of the notebooks would soon be unmasked to those she knew.

In March 1964 Highsmith's mother sent her a twenty-nine-page letter laying out, in her opinion, her daughter's history and character: a compulsive perennial liar, a sadist (her malice directed only in part towards Mary and Stanley), immune from the emotional pain she caused for others, and, worst of all, a sexual pervert. Mary, as a person of liberal disposition, was tolerant of gays and lesbians but she accused her daughter of marshalling her sexual inclinations as a weapon for unhappiness. For Highsmith it felt as though her curious love–hate relationship with her mother had returned with a vengeance and a week later this sense of the past as her nemesis turned into an exercise in black comedy. Mary would follow her vituperative letter by visiting her daughter in person.

Via her various contacts in the London literary establishment Highsmith had sometimes been invited to book launches and to cocktail parties and dinners hosted by figures in publishing. Charles Latimer, for example, was head of sales at Heinemann, had a cottage near Earl Soham and often played host to Highsmith in his mews house in the West End. Barbara Ker-Seymer – a well-connected society figure and arts photographer since the 1930s – regularly provided her with a spare bedroom in the chic Regency house in Islington she shared with her partner, Barbara Roett. Ker-Seymer later disclosed to Schenkar that knowing Highsmith was like walking from 'grass to glass'. She would at first seem a benign, harmlessly enigmatic figure, but once upset by a statement or suggestion would become especially malicious. 'Quarrelling with Pat ... would be like quarrelling with a dog with rabies. You could get bitten.' Latimer recalls enjoying her company while being perplexed by her sudden shifts between helpless anxiety regarding her love life and reputation as a writer and her taste for loutish humour. One day she brought to his office a week-old edition of *Le Monde* which contained a typographical error that had escaped the attention of the French copyeditors. 'Look at this!' she announced. 'Graham Greene has written my biography, *Travels with My Cunt*.' Latimer too found this amusing but was dismayed by Highsmith's insistence on referring to it every time they met for the subsequent few months.

Highsmith was once doing a radio interview at BBC Broadcasting House while staying in London at the Kensington home of a friend of Ker-Seymer's, to whom Schenkar awards the pseudonym of Camilla Butterfield. When Highsmith was at the interview Butterfield took a phone call for her from a woman who did not introduce herself but who sounded as though she was auditioning for *Gone with the Wind*. Butterfield had heard from Highsmith unflattering stories about her mother and guessed the identity of the caller while remaining puzzled by how Mary knew where her daughter was staying, let alone how she had obtained the number. When Highsmith returned from Broadcasting House Butterfield tried to lighten the situation. 'Brace yourself,' she said. 'The deep south has arrived.' According to Butterfield, 'Pat fainted right on the doorstep ... It was incredible and it was more than a faint. Her legs just gave way. She just crumpled into a heap on top of herself, like a doll...' (Butterfield to Schenkar, 17 December 2003). Mary had flown in from New York without warning and taken a taxi to the Cavendish Hotel, which Highsmith had referred to often in her letters. It had achieved minor fame for its mention in Wilde's *The Importance of Being Earnest* but was, in 1964, as Mary's taxi driver informed her on their arrival, a bombsite. Seemingly, Highsmith had provoked her mother with reports on her affection for a hotel enjoyed by another celebrated homosexual writer, without mentioning that it no longer existed.

The Butterfields had arranged to go to the theatre and Highsmith asked them if they would allow her to use their house as an interim stay-over before she drove her mother to Earl Soham. They agreed to do so but when they arrived back it seemed as if their living quarters had been visited by well-mannered vandals. Pieces of furniture were upside down or at bizarre angles to each other, sandwiches – origin unclear – had been bitten into but left uneaten at various places around the room, some glasses contained mixtures of alcohol of various types from the Butterfield cabinet, others were standing next to them, empty, ashtrays contained liquids and fragmented foodstuffs while cigarette ends floated in what was left of the brown liquids of coffee cups. It was, recalled Camilla, the apparent site of a mild skirmish but with no object broken or moderately damaged. She told Schenkar that before she left Highsmith and her mother in their sitting room 'the air quivered' and that once in the taxi her husband had commented that 'you look like you've been through an earthquake.'

Highsmith drove her mother to Earl Soham but closed her house to incomers for the subsequent week. She telephoned her general practitioner, Dr Auld, stating that both she and her mother required sedation, given that Mary had threatened to strangle her with a coat hanger, and that she was contemplating murder as a defence. Others who knew her in the area recalled that her strangeness went much further than her tense relationship with Mary. Highsmith wrote to her cousin Dan that her mother had gone mad, and that she had gathered together all of her ongoing writings and locked them in a wardrobe, certain that Mary was intent on burning them.

Highsmith's eccentric habits were not limited to the human world. Her fascination with snails dated back to the mid-1940s when she had spent an hour watching two try to mate. She read copiously on their lifestyle and breeding habits and in England attempted to recreate a snail colony in her back garden. Peter Thomson, an artist she'd met in the late 1950s, visited her in Suffolk and was horrified to find that not only did she breed snails outside the house but she also kept around a hundred in her handbag, permanently. He assumed that she had decided to protect a selection of them from the potential ravages of the East Anglian climate, at least until he met with her again at a dinner party in central London. Highsmith, according to Thomson, 'walked in with this [same] gigantic handbag, which she then opened with pride and which contained a hundred snails and an enormous head of lettuce'. She announced that 'they were [my] companions for the evening'.

Three years later when she was moving from England to France she proudly confided in her Doubleday editor, Larry Ashmead, that she had carefully selected a number of her most prized slimy pets and secreted them beneath her bra in the hope that they would breed and provide her with as copious a flock as in Earl Soham, though she also confessed that the French habit of eating them seemed to her to border on cannibalism. In 1966 the short story 'The Snail Watcher' was published in *Nova* magazine, whose protagonist Peter Knoppert has an obsession with gastropods – he fills his apartment with them from floor to ceiling – which results in them destroying him. They gradually block his means of contacting the outside world and staying alive, swamping his eyes, throat, nose and ears. A year later she wrote 'The Quest for Blank Claveringi', involving Professor Clavering of the University of California, whose quest for the legendary giant snails of a remote Pacific island ends with him meeting a fate similar to Knoppert's.

Her snail fixation was both a private idiosyncrasy and a public embarrassment, which she turned into grotesqueries reminiscent of Poe, but the autobiographical element of the stories is even more disturbing than that. Knoppert and Clavering at first treat snails as a zoological interest, respectively an eccentric hobby and an academic specialism, but other factors intrude on scientific impartiality. Feelings that we would usually associate with human-to-human interactions – affection, eroticism, voyeurism, even love – begin to cause their attachment to snails to become something like a clandestine love affair. Each man senses that they are indulging a perversion and are addicted to it all the more for that. Knoppert, like Highsmith, begins to treat snails as creatures with private, even sensual existences when he witnesses two of them having sex. When the eggs hatch, 'Mr Knoppert was as happy as the father of a new child.' On his first encounter with a giant snail, Clavering exclaims, '"You are magnificent" … in a soft awestruck voice'. Unlike its tiny counterparts the fifteen-foot snail makes Clavering feel slightly inferior, to his evident delight. 'It was pleasant to think he could skip nimbly about, comparatively speaking, observing the snail from all angles.' But he finds that the enormous creature can outrun him. It gnaws at him with its 20,000 teeth and the story closes with him facing a choice between drowning himself and being ripped apart.

Both pieces echo Highsmith's notebook entries on her first year with Caroline. The fact that the two of them, like Knoppert, Clavering and their snails, are entering a relationship that much of the rest of the world would treat as unacceptable increases Highsmith's love for the Englishwoman almost immeasurably. There is little doubt that Caroline meant more to her than any of her other lovers, at least if we accept her notebook entries as authentic. Yet the depth of her attraction to this woman whom she knew would be only occasionally available to her caused her, even in the first weeks, to treat love as the equivalent of suicide, or at least the weary acceptance of annihilation. The short stories on the snails were Highsmith's exploration of the nature of lesbianism and same-sex love. It was a secret experience – passionate, confidential, and seen from the outside in the same way that 'normal' people would judge others who formed a seemingly special feeling for snails. Similarly, in her novels, she projected her grotesque character defects, especially involving those to whom she declared love, into stories of murder. None of her killers acts out of malice or vengeance, let alone greed, but each shares a sense of being unable to explain why they have behaved as they have. And so did Highsmith. She invented terrible inexplicable acts in her fiction as a means of displacing – avoiding – a private world that was becoming ever more bizarre with each passing year.

One of her closest friends in Earl Soham was Ronald Blythe, roughly her age but in other respects a figure who might have felt more at home in England at the turn of the nineteenth century or in a novel by Barbara Pym. He loved churches, vernacular rural architecture and an idyll of the English countryside unpolluted by motor cars. His most famous book, *Akenfield: Portrait of an English Village* (1969), came out shortly after Highsmith left the region but he had been working on it since the mid-1960s and spoke to her of what it meant to him. It is based on interviews he conducted with local residents who told him of stories passed on to them by their relatives and ancestors. It is a partly fictionalised study of Aldeburgh going back over two centuries, based on legend, myth and recollections preserved in the local community.

Aside from both being writers, Highsmith and Blythe had absolutely nothing in common. He was a lay reader for the Church of England and eventually lay canon at St Edmundsbury Cathedral in Bury St Edmunds. He never once dated a woman and was effectively an unordained, largely celibate clergyman in the Anglican High Church, drinking only small amounts of ale in the local pubs and dry sherry with friends. During this same period Highsmith was partaking of her private stock of gin from breakfast onwards. Nonetheless, they met regularly for afternoon tea. Disclaiming the use of cars, he always cycled to her house, often with biscuits and cakes. One night, when he stayed for supper, he noticed that the glass bowl of the light fitting above the dining table was filling with water from a leak through the ceiling. Highsmith told him to ignore it, but he took it upon himself to go upstairs to free up the jammed ballcock in the lavatory. Following his return, she treated him with a mixture of contempt and disdain, seemingly because he had disobeyed her instructions but just as likely, as he later reflected, because when drunk, which she was, she became infuriated by good sense in others. Blythe's account to Wilson of their more intimate associations shifts between innocence and incomprehension. 'We weren't lovers,' he declares, 'but we did sleep together once or twice.' By them not being 'lovers' we can assume he means that they did not have a lasting relationship, but they did have sex. 'Sex with her was like being made love to by a boy. Her hands were very masculine and she was very hipless like an adolescent boy. She wasn't at all repelled by the male body, she was intrigued by it' (Wilson, p. 255).

She had seduced a (possibly gay) man who preferred quiet celibacy and whose world was made up of English rural idylls and quaint religiosity. As fiction, the story would have come across as improbable yet strangely alluring: Blythe was another human version of her snails.

On one of the few occasions that Caroline went out with Highsmith to a social event in Earl Soham it was clear to her that her lover had alienated herself from the conventions of social discourse. They had been invited to a local hotel, to a drinks party attended by local bohemians who for financial and other reasons had decided to decamp from London. Caroline recalled that Highsmith 'was given so much leeway – and had it been anyone else she would have been thrown out the door. It wasn't sympathy, exactly, it was some sort of feeling that she must somehow have got something wrong with her. But no, you couldn't do anything…' (Interview with Schenkar, 6 November 2003). Again, Caroline seems more to be commenting on someone beyond her reach than describing her ex-lover. In the hotel Highsmith had decided to sit alone in the hall and the owner of the premises was approached by a member of the party, a psychiatrist who, after studying Highsmith for a few moments, advised the landlady that 'You do know you have a psychopath in the hall.' Caroline adds that 'I remember Pat sitting there with a hard, baffled look on her face. She was lost; these people were all very sure of themselves. A heavy, a really heavy look, full of hatred.'

The journalist Bettina Berch interviewed Highsmith almost twenty years later and observed that by the early 1980s her sense of detachment from the rest of the world had become even more pronounced. She was against feminism not because she objected to it on ideological or even personal grounds. She regarded it simply as something inexplicable from which she was happy to be alienated: 'it was symptomatic of the fact that she lived in her own self-created world'. She adds that 'I remember spending about an hour with her trying to explain how to use an ATM card.' Highsmith didn't have one but felt she needed to include some reference to them in a novel to be set in the present day, when most people used them routinely. 'I think the last time she had really been in the world was probably back in the fifties' (Interview between Wilson and Berch, 19 May 1999). Berch corrected herself, adding that she had caused time to stand still. She 'would talk about [Ripley] like he was a person who was very close to her ... He was very real to her.'

It is clear enough from Caroline Besterman's accounts of Highsmith towards the end of their relationship that, for her at least, the woman she thought she'd fallen in love with during their first encounters in London and Paris didn't really exist. Highsmith had briefly allowed herself out of what Berch refers to as her 'own self-created world' but when some friction between this and the life led by others, Caroline included, became apparent she would retreat again into a universe of her own. This explained the figure in the hall of the hotel, 'lost ... a hard, baffled look on her face...'

This brings us to one of the most significant novels of Highsmith's career. It received mixed reviews and subsequent commentators have classed it politely as yet another of her non-Ripley curiosities. *A Suspension of Mercy* (1965) was written during her years at Earl Soham and is probably the most openly confessional of her works.

The main character is Sydney Bartleby, an American novelist living in rural Suffolk, struggling to repair the damaged relationship with his English wife Alicia, working to complete his seemingly hopeless novel and collaborating with his writing partner, the Englishman Alex, to sell a crime serial to a recently established British commercial TV network. Sydney is Highsmith, Alicia is Caroline and Alex is Richard Ingham, a school teacher and aspiring writer who lived nearby. Highsmith felt more comfortable with Ingham than with the London expatriates from whom she'd fled to the hall of the hotel. When they met, he had published nothing; she was effectively his mentor. They worked together on a screenplay for a television thriller called *It's a Deal*, which would be rejected by the BBC and ITV. I will not trouble you with the plot of this, except to say that it is a close replica of what happens in the novel and, as we shall see, the novel is a thinly disguised version of key aspects of Highsmith's life during and shortly before the period in which she wrote it. While Ingham was fully aware of the problems the two of them struggled with day by day as they rewrote drafts of *It's a Deal* in an attempt to make the show credible and saleable, he did not know that he featured in another project, Highsmith's novel, which also incorporated aspects of her life with which she felt dissatisfied and which she thought she might improve by rewriting it.

In the novel Alicia suggests that their marriage might benefit from a trial separation. Sydney agrees and after she leaves, he attempts to turn his marital problems into a means of energising his directionless novel. As an abandoned husband he puts himself into the mind of a fictional character who wishes to dispose of his wife, imagining each scenario precisely: the morning after Alicia leaves, he carries rolled-up carpet out to his car, wondering if his neighbours will connect this curious spectacle with the unexplained absence of Alicia. They do and he becomes a suspect, her potential murderer. All the time Alicia has been living with her extra-marital lover, Edward Tilbury, in Brighton. As with most of Highsmith's novels the ensuing narrative twists are arbitrary and often far-fetched, but to simplify things: Tilbury dies, at the hand of Sydney, and Alicia seems to have killed herself by leaping from a cliff. Sydney is cleared of involvement in Tilbury and Alicia's deaths, but at the close he considers recording what actually occurred in a private notebook: 'the notebook was, after all, the safest place in which to write it' – just as his author might have put it in her *cahier* or diary.

Sydney's notebook is all that allows him to disentangle the life he lives from the one he invents and during the period she wrote the novel, so it was for Highsmith. From the beginning of her time with Caroline she recorded in her notebook that it was a suicidal enterprise, while keeping alive the fantasy of something different, glorious and lasting for Caroline herself. Multi-layered novels within novels have become something of a commonplace, particularly following the rise of modernism, but there is none quite like this. It is a confession and a retreat from the truth, a self-referential literary artefact and an admission that invention will always override fact, a love affair with the opportunities of fantasy and a contrite expression of loathing for escapism. It reflects Highsmith's mental condition far more astutely than anything else she wrote and most of all it is a tortuous re-enactment in literature of her affair with Caroline.

For her, the thing that made the relationship so electrifying also destroyed it. From the moment they met they would become more and more like figures in the multi-layered novel that would commemorate their time together. Like Sydney, Highsmith shifted between states of disclosure and subterfuge, her private world with Caroline and the one the two of them shared with figures they encountered on the street, at parties, in hotels and restaurants. Caroline's husband witnessed this, but he too was their partner in their drama of private sensations, hints and concealment. He indulged their secret affair but despite his liberalism connived in it as something that should be kept from others. In Earl Soham Highsmith's friends and neighbours, including Blythe and Ingham, witnessed Caroline's arrivals and departures, but never knew for certain what the 'friendship' between the two women actually involved.

When Sydney moves the carpet to his car only he knows that the roll is empty. But his neighbour Mrs Lilybanks allows herself to speculate on what might be inside, given that she has taken note of Alicia's recent absence. Throughout the book characters protect their private worlds by inventing others and seem obsessed with spinning truth into a web of deception, and eventually their masquerade collapses tragically. Sydney is cleared of any criminal offences, but we leave him at the close of the novel as a character hollowed out, having lost all he thought he loved and all he hoped to become.

11

FRANCE

Highsmith and Caroline separated for good in October 1966, though which of them instigated the break-up is unclear. All we know, from third-party accounts, is that following one of their routine arguments they spent the night in separate bedrooms in the Earl Soham house. Caroline left very early next morning, never to return.

During the previous year their time together was made up of a catalogue of disasters. In May 1965 Highsmith suggested that as a means of reigniting what had first drawn them to one another they should take a long holiday in various parts of continental Europe. Given the proposed destinations and their previous resonances, and Highsmith's profession, this was the equivalent of the murderer revisiting the scenes of the crime.

Their first stop was Paris where things had begun for them three years earlier, but the city had also been the source of distress for Caroline in March, seven weeks before they were due to arrive. Highsmith had flown there for a long weekend with her ex-lover Daisy Winston, one-time Midwestern waitress and bar-room singer, who had never previously left the United States. Highsmith paid for her flight across the Atlantic and cautiously allowed details of the excursion to reach Caroline, stating on her return that 'she had no emotional involvement' with Daisy while offering no other motive for seeing her. As Caroline knew, Daisy had no interest in literature or the arts and it would have seemed as though Highsmith had planned the assignation as an act of arbitrary provocation.

Nonetheless their May holiday went ahead and after a few days in Paris they took the train through eastern France and Provence to Italy and a room in a comfortable though not grand hotel in Venice on the same street as La Calcina, Ruskin's home during the 1870s. We have no record of whether their relationship was improved by their time in the city. All we know is that Highsmith explained to Caroline that she had contacted Peggy Guggenheim, her 'old friend', to arrange a meeting with drinks but had been 'snubbed' by the society matriarch. Previously Highsmith had, as with others, impressed Caroline with stories of her legendary past, Guggenheim included, but whether she had indeed snubbed the author or failed to respond to a message from someone she did not know remains open to question.

What happened next certainly involved real visitors from the past. The subsequent part of their trip was supposed to involve a visit to Positano, to which Highsmith had introduced Caroline briefly in 1963. Before they left England, Caroline knew that this coastal village, Highsmith's creative and emotional Bethlehem, would feature prominently in their itinerary. She held her peace on how well, or otherwise, their time there might affect their relationship, at least until shortly before their departure from Venice, when Highsmith disclosed to her that a third person would be staying in their villa: Ellen Blumenthal Hill. Highsmith had in the past informed her of her affair with Ellen but this sudden announcement, without explanation, seemed to Caroline further evidence that her partner was by parts sadistic and mentally unstable.

Caroline packed her bags and returned to London. Highsmith went to Rome where she stayed with Ellen for a week and then travelled south to Positano alone, for no other reason than she felt it proper to pay a brief tribute to the site of her numerous catastrophes, and the birthplace of Tom Ripley. He too would soon return to her life.

That Caroline put up with her for a further eighteen months testifies to something commendable. It might be tolerance, or possibly pity for a woman she thought she loved but who had become a dreadful inversion of their first encounter.

At a dinner party in London hosted and attended by writers, artists and wealthy cultural philanthropists, Caroline watched as her lover embarrassed and mortified everyone present. As she fell forward over the candles on the table her long dark hair caught fire and there followed a quintessentially English spectacle of charity and good manners. Guests closest to her did their best to prevent her from going up in flames while the rest behaved as though nothing had happened, reserving their observations for later. Highsmith was outrageously drunk. At another prestigious event, also attended by Caroline, Highsmith opened her handbag and released onto the table around thirty of her beloved snails, which left silky stains across the expensive linen tablecloth as they crept away. Fellow diners pretended not to notice while Caroline was confirmed in her suspicion that her lover was unusual, to say the least. While Caroline belonged in the same privileged circle as the other guests she could not, like them, regard Highsmith as an acceptable eccentric because she had privately experienced her less amusing, often brutal, inclinations.

Highsmith wrote *Plotting and Writing Suspense Fiction* in little more than six months and it appeared in 1966. It falls into the category of a 'how to' book, whose sales are boosted by the reputation of an author with a proven record of success in the field. For an aspiring crime writer, it offers little more than could be gleaned from reading the more impressive novels of the genre, but more perversely it can be read as a classic case of the criminal covering her tracks and creating what amounts to a convincing alibi. It is autobiographical in that she refers to how she came up with ideas for her more celebrated novels and in every instance she tells blatant lies.

She claims that all elements of her fiction, from characterisation through overarching themes to the storyline, are formed from an alchemical imaginative source, entirely unpolluted by external factors, particularly her experiences in the real world. For example, she affirms that actual relationships or our perception of social interactions based on watching people or listening to their conversation should be excluded from the creative process. 'The plane of social intercourse ... is not the plane of creation, not the plane in which creative ideas fly...' The wannabe crime novelist might begin to wonder that if observation of the actual world is an unsuitable source for good fiction writing, then where might inspiration be found? Compared with Highsmith, adherents of Wordsworthian visionary purism sound like reactionaries. Her model of literary creativity sounds ludicrous because she does not believe it. She continues: '[S]ometimes the very people we are attracted to act as effectively as the rubber insulators to the spark of inspiration.' As we have seen the people to whom she was attracted or with whom she claimed to have fallen in love were the only inspiration for much of her fiction. Why cover this up? Perhaps because she felt uneasy about transforming the pain that was an inevitable outcome of her relationships into suspense stories. Who would admit that their success as a crime writer was based on their career as an emotional vandal?

The timing of this hastily prepared note of denial is significant. It followed A Suspension of Mercy, her most autobiographical novel, in which she comes close to confessing to the destruction of her life with Caroline, and shortly after she completed it she began Those Who Walk Away (1967). In fact, she put together a synopsis of the plot and some drafts of dialogue and narrative during her eleven-day stay in Venice with Caroline.

The two principal characters are Ray Garrett, whose wife, Peggy, has committed suicide a few days before the story begins, and Ed

Coleman, Ray's father-in-law, who is convinced that Ray has murdered his daughter and spends much of the novel seeking vengeance in several attempts to kill him. The plot is meandering and inconclusive in that the two men are involved in a struggle over the true cause of Peggy's death and which of them bears most responsibility for it: Ray did not actually kill her but feels responsible for causing her suicide while Ed sets aside circumstantial evidence to bring himself some kind of venomous satisfaction in not allowing Ray to survive while his daughter is lost. Some reviewers treated it as an Iris Murdoch-style novel of ideas where murder does not create a prurient thrill for the reader but rather induces philosophical reflections on existence and morality. In truth, it was another example of Highsmith spinning out her private sense of guilt and bitterness into a genre that perfectly accommodated it, in which people were caught in a seemingly perpetual web of fear and avoidance: once more crime fiction was her self-administered talking cure. Ray and Ed chase each other across Europe. Neither is certain of whether one or the other is responsible for the destruction of the person they both loved and the only certainty is that what they have lost can never be returned to them. Their pursuit of each other takes them through each of the locations visited by Highsmith and Caroline during the trip through Europe that effectively ended their relationship.

It is not a coincidence that Ray's wife shares her first name with the woman who had possibly snubbed Highsmith in Venice when she hoped to impress Caroline with her cultural associations. Peggy Garrett and Peggy Guggenheim seem to inflict a fair degree of pain through their absences. Just as intriguing is Ray's rather guilty but uncontrollable obsession with Inez in Venice, a waitress of simple and unpretentious character. Hello again Daisy Winston, who at Highsmith's instigation had almost ruined her relationship with Caroline shortly before it reached its eventual cessation.

It is a book by parts dreadful and compelling. If we did not know of its autobiographical links it would forever be a novel that is infuriatingly directionless. But because we do it becomes a blend of a flawed artwork and a cry for help. The prose is pretentious, with Ray and Ed regularly citing passages from Plato and Proust and speculating on what caused the likes of Bosch and Cézanne to paint as they did. It is as though Highsmith is apologising to Caroline for her grandstanding public philistinism, her embarrassing behaviour at numerous events and dinners, and offering her the woman she once thought she knew, who would talk easily about books and with whom she would spend afternoons in art galleries. In 1968 she entered in her *cahier* that 'It is obvious that my falling in love is not love, but a necessity of having to attach myself to someone… Perhaps a great source of shipwreck in the past has been to expect a physical relationship (7 August 1968). Madeleine Harmsworth, with whom she later had a relationship, who knew nothing of her private notebooks, offered a shrewd echo of the *cahier* entry based on her time with Highsmith. 'She was an extremely unbalanced person, extremely hostile and misanthropic and totally incapable of any kind of relationship, not just intimate ones. I felt sorry for her, because it wasn't her fault. There was something in her early days or whatever that made her incapable. She drove everybody away…' (Interview with Wilson, 12 August, 2000).

The end of Caroline meant also the end of England and in December 1966 Highsmith took the first of her trips to the areas around Paris to look at properties. She began a proper search in January, sharing a car with Elizabeth Lyne, who had retired from designing for Hattie Carnegie and was now renting an apartment in Paris's fashionable 6th arrondissement. It was not a random encounter. In early summer 1966, before her disastrous travels with Caroline, she had made contact with Elizabeth and the two of them had taken a short holiday in Tunisia. They had also met before that and Highsmith's reintroduction to her old acquaintance is curious given that their most memorable evening in New York involved her making a pass at the older woman and Elizabeth treating her with amused disdain.

Highsmith had visited North Africa before her various excursions through Europe, mostly Morocco, but the visit to Tunisia was a puzzling choice for both women, especially since Elizabeth, a resident of Paris, was under no illusions about the state of the country since it had gained independence from France ten years before, in 1956. It was a corrupt dictatorship with police turning a blind eye to one of the major tourist industries of the capital: young Arab men and boys selling themselves to or being pimped out to men from Europe and America. This had gone on for some time when the country was a colony of France and had now become a vile extension of colonialism in the tourist industry. Mexico had provided Highsmith with a glimpse into the contrast between Americas, North and South, which emphasised how the United States had sanitised its own past as an imperial outpost, but Tunis involved something far more grotesque, as if the colonised had extended their range of oppressors far beyond France. For some reason, it had become the accepted custom for young men to defecate in the women's lavatories in restaurants used by Westerners and make a point of not flushing the toilets. Perhaps a bizarre variation on the Islamic notion of women as not being allowed independence, even when they went to the loo? Who knows? Their luggage was burgled, they were blatantly overcharged for their rooms and meals and even when they sought refuge in a villa beyond the hotel their complaints about the faulty plumbing and electricity were treated with indifference by the owners. For Highsmith, the most unsettling spectacle was of impoverished boys as young as twelve, along with their mature counterparts, displaying themselves on the streets and offering themselves for sex with visiting Western men. The underground culture of lesbianism, particularly in New York, had been necessarily discreet and because of that it provided for its members a kind of clubbable hospitality. Now she encountered the opposite of what gay exclusion could involve: sex for money and mutual contempt. The experience of Tunisia would provide her with material for *The Tremor of Forgery* (1969) which she would write in her new French home.

Elizabeth had given Highsmith a guided tour of the wooded countryside surrounding Paris, France's version of the English home counties, introducing her to villages that seemed unchanged for centuries despite their proximity to the capital. They took notes and in March Elizabeth sent her details of a charming 200-year-old two-bedroom furnished property to rent on the walled estate in Bois Fontaine. She moved in in June but stayed only three months. The antique appeal of the cottage belied the discomfort of no central heating, draughty chimneys, broken electrical fittings and a lavatory that flushed directly into a shallow septic tank.

Highsmith had recently received $29,000 from Columbia Pictures for the film rights to *Those Who Walk Away* and used around half of this to co-purchase 20 rue de Courbuisson, in Samois-sur-Seine with Elizabeth. It was a converted farmhouse only a few minutes' walk from the river, where an artificial sandy beach, constructed by the commune, served local bathers. The building was an improvement on her rented house. Samois-sur-Seine was the town to which the jazz musician Django Reinhardt retired in the early fifties. Earlier it had been a magnet for impressionist painters such as Signac and Guillaumin and its only other claim to fame was its mention in Anne Desclos's notorious sadistic-pornographic novel *Histoire d'O* (*Story of O*, 1954), as the site of the fictional mansion run by Anne-Marie, a lesbian dominatrix.

Elizabeth kept her Paris apartment but shared the Samois house with Highsmith for periods of up to five days. The question of why the two women decided to almost cohabit will remain unanswered.

It is implied from those who knew Elizabeth that she was attracted to the notion of a second home in the countryside, within commuting distance of the capital. Yet each of them was aware of their incompatibilities well before they bought the house. Elizabeth had conditioned herself to a regime of order and regularity; she enjoyed food and drink but neither to excess. A lifestyle that was determinedly erratic and slovenly was Highsmith's preference: unwashed glasses, cups and plates juxtaposed with disordered items of clothing. The contrast was hardly noticeable, often the cause of amusement, when they had taken holidays but in Samois it created problems. Their respective bedrooms – the house had two, generously sized – allowed them a degree of autonomy but they shared, day by day, the sitting room, the kitchen/dining room and crucially the bathroom.

Highsmith wrote to her friend Alex Szogyi (undated; in the Bern archive), reporting that Elizabeth accused her that 'the state of your room indicate[s] a disorderly mind!' She was, allegedly, 'juvenile, self-centred, selfish, not mindful enough of work other people do for me, and in the last five years I have had a temper on occasion, especially when "Baited".' Elizabeth's longest period away was during her visit to New York in late summer 1967. In her absence Highsmith invited her ex-lover Rosalind Constable to Samois, who found that the woman she once thought she knew had become a recluse who seemed unable to decide on whom she loathed the most: herself or those who criticised her. She was, Rosalind noted, drinking from morning until she retired to bed.

By April 1968 Highsmith had found another house, in the village of Montmachoux, some twenty miles away. She made an offer on it and asked Elizabeth to agree to selling the Samois property and halving between them the amount received. The issue resulted in a costly court case, because Elizabeth felt she had been forced into the sale without her consent and also because she regarded the fifty-fifty division as a disproportionate outcome of what each had paid. The case rolled on for two years in total costing both of them in lawyers' fees more than they could have hoped to have gained from the sale. Nonetheless, Highsmith used her other savings, mainly from the sale of film rights, to purchase the house in Montmachoux before the Samois sale was settled. 'I shall be living alone, thank God,' she wrote to Barbara Ker-Seymer (17 May 1968). The Montmachoux house was tiny but it suited her increasing perception of the outside world as unwelcoming. She would live in it for longer than anywhere else.

Throughout these months of moves she was working on the draft of *The Tremor of Forgery*. The original thoughts for the book had come from her impressions of Tunisia when she and Elizabeth had gone there in 1966 but while she was struggling to forge a narrative from her impressions of the place – mostly revulsion – something devastating occurred involving the Muslim states of North Africa and the Middle East. The Six-Day War took place in June 1967, a conflict in which Egypt, Syria, Jordan and Iraq, with minor assistance from Lebanon, attempted to destroy Israel. Most of the Arab nations had been supplied with weapons from the Soviet Union but even though their forces outnumbered those of Israel they were driven back in less than a week and Israeli forces occupied land previously designated as Arab/Palestinian. It was a conflict which, by its electrifying brevity, diverted the attention of the world's media and political class from the war in Vietnam.

Highsmith was fascinated and once the war was over, she made use of accounts of what had occurred, alongside polemical articles on the moral standing of the various nations involved, in a rewriting of the draft. In the original Ingham, recently divorced, visits Tunis supposedly to write a piece on North Africa. In reality he is bisexual and is following rumours that Arab boys as young as twelve can be bought for sex for as little as a pack of cigarettes. He shares a surname with Highsmith's Suffolk neighbour Richard, also a writer. We have no record of Richard's feelings on this but had the novel appeared in its first draft we should assume he would not have been pleased.

After the Six-Day War Highsmith, while not entirely dispensing with sex in the novel, focuses far more on politics. The Western visitors to Tunisia hear of the war via European and US news media, mostly the radio. Jensen, a Dane, takes over from the original Ingham as the homosexual character, in the country to buy cheap sex from the young indigenous population. We learn of Jensen's opinions on Arabs when his dog disappears and he expresses contempt for the idea of his pet's '*bones* being in this goddamn sand', as if the memory of their mutual affection is spoilt by North Africa being his pet's resting place. 'Am I glad the Jews beat the shit out them!' he observes. Francis Adams, another character, is an American conservative but rather than supporting the state of Israel, he rails against it as an example of undeserving nationhood. In his view it is a country with no moral compass, which judges its actions only in terms of its own interests: 'the hallmark of Nazi Germany, and for which Nazi Germany at last went to her doom'. An oft-repeated mantra for antisemites who deny that they are antisemitic is that Israel has become a replica of the regime that carried out the Holocaust. Those who campaigned first against the foundation of Israel and later against its occupation of Arab/Palestinian territory – following its victories in the Six-Day War and, in 1973, the Yom Kippur War – were, in the West, aligned with radically left-wing parties and causes that were united in treating Israel as an instrument of US-sponsored capitalist-neocolonialist expansion.

Adams is an unapologetic advocate of this anti-Israel stance but he is also a vociferous supporter of the Vietnam War as an extension of the American way (notably God, democracy, freedom of speech, etc.) which seems weirdly inconsistent with his perception of Israel as a form of Nazism reborn. It was, as he was aware, then the only democracy in the Middle East. Ingham, privately, is repulsed by Adams' opinion on Vietnam. He sees it as a means of 'introducing the Vietnamese to the capitalist system in the form of a brothel industry, and to the American class system by making Negroes pay higher for their lays'. Add to this Ingham's killing of an Arab teenager who seems to have broken into his rooms. He batters him over the head with his typewriter. Perhaps this is Highsmith's only honest moment in the book. An instrument of writing becomes the cause of fatal violence. The attack is unplanned, confused, motiveless, but in the description Highsmith excluded from her description of Ingham's state of mind any hint of guilty, erotic pleasure; a notable revision of the first draft.

We might, just, treat *The Tremor of Forgery* as a novel of ideas: ideas in conflict with instinct, ideas incompatible with each other and ideas that could assist a world beset by tensions which resisted resolutions. But we would be deceiving ourselves. It is, rather, a reflection of an author who was not intellectually resourceful enough to make up her mind about what she observed and reconcile her confusion with what, privately, she felt.

Within two years of writing the novel she would reveal herself to be a racist, and antisemitic, and utterly confused on her opinions regarding Vietnam. Jensen, Adams and Ingham are versions of their creator, each at odds with the other and each uncertain about what they actually feel about major issues – apart from sex.

On 5 January 1970 she admitted in her *cahier* a hatred of black people, which she acknowledged was at odds with her 'social democrat' inclinations. In June 1969 she wrote to Alex Szogyi of how she abhorred the introduction of studies involving the history, even writings, of black Americans into the degree curriculums of the more radical American universities. These, she contended, ignored a few uncomfortable facts such as the absence of a written language among their pre-Americanised antecedents (save for some scribbling by the Zulus, apparently) and the fact that their own chieftains were very helpful in herding the slaves onto the boats (Letter to Szogyi, 25 June 1969). In a letter to Ronald Blythe she commented that blacks and Latinos 'enter college without high school diplomas now, and when they take one look at those books ... they say to themselves cripes, I'll never make it ... so they attack the professors and so on and so on. It's a hell of a way to cover up lack of brains' (16 August 1970). She wrote to Barbara Ker-Seymer that soon a common spectacle in New York would be 'coons hanging from 50th story windows, plugging their neighbours (other coons) before taking the lift downstairs to fleece their pockets' (9 May 1971).

In her *cahiers* Jews became the equivalent of African Americans, an inferior race that had somehow come to exert power in global politics, just as blacks seemed to her to have taken over the nation that had once enslaved them. A mild example is her observation that Jewish men give thanks in daily prayer that they were not born women. 'The rest of us give thanks that we were not born Jews ... If the Jews are God's chosen people – that is all one needs to know about God' (*Cahier*, 5 June 1971). Included in her observations are comments on how American lives were being wasted in an attempt to rescue a racially inferior people from communism, in Vietnam.

Her erratic, scatter-gun prejudices and political biases might appear symptomatic of an individual on the brink of a nervous breakdown, but look back to *The Tremor of Forgery* and witness how she used fiction as a buttress against mental imbalance. The states of loathing against others that crowded into her own mind and threatened her ability to make sense of the world were shared out between Jensen, Adams and Ingham. Each was, in their own way, slightly mad and despairingly unpleasant. Imagine them as features of the same person and you have a recipe for something extraordinarily foul. As always, Highsmith used her novel as a means of projecting into her characters elements of herself that privately she found difficult to bear. In her September 1970 diary she paraphrased Oscar Wilde: 'Work [writing] never seems to me a reality, but a way of getting rid of reality.'

While she was still in the Samois-sur-Seine house Highsmith was visited by a young journalist who had been sent to do an interview for *Queen*, a society magazine that at the time served the appetites of the London-based gentry, with hedonism disguised as radical social insight. Madeleine Harmsworth was twenty-six when she met Highsmith, and was a scion of the famous Harmsworth family, which owned many of the most profitable newspapers in Fleet Street. Their aristocratic titles – Northcliffe and Rothermere, usually Viscounts and Lords – were bestowed by politicians who had bought favours from their news media outlets, and Madeleine's relatives had used their influence to find her a position at *Queen*. The Highsmith interview would be her first big break, an exchange with one of the most puzzling, controversial crime writers in America and Britain who had inexplicably exiled herself to rural France. Madeleine later stated to Wilson that she felt it 'flattering' to be allowed into Highsmith's company, indeed her home, confessed that she was 'young and impressionable' and anxious about the nature of her encounter with a literary celebrity. She found herself surprised that halfway through their predictable question-and-answer session on writing, its inspiration and significance, Highsmith paused, stared at her and asked if she would care to stay the night, for sex. 'I wasn't averse to trying a bit of bisexuality,' she recalled, and she stayed in Samois for four days.

Their relationship lasted for around eighteen months, until early 1969, by which time Madeleine, originally thrilled by the prospect of an affair with a writer she idolised, recognised that Highsmith suffered from something close to bipolar disorder, or at least a simplified version of it: a split personality aggravated by alcoholism. Madeleine only realised that Highsmith drank constantly when she saw her, openly, pouring a generous shot of gin into a glass at breakfast time. Unlike other drunks she had come across Highsmith exhibited none of the more conspicuous indicators of the condition: physical imbalance, slurred speech and so on. Instead she appeared to Madeleine to regard drink as the fuel for behaviour that was deplorable yet measured and calculated. 'It seemed to me as if she had to ape feelings and behaviour, like Ripley. Of course, sometimes having no sense of social behaviour can be charming, but in her it was alarming' (Interview with Wilson, 23 August 2000).

At a dinner party in Highsmith's house in France, attended by Alex Szogyi and his long-term partner, Philip Thompson, Madeleine and Thompson seemed to discover in each other shared interests in all manner of things – social, cultural, political and amusingly inconsequential. They made each other laugh and outwardly at least, this appeared to be a man and woman going through the routines of mutual attraction. Except that everyone present knew that Thompson was gay. Nonetheless, Highsmith played out a pantomime of insulting Thompson for attempting to seduce her partner which concluded in her bringing down from the wall her two 'Confederate' swords and challenging him to a duel to death. Most regarded the episode as a joke but both Thompson and Madeleine recalled that, throughout, Highsmith displayed a level of virulence that was far from comedic.

Ker-Seymer recalled that once at a party in her London house in early 1968 Highsmith interrupted the conversation to ask if she could use the telephone. She then dialled a number which as Ker-Seymer saw was a random sequence of digits and pretended to hold a conversation with the dial tone. She was, apparently, calling another lover and making excuses for her absence because of her regrettable but unavoidable arrangement with Madeleine. In her interview with Wilson Madeleine offered one of the shrewdest assessments of Highsmith's twisted personality.

If she hadn't had her work, she would have been sent to an insane asylum or an alcoholic's home ... It took a while for me to figure this out, but all those strange characters haunting other people, and thinking and writing about them – they were her. She *was* her writing.

In Madeleine's view *This Sweet Sickness* is the novel 'which most closely represents her' with its story of a man creating an alternate identity as a means of escaping his true self. Madeleine also commented that her lover was 'like Ripley' and shortly after the two of them broke up Highsmith resurrected her most famous literary psychopath.

12

ANIMALS AND US

Peter Huber, a retired teacher, introduced himself to Highsmith in 1974 at a week-long series of seminars held in Holstein, Switzerland. Other writers present included Michael Frayn, and Stanley Middleton, who had won the Booker Prize that year for *Holiday*. In attendance were schoolteachers, academics and those who held to the questionable maxim that creative ambition could be realised by listening to advice from writers. Huber had published nothing and never hoped to do so, but for some reason he and Highsmith struck up an immediate friendship, began to exchange letters and remained in contact for the rest of her life. He did not fall into any of the categories that usually ensured a lasting friendship with her, fraught or otherwise: he was not part of the literary establishment, neither moneyed nor of moderately gentrified background, and expressed no conspicuous interest in sex. Some explanation for their long-term association comes from an exchange between Huber and Ellen Hill at least ten years later. 'What do you see in Pat's books?' asked Hill. She was surprised by his reply, which amounted to puzzlement at why such a question might be posed at all (Interview between Huber and Schenkar, 18 April 2003). As Hill suspected, Huber was an unquestioning devotee of Highsmith's work, certain of its importance but disinclined to ask if it deserved its ranking. It is likely that when they first met Highsmith too discerned this same feature in him: an idolater reluctant to tarnish the thing he adored by asking why or if it was any good.

Hill, when she met Huber, their single encounter, no longer had any great affection for Highsmith, but there is no evidence that her enquiry on what he thought of her books was driven by private antipathy. A few years later she spoke with the artist Dédé Moser, who said she admired *This Sweet Sickness*. Hill replied that '[she] rewrote this thing so many times!', meaning not that she had studiously revised drafts of this book, but rather that Highsmith was capable only of reformulating versions of the same model in all of her work, time and again (Interview between Schenkar and Moser, 2 August 2004). Even Kate Kingsley Skattebol, her devoted friend from Barnard onwards, confessed that she either gave up on Highsmith's books after several pages or, based on such regular disappointments, didn't attempt to read them at all. She never admitted this to Highsmith, preferring to accept public acclaim as a guarantee of her qualities without wondering why she herself did not like her work. Towards the end of her life Highsmith became a magnet for journalists and interviewers – Lorna Sage, Craig Brown, Ian Hamilton and Melvyn Bragg amongst others – and the characteristic feature of their exchanges and articles is a sense of evaluative apathy. These scrutineers are, in their own way, fascinated by why she was prompted to concoct such weird stories but respectfully unquestioning of whether they qualify as good books. Craig Brown called *Deep Water* 'the book of a lifetime' but the description is facile. She seems to deserve their attention because of her curiosity value, as a figure seemingly addicted to the macabre, rather than her merits as a writer.

This question of her literary abilities, or otherwise, is significant at this stage as 1970 was for Highsmith a turning point. *Strangers on a Train* and *The Talented Mr. Ripley* launched her, and some of her other books in the 1950s and 1960s deserve interest as examples of private disturbance distilled into modernisations of Poe. After that, however, she drifted between works of genius and (arguably) some of the most dreadful pieces of suspense fiction ever to go into print. *Ripley Under Ground* (1970) was begun when Highsmith was in the middle of her relationship with Madeleine. It received mixed reviews, mostly positive, but what its assessors seemed to ignore or tolerate, in my opinion, is the fact that its plot is arbitrarily tortuous. It does not use difficulty as an intellectual or moral challenge but rather as an act of bloody-mindedness.

Ripley, now in his thirties, is living on an estate in France, Belle Ombre, with his wealthy heiress wife Héloïse Plisson. Aside from Héloïse's money he has inherited much of Dickie Greenleaf's estate, having forged Greenleaf's will to make himself the recipient. One might assume from this that he would be content with the outcome of his previous dreadful behaviour, murder included. But no. He becomes involved in the forgery and sale of works by the painter Derwatt who had committed suicide more than a year earlier. So, here is a brief version of what happens next: Ripley, at various points, pretends to be someone else – an activity his debut novel has prepared him for – commits murder, fakes suicide, burns and buries bodies, and at the close seems content to be in bed with Héloïse; which is odd since prior to this he has shown no sexual interest in his wife. The police note that people tend to die following encounters with him but have no evidence to follow up on this eerie observation.

Throughout the book Ripley's behaviour seems by equal degrees motiveless and implausible. For example, he does not really need to murder the American collector Thomas Murchison, who suspects that one of his Derwatts is a forgery. Even if it is proved to be a fake, he has no evidence that Ripley is behind the scam. Ripley does so not because he fears that he might be exposed nor even because he is psychotically addicted to killing. He is not a character at all, at least in the customary sense of a fictional creation who shares characteristics with figures in the real world, even the worst and most bizarre. With one exception: he is a projection of his creator, who shares his nihilistic hopelessness. He is an autobiographical instrument, the activating feature of a series of novels that appear to be driven by a double maxim: that life is inconsequential and representing it in literature is a fruitless endeavour.

I do not wish to present Highsmith as a crime-fiction version of Samuel Beckett. Beckett's work is an extended quarrel with the assumed purpose and mannerisms of literature. He wanted to dismantle the assumption that by writing about life we could reframe and make sense of it. Highsmith's books, particularly her later ones, are possessed of a selfish disregard for anything but themselves.

There is in *Ripley Under Ground* an episode in which Tufts, the Derwatt forger, tries to kill Ripley by hitting him over the head with a shovel and, thinking he has succeeded, buries his unconscious victim in a shallow grave (from which he escapes). Ripley has already killed the art dealer Murchison and after entertaining his widow at Belle Ombre begins to suspect, for no obvious reason, that Tufts is contemplating suicide and pursues him through Paris, Greece and Salzburg – though it is unclear as to whether he wants to prevent him from killing himself or assist him. Ripley finally locates Tufts in Salzburg, where Tufts thinks that Ripley is a ghost, believing he killed him in France. Tufts flees from the spectre and leaps from a cliff to his death. Ludicrous would be a generous estimation of this plotline. At every point logic, believability and common sense are excluded from the mindset of the characters and the narrative that contains them.

The Times's anonymous review presented the novel as a self-consciously literary exploration of the relationship between aesthetics and existentialism. 'By her hypnotic art she puts the suspense story into a toweringly high place in the hierarchy of fiction' (21 January 1971). But he or she would say that, wouldn't they. Literary experimentalism was in 1970 still sacred and protected territory, Highsmith already had a reputation as a radical in a popular genre, crime writing, so she could do no wrong.

When Highsmith produced *Ripley Under Ground* it seemed she knew that its predecessor and her reputation would guarantee promotion and esteem. However, when she wrote passages such as that in which Ripley is buried alive by Tufts and then pursues him across Europe, reappearing to him as a ghost, one has the impression that she was laughing behind her hand. That she knew it was inane but she did not care because she was also aware that her prestige, if only as an enigma, protected her from critical abuse.

The novel is significant to the extent that it is Highsmith's private note of confession; private to the extent that even her most intimate friends would be unlikely to recognise Ripley as her admission of self-loathing. When he has sex with Héloïse, often reluctantly, he regards her as 'inanimate, unreal … a body without an identity', and he treats everyone else, irrespective of whether or not he kills them, with a resolute lack of compassion. Tom Ripley lives in a world occupied exclusively by Tom Ripley. Outside it there are individuals he can pretend to treat with affection or respect but for whom he reserves lazy contempt. His only interest is in faking things: paintings and feelings. He persistently evades any confrontation with reality and he is an exquisite portrait of his creator.

Vivien De Bernardi reported a conversation she had with Kingsley Kate Skattebol. 'Kingsley told me – which I think is a perfect phrase – that Pat was an equal opportunity offender … You name the group, she hated them. She saw awful things about everything and everybody, but it wasn't personal. It sounds bizarre but although she said terrible things, she wasn't really a nasty person' (Interview with Wilson, 23 July 1999). This raises the question of how it is possible for someone to be offensive to everyone while not being a 'nasty person'? Like Ripley she was capable of behaving in a way that caused others distress, in his case sometimes their loss of life, but avoided feelings of contrition because she had no reciprocal notion of the effect of her actions. Sadists obtain pleasure from hurting others, while violent, prejudiced or abusive people (or indeed career criminals) have the capacity to remain aware that they have inflicted pain. Highsmith and Ripley fall into the rare category of neither enjoying the distress they cause nor being able to acknowledge that they have caused it. In a 1970 *cahier* she reflected on how the tensions and bitterness of her early family life had affected her permanently as an adult. 'I learned to live with a grievous and murderous hatred very early on. And learned to stifle also my more positive emotions' (12 January, 1970).

While she was writing *Ripley Under Ground*, she reflected on why her books were failing to sell in paperback in America. Her US agent, Patricia Schartle Myer, wrote to her and suggested politely that perhaps her fiction was 'too subtle', shorthand for too difficult to read by people with an appetite for standard crime fiction. Highsmith did not reply directly but entered a private reflection in her *cahier*. 'Perhaps it is because I don't like anyone' (28 January 1967). She meant that her own immutable misanthropic condition informed her work. Later in her *cahier* she concluded that the vast majority of human beings were 'morons'. 'How about training them as casual servants, people who empty ashtrays, polish brass, make beds, wash dishes and generally go about picking up?' Occupying the 'morons' with menial tasks would not, however, stop them breeding and as a solution to overpopulation by the lower orders she recommended infant genocide. The babies of the 'morons' should be 'killed early, like puppies or kittens' (3 February 1968; 11 March 1968).

She does not describe the kind of people who belong in the non-moronic natural aristocracy, those who would be served by individuals deemed unworthy of doing anything else. But when she recorded these thoughts privately, she was sharing them with her creation, Tom Ripley, who behaved not so much as a part of some kind of elite but more as its only member, immune from the regulations, let alone the moral inhibitions, observed by the rest of humanity. She was well into the novel when she wrote: 'the moral is: stay alone. Any idea of any close relationship should be imaginary, like any story I am writing. This way no harm can be done to me or to any person' (23 June 1969). The phrases seem oblique and ambiguous, except if we treat the words as written both by Highsmith and by Ripley. Throughout the novel Ripley behaves as if he is the narrator of a story in which other, mostly unfortunate, figures are involved, but from which he can detach himself. He avoids 'any close relationship'; even his marriage is an emotionless performance, or as Highsmith puts it, 'only imaginary'. 'No harm can be done to him' because in his 'imaginary' world he can forever escape the consequences of his actions, and although he can do actual 'harm' to 'any person', he is remote from their suffering. Ripley was Highsmith but more importantly he was her protection against a potential nervous breakdown.

On the page, in the book, he is soulless, a man with no moral compass, but he is also possessed of almost supernatural strength of character and ingenuity. He knows, and we know, that he will never be caught, brought to justice and exposed as the twisted maniac that he actually is. So long as he lived on in her books, he provided Highsmith with a security blanket against her actual personality. While she wrote the book, she behaved in a manner that was, to say the least, bizarre; as if she had become a real version of Ripley, murders excluded.

In February 1970 Highsmith flew to New York and spent three weeks in the city, staying at the Chelsea Hotel in Manhattan, magnet for numerous high-ranking literary guests (ranging from Mark Twain through Arthur Miller, Tennessee Williams, Allen Ginsberg and Thomas Wolfe, to Dylan Thomas, who died there). She was declaring herself as one of the first team, and during her stay she visited parts of the city and its outskirts that had marked out the narrative of her life from Barnard through to her successes with *Strangers on a Train* and *The Talented Mr. Ripley*.

Then she went south to Fort Worth to spend time with her mother Mary and stepfather Stanley. The disastrous week there opened with a buffet party which her parents arranged to celebrate her fame as a writer, the first formal acknowledgement by the family of her status. A local preacher asked if *The Price of Salt* was by her and not its pseudonymous author. He was not accusing her of anything but her reaction is recorded in a letter written to her by Stanley after her return to France: '... you started wrecking the kitchen, throwing a big container of milk all over the place and breaking the louvred door, like a mad woman!' (23 August 1970). During the twelve months following her arrival in America and her return to Europe Highsmith bombarded Mary with letters so abusive that Stanley accused her of deliberately attempting to cause her mother to have a nervous breakdown.

Soon after Willie Mae, her grandmother, died in 1955 Highsmith, with no legal grounding, claimed that she was the rightful heir to the family home. This contradicted the fact that Willie Mae had specified in her will that it should go to Mary and her brother Claude. Highsmith was fully aware of this and her demand was specifically designed to cause distress to all involved. She was consistent in her leech-like demands. In November 1970 Stanley died from the side effects of Parkinson's disease. Highsmith did not send a note of condolence to her mother and the virulence of her letters to her after Stanley's death increased considerably, including claims that she had rights to the estate. Mary consulted a doctor and spoke confidentially to several of her friends who knew her daughter, on the question of why Patricia had subjected her to 'inhumane treatment'. She wrote to her daughter reporting that the doctor said that in his view if Patricia had stayed 'three more days' in Fort Worth 'I would be dead'.

In her *cahier* of 20 December 1971, she reflected on Mary's personality. 'My mother is the type who fires a shotgun and then wonders why some of the birds are killed, others wounded, and the rest scared. "Why don't the birds come back?" I came back several times…' There is no record of Mary having ever used a shotgun and Highsmith's analogy of her hatred as the equivalent of randomly killing, wounding and frightening birds is prescient. As is Highsmith's remark in her 1968 *cahier* that the children of the 'low-life general population' should be 'killed early, like puppies or kittens' because throughout the late 1960s and 1970s Highsmith's sense of the boundary between the animal world and the human began to blur alarmingly.

In *A Dog's Ransom* (1972) Lisa, a black poodle owned by a wealthy Manhattanite couple, Ed Reynolds, an advertising executive, and his wife Greta, is kidnapped and one thousand dollars is demanded for the dog's return. Ed and Greta send the money to a place specified by the kidnapper without realising that their pet is dead, her head smashed in with a rock shortly after her abduction. The kidnapper/dog-murderer is Kenneth Rowajinski, unemployed, slightly physically disabled and referred to on several occasions as 'the Pole', and Clarence Duhamell is his nemesis. Duhamell is a police detective, educated at Cornell, who treats his job with a mixture of distaste and hopelessness. He is, supposedly, duty bound to uphold values of decency and order in a city that he sees as riven with venality and corruption, especially within its police department. A righteous liberal despairing of what his country has become – as a student he campaigned against the Vietnam War – he is the quintessence of the moderately left-leaning conscience of Western democracy. Which is fine, except that it does not explain why he becomes obsessively concerned with the plight of a middle-class couple whose beloved poodle has been kidnapped.

Eventually he tracks down Rowajinski and kills him for no other reason, it appears, than that the dog-murderer deserves it: it is also implied that 'low-life' second-generation Eastern European immigrants are the sorts who have undermined the American ideal. As she was drafting the book, she wrote to Alex Szogyi and

Ronald Blythe regularly about her dilemmas. Specifically, she was uncertain of whether it should become a political polemic with Duhamell as her means of delineating the contradictions and hypocrisies faced by those who lived in – and felt they should support – the country which saw itself as the principal defender of the free world. She admitted to Blythe that she would not resolve the dilemma (Highsmith to Blythe, 16 August 1971), indicating that while this was indeed the direction the project seemed to be taking, she was temperamentally averse to literature as a form of virtue-signalling.

Some of the early drafts were too bizarre and grotesque for her to have let them come to fruition. First of all, Highsmith has Duhamell concentrate exclusively on finding and rescuing the dog and only later feels that he should bring the kidnapper to justice. He appears to share the Reynolds' sense of Lisa as the equivalent of a human child. The Reynolds had lost their daughter in a car crash but would they really involve themselves in the emotional trauma of the first draft – played down in the revision – in the unlikely hope that their pet will be returned? Had Lisa become an emotional replacement for their late daughter? Perhaps, but in the first draft Highsmith presents Ed as having a far more intimate relationship with Lisa: he has sex with her. This is left out of the finished version, but there are parallels between Highsmith's description of Ed's sensations when he has sex with the dog and Duhamell's at the close of the printed draft. Duhamell, despairing of his fellow officers, takes out his anger on a passing drunk by knocking him unconscious. 'The act exhilarated Clarence,' writes Highsmith, as does his subsequent killing of 'the Pole', for which he feels no guilt or remorse. When he sees the report of it on the TV all that registers for him is his loss of appetite for his mother's apple pie.

There are residual hints at the novel being about the social decay of America, New York City in particular, but this was a ruse: beneath the surface is something far more privately grotesque, something that, as we shall see, Highsmith revealed in her own behaviour.

Snails were her favourite creatures mainly, as she disclosed to
Ellen Hill, because they seemed to undermine, in her view,
the anthropomorphic delusion that animals share any of our
characteristics. She was attracted to them initially when she saw
two of them copulating, apparently without emotion, pleasure or
even of any evident notion of what was happening between them,
and this is echoed in the early draft of *A Dog's Ransom*. Her *cahier* of
17 July 1971, just as she was completing *A Dog's Ransom*, is quite
horrifying. She begins by observing that in France it is thought
proper that humans should butcher, sell and eat horsemeat while
this same foodstuff is cooked and fed to pets in French households,
specifically dogs and cats. In other circumstances, she adds, it is
thought improper for humans to eat the same meat as animals, so
why are horses an exception, especially given their exalted status in
art and culture? Here we are reminded of her original plan for Ed's
attachment to his pet to go beyond affection. Sex is not involved
but a similar question is raised: are the rules on the relationship
between different species arbitrary? Next in the *cahier* she reflects on
how, in her view at least, the conventions of butchery, cooking and
eating reflect and raise questions about our sense of ourselves as the
superior species. She notes that we are particularly attracted to the
consumption of parts of animals that, for us, are the most private,
intimate and sacred, notably the testicles of bulls and other animals.
We seem not to concern ourselves with the dignity of bulls and
sheep, she comments, so perhaps we should compensate our fellow
mammals by feeding them the foetuses of aborted babies. 'After all
it [foetal matter] is protein, [which] is becoming increasingly scarce
as the world's population increases.'

There are numerous stories of how pets (particularly dogs) and
their owners bond emotionally in a manner that equals relationships
between humans. Ed and Lisa obviously fall into this category:
he is happy to pay any amount for her return – evidenced when
Rowajinski demands more money – just as would a husband with
a wife or a father a daughter. So, Highsmith, at least in the original

draft, poses the moral question of why such a loving relationship should not also involve a physical one. In the *cahier* and the novel, she constantly questions standard conceptions of the moral seniority of human beings.

Barbara Ker-Seymer and her partner Barbara Roett visited Highsmith in Montcourt, her third and final French house on the Seine, in 1971, when she was completing *A Dog's Ransom*. Roett noted her curious engrossment with animals. Usually her diet involved the standard American blue-collar combination of cereal, bread, bacon and eggs but she did her best to provide her guests with dishes put together from local market produce. Roett was surprised by her account of how a year earlier she had found a way of alleviating thyroid problems and fatigue by consuming raw beef. Roett assumed that she had acquired a taste for the quintessentially haute cuisine dish of steak tartare involving the highest quality fillet of beef mixed with onions, capers and other seasonings. But no, Highsmith explained, she had eaten standard cuts of beef from the local butcher as they came, seemingly proud of being able to consume raw meat with the same untroubled relish as dogs and cats.

Roett also recalls that one afternoon when she and Ker-Seymer were chatting in a spare bedroom they were startled by a thud on the wooden floor. Highsmith had battered a large rat to death in the garden and introduced the corpse to her friends by throwing it through the open window. None of the women remarked on the gesture but the two guests agreed that it resembled the tendency of domestic cats to triumph in the killing of rodents by bringing them to their owner.

Highsmith had a cat, and, as recalled by Roett, Ker-Seymer and Skattebol's daughter, Winifer, who was visiting France for two weeks, she treated the animal with a mixture of close tactile affection and disdain, often forgetting to feed it and leaving it to fend for itself. The most disturbing account comes from Roett and Ker-Seymer.

Roett states that 'Pat really did love animals', but admits that she and Ker-Seymer were perplexed, horrified, by her regular habit of placing the animal in a hessian sack and swinging it around the room. Roett said to her, 'You're going to make that poor thing dizzy', and that evidently was her intention. On releasing it she would watch, fascinated, as the cat staggered in a daze around the room. Highsmith repeated this bizarre ritual daily and only once confided in her guests that she enjoyed being drunk so much that it seemed unfair to deny her pet a similarly disorientating experience. Roett later reflected, 'She didn't know how to be gentle with it and that was something she really cared about' (Interview with Wilson, 5 May 1999). Clearly Highsmith's friend remained confused by the bizarre conflict between the author's self-evident love for the animal and her inclination to cause it distress. Roett continues, 'It was hard to gauge her normal behaviour, because she was never normal around people.' Essentially, her inability to appreciate that she was harming the cat showed Roett something of her lack of feeling for humans, too. Her anthropomorphism was neither discriminating nor condescending, indicating as she did that if animals deserved a share of our love for each other, then it should come with a flavour of man's inhumanity to man.

In her *cahier* of 25 August 1971, just as she completed the novel, she imagines a character who is oblivious to the foulness of existence, who indeed takes pleasure in existing alongside, often eating, human detritus: the foulest of waste, emptied toilets and bedpans, nappies, hysterectomies, aborted foetuses. 'I need a character obsessed with all this ... I've got one, myself.' Perhaps her obsessive concern for animals was conversely related to her loathing for human beings, or at least herself as an example of the species.

While writing *A Dog's Ransom* she was also completing short stories that would make up the 1975 collection *The Animal Lover's Book of Beastly Murder*. She had been working on some of these since 1967 and the consistency of the project reflects her general opinion on the relationship between humans and animals. In each story an animal, representing their species, assumes the role of the unjustly repressed and takes revenge on their oppressor, members of the human race. Battery chickens peck to death the owner of the farm in scenes resonant of Hitchcock's *The Birds*; Ming the cat kills his owner's lover because he has intruded upon their special relationship; Baron, an aged poodle, devises a way of getting rid of his owner's boyfriend; a goat gains sadistic revenge for his mistreatment by the owner of an amusement park; and even a cockroach, that most derided creature, gets its own back on humans seemingly determined to exterminate his species.

Throughout, the stories bring us back to the question raised in *A Dog's Ransom*: if we compare humans with animals can we come any closer to a sense of the purpose of our existence? In each of the short stories the answer is profoundly unambiguous: we as a species are inherently flawed and inferior to animals.

Everyone who knew Highsmith in her later years has stories to tell of her love of animals. In December 1970, the local stray cat in the village had had its tail docked and, in her *cahier* (13 July 1970), she plots a detective investigation, seeking out the perpetrator and purchasing a shotgun – a relatively easy task in France – and shooting them. When she was sharing a house in Samois-sur-Seine with Elizabeth Lyne, she wrote regularly to Ronald Blythe of how her cat was her protection against Elizabeth's aggression and animosity. 'There are perhaps more brains in those tiny heads than we think.' Kate Kingsley Skattebol commented that 'As for animals in general, she saw them as individual personalities, often better behaved and with more dignity and honesty than humans' (Letter to Wilson, 13 February 2002).

The problem with the collection and Highsmith's inspiration for it is that each of the protagonists is, aside from its physical characteristics, a human being. The goat, the cat, the monkey, even the cockroach are, in terms of their emotional registers and their linguistic, intellectual and moral compasses, indisputably reflections of us. They also display the most regrettable aspects of the human condition: an inclination towards malice, a desire and ability to do harm to others. Highsmith didn't love animals. She was obsessed with them as destined to lose out in a world controlled by humans, and she blinded herself to the fact that if the roles were reversed all non-humans, from the cockroach to the hen, have an extraordinary potential for pitiless brutality. The premise of the stories is self-contradictory: in order to take revenge on us animals have to acquire precisely the same distasteful qualities – notably the capacity to kill without emotion – that cause us to be horrible to them. Marghanita Laski in her review in the *Listener* stated that it seemed to her that the collection had less to do with pity for animals than 'distaste for men' and much later her carer in Switzerland, Bruno Sager, observed that her affection for everything from spiders to cats was due to her sense of alienation from the rest of humanity. 'For her human beings were strange – she thought she would never understand them...' (Interview with Wilson, 25 September, 1999).

When she completed *A Dog's Ransom* in late 1971 she was suffering a period of depression, made worse by bouts of flu, lethargy brought on by alcohol abuse and a particularly lengthy, painful case of toothache. Her outlook on life was not beatific and this probably contributed to the formation of Ripley, in his third novel, as a loathsome misanthrope. In the midst of this on 20–21 January 1972 she wrote to Ronald Blythe on how her ex-lover Daisy Winston seemed to be striving for a sense of purpose. Highsmith had already reached her own conclusions on this. 'She cannot realise that life is about nothing.'

Vivien De Bernardi recalls that Highsmith once said that if she came upon a kitten and a baby, both starving, she would feed the former. Her neighbour in France, the painter Gudrun Mueller, told of how they once accompanied her to the local vet, because a cat, having been hit by a car, was terminally injured and needed to be put down. Mueller reported that Highsmith almost fainted with despair. She later told the writer Neil Gordon that 'it affected me very much because it was much more important than a member of my family who might die of old age ... I had the power to do it [order the cat's death] ... It's terrifying to have that power. I don't go to jail for it, [but] the cat is dead ... They have a great right, these animals' (Interview between Gordon and Wilson, 9 November 2001). Horrified at the prospect of being able to end the life of this harmless creature, or at least to allow the vet to do so, she seems to turn her distress against human beings, ostensibly those closest to her, who in her opinion are more deserving of the same fate.

In July 1973 she visited Germany, partly to visit individuals who were promoting her work in the country but also to compare the parts of it worst affected by the war with Munich, where she'd lived, and which had been far less seriously damaged than urban areas in the north. First, she stayed for a week in Hamburg with her German translator, Anne Uhde, and then went on, alone, to Berlin, where she obtained details on how to enter the East. In her *cahier* (19 July 1973) she records the delay at Checkpoint Charlie, the dreary yet unforgiving appearance of the Wall and a city, like its people, deprived of soul and character. Not once, however, does she comment on the regime that presides over this or on global politics as a whole. The cause of the divide between West and East is conspicuously absent from her account of leaving the democratic West for a world of totalitarianism. Even left-leaning observers would have noticed that much of East Berlin in 1973 was poorly repaired, with buildings ruined by carpet bombings still inhabited. The two halves of the city seemed to be in different universes. But it is only when she visits the Tiergarten that she begins to pick up on acts of cruel iniquity. She wonders how those who run the place would feel were they were 'forced to defecate and make love in the presence of spectators [their captors] who laugh, point and stare'.

She was not, however, referring to the dehumanising treatment of the general population in the East by the Stasi. She was in the city zoo, which caused her, briefly, to empathise with the captives of a quasi-police state. For her, the animals behind the wire suffered far more than the citizens imprisoned by the Wall. There are clear parallels between Highsmith's individual dilemmas and their manifestation in her next Ripley novel. He slaughters other characters in a particularly cruel manner, ensuring that pain and humiliation are overtures to death. He exists in an emotional vacuum, without anything close to guilt or remorse, let alone compassion, and he is his creator's means of seeking revenge upon those who share her state, which disgusted her: being human.

13

'IT'S GOOD YOU NEVER HAD CHILDREN'

Shortly before *A Dog's Ransom* went to press Highsmith began work on the third Ripley novel, *Ripley's Game* (1974). The esteemed German director Wim Wenders adapted it for a film in 1977, a considerable achievement given that the book surpassed its predecessor as a masterpiece of incoherence and implausibility. Ripley, still in Belle Ombre with Héloïse, is approached by his occasional fence, the minor criminal Reeves Minot, who offers him $96,000 to kill two men in Germany. The question of why exactly Minot feels that Ripley is a suitable hitman is left unanswered, and we have to ask also why Minot assumes that his offer will convince this immensely wealthy man to potentially ruin his life by killing people.

Ripley declines and recommends to Minot Jonathan Trevanny, an indigent British picture framer suffering from leukaemia, as his replacement. Trevanny has insulted Ripley at a party in Fontainebleau and Ripley feels it appropriate that this decrepit figure should be approached by criminals and offered money to resolve his own financial and medical problems. It is, perhaps, an act of twisted philanthropy, though we should note that while Trevanny's illness is serious Ripley persuades him by various means that he has no more than six months to live, ensuring that he will take on the contract killings to provide money for his wife and child following his imminent demise.

The mild slur delivered by Trevanny is not convincing as the motivation for Ripley's subsequent behaviour. Rather, he seems to relish his status of manipulator and choreographer of events, as if he has taken control of the novel in which he appears. Trevanny successfully shoots dead his first victim and then, through a mixture of fear and remorse, decides that after the second he will commit suicide, certain that Minot will have transferred the money to his wife. Ripley has followed him onto the train where he is due to execute the mafioso, Marcangelo, and takes on the task himself. Once more, Ripley seems to be monitoring the direction of the narrative, ensuring that events he has set in motion do not shift quite beyond his control. Minot has provided Trevanny with two weapons, a handgun and a garrotte, and he chooses the former as the one which will lessen his proximity and contact with his victim. Ripley, however, makes a point of using the garrotte, executing Marcangelo in the humiliating, confined space of the lavatory.

Francis Ford Coppola's The Godfather (1972) was released just as Highsmith began her novel and its influence is tangible. The film was revolutionary in that nothing had come close to its brutally realist representation of organised crime. Particularly memorable and shocking are the director's set pieces depicting the ways in which members of Italian-American gangster organisations, the Mafia, dispose of their enemies and the traitors in their own families. Shootings involve heads and torsos being shredded by bullets and garrotting is a particular favourite reserved for those who have betrayed their own, given that it involves extreme pain and indignity. Highsmith's episode in the train lavatory carries the discernible influence of Mario Puzo (the original Godfather novelist) and Coppola. The victim's death is described in excruciating detail, including the choking and gurgling sound that comes as his vocal cords are paralysed and he tries unsuccessfully to draw air into his contracting throat. His eyes bulge, his swollen tongue protrudes from his mouth and in a final attempt to draw in breath he expels his bottom set of false teeth which clatter onto the metal floor. Ripley picks them up, drops them into the lavatory bowl and presses the foot-pedal to expel them from the train. Then, 'He wiped his fingers with disgust on Marcangelo's padded shoulder.' When the corridor appears to be clear he opens the door and despatches Marcangelo's body at a point several kilometres beyond the final resting place of his false teeth. After returning to his seat he orders a bowl of goulash and a glass of chilled Carlsbad beer.

Between Germany and Belle Ombre four more mafiosi are disposed of and though the descriptions of each death are a little more economical than Marcangelo's, Highsmith allows sufficient space for us to note Ripley's appreciation of the inflicting of pain. One is bashed over the head with a log and then sent to oblivion as the steel butt of a rifle noisily shatters his skull and releases blood in all directions. 'Mind the rug with that blood!' Ripley tells Trevanny as they move the body. Watching the bodies of two more gangsters being incinerated in their car Ripley relaxes by whistling a marching song from the Napoleonic Wars. Then with the precision of a butcher he smashes a hammer through the forehead and into the frontal lobe of his next victim, 'straightforward and true, as if he had been an ox in a slaughterhouse'. During their final exchange with the mafiosi Trevanny is shot, seriously injured and dies in Ripley's car as Ripley attempts to drive him to hospital. Throughout, Trevanny is presented not so much as Ripley's accomplice but as his unwitting and rather feckless apprentice, drawn into a catalogue of nightmarish events that causes him to wish for suicide. Ripley's victims are themselves part of a world in which murder is common currency, so we are hardly expected to sympathise with them, though the pleasure that he takes in causing their deaths to be as inhumane and painful as possible has nothing to do with the exigencies of gangsterism. The question remains as to why Ripley feels it appropriate to subject the villains and Trevanny to several weeks of unceasing torment. This version of Ripley was born out of the book that immediately preceded him, *A Dog's Ransom*, and the one that Highsmith was preparing while *Ripley's Game* progressed, *The Animal Lover's Book of Beastly Murder*. He kills like an animal, without conscience, but his theatrical sadism is uniquely human.

Virtually everyone who met her during the early 1970s could testify to Highsmith's loathing of France. The French were, in her view, insular, systematically corrupt and selfish, and wedded to an administrative system that outranked any other in the world in its addiction to utterly pointless bureaucratic regulations. Her house in Montcourt, her final residence in France, struck everyone who visited it as a recipe for depression. It spoke of a decent heritage, minor gentry, but those who built it in the eighteenth century seemed more concerned with the costive retention of fireside heat than with sunshine. The beamed ceilings were low and the windows admitted little light. Its back garden was spacious enough, but it too carried the atmosphere of a prison yard; a ten-foot-high stone wall sealed it off from the rest of the landscape. In 1977 the journalist Joan Juliet Buck visited to do an interview: 'It is an austere place: lived in but empty at the same time.'

It was from here that she projected Ripley into the spacious, beautifully sunlit Belle Ombre château. During the autumn and winter of 1973 Highsmith suffered from an eclectic malady of conditions: pains in her arms, which friends said might be due to angina, but she dismissed as the results of digging in the garden, persistent nausea, abdominal cramps and diarrhoea, plus bouts of dizziness and a severe, painful hardening of her calves after long walks. In December she was recommended to a heart specialist in Wimpole Street, London, who advised she would have to alter her lifestyle if she hoped to live beyond her mid-fifties. She had been candid about her habits. She despised fruit and vegetables, preferring fatty bacon and occasionally eggs to bulk out her intake of alcohol. Aside from gin and beer she now consumed a bottle of Scotch every three or four days. Even though nannyish advice from physicians and the state was moderate compared with today it was evident to all, Highsmith's friends and medical advisers included, that she had chosen a route to oblivion. In 1973 most people smoked cigarettes but Highsmith's determination to get through forty a day of the most famously tar-ridden brand, Gauloises, seemed a loud refutation of instructions on what might or might not be good for you.

In the New Year, she accepted an invitation from her friend, the publisher Charles Latimer, to stay with him and his partner, the concert pianist Michel Block, in their country house in the Lot, southwest France. The region in summer could be as hot as the Mediterranean but even in midwinter it provided blue skies and icy sunshine. Unlike the Mediterranean coast, Paris and parts of the Loire Valley it was not, in the 1970s, an area well known to non-French holidaymakers and very few of its beautiful sandstone manor houses and small châteaux had been bought by northern Europeans or Americans. It is a superbly attractive area largely unchanged over the previous century. But, to Latimer and Block's surprise, their guest seemed oblivious to her surroundings. Irrespective of their opinions on the nation as a whole few people would fail to find the Lot physically captivating, but Highsmith could not be persuaded to leave the house. 'She was not your typical American expatriate. She was, in my opinion, an "exile", or maybe she was "in exile"' (Letter from Block to Wilson, 7 May 2002). Block recalled that almost ten years later he, Highsmith and Latimer stopped for petrol when driving through the Pennsylvania countryside. She got out of the car, gazed at the forested hills speckled with small white-painted houses and churches, and began to weep uncontrollably. He comments to Wilson, 'I really think Pat sacrificed her "every day" life to her reputation to be an artist ... I think she would have been much happier living in the States.' At the beginning of her career Europe proved exotic and irresistible but by the time she had established herself the country of her birth seemed to have taken an obtuse form of revenge for her affair with the Old World.

Larry Ashmead, her US editor at Doubleday, suggests that she felt let down by her American audience. 'Her books were invariably well received in the US ... often in important journals and by important critics ... but the core audience was consistently small

... She didn't appeal to the mass market because her books were dark, often terrifying and the reader had to pay careful attention.' Gary Fisketjon, who dealt with her for Knopf: 'She defied categorisation', in that she was not mainstream crime-suspense but the moral-philosophical aspect of her work – 'a cynicism about human transactions' – wasn't 'particularly user-friendly'. Hard-boiled crime fiction of the kind practised by Hammett, Chandler and Cain was born in America in the 1930s and lived on there with the likes of John D. MacDonald and Joseph Wambaugh. Some associated her with the genre but most in the serious magazines and journals found that Highsmith lacked, or avoided, the inclination to turn bad behaviour into a credible and entertaining narrative.

Her Heinemann editor Roger Smith found that her avoidance of the vulgarised tradition of the bestseller appealed to the British and European taste for fiction, even suspense fiction, as a platform for philosophical speculation. In America she was an enigma and curiosity, an outsider, but in Europe, for the same reason, she became something of an intellectual celebrity. She preferred the intellectual celebrity but by the time that Block and Latimer invited her to the Lot she was beginning to regret exchanging her home for acclaim. She was delighted when in 1967 Daniel Keel, founder of the Swiss publisher Diogenes Verlag, offered to deal with her rights for continental Europe and the rest of the world beyond America and the UK. To shift genre, it felt to her as if she had traded in the coarse extravagance of Hollywood for the high-art contexts of Szabó, Godard, Herzog and Fellini, despite the fact that the Europeans did not make much money.

At the end of summer 1974 America called her back, specifically with a letter from her cousin Dan Coates who reported that her mother, now living permanently in Fort Worth, was incapable of looking after herself. According to Coates she lived on uncooked food, from tins; refused, or was unable, to clean a house or herself; and often appeared to be incoherent. When she arrived in Fort Worth Highsmith found the situation to be even worse than Dan had described it. The door was locked and blocked with heavy furniture and after she broke in through a window to the kitchen she retched at the smell. The sink was full of unwashed pots, uneaten food – in tins, parcels and on plates – covered every surface, and the fridge had become an incubator for rot and decay, with various forms of cheese, meat and vegetables turned green, some nurturing insects. Mary, upstairs, had not washed or taken a bath for some time and although she recognised her daughter she seemed to resent her intrusion. According to her neighbours and local shopkeepers Mary veered between periods of normality and bouts of distraction and forgetfulness but they saw this as no more than one might expect of a woman in her seventies. Highsmith and Dan Coates, who knew her better, suspected a condition more unsettling than age and tried to acquire power of attorney. They failed but Mary was clear enough of mind to gather her contempt for her daughter's act into a letter.

> Well you've done it – broken my heart – yet gave me freedom I've not felt in many years. How sorry for you I am … Stanley and I made a great mistake – giving you everything we could … It's good you never had children – they'd be forever criticised and then never come up to your demands. You can think of no one but yourself … Don't write – I shan't. (30 September 1974)

The manner of the letter seems to belie Highsmith and Coates's view that Mary was becoming incapable, mentally, of looking after herself. Throughout it reads as the case for the prosecution, laid out meticulously and convincingly. It was the last letter she would write to her daughter and it is the only one that is not signed off with something familiar such as 'Mother' or 'Mom'. This time she signed herself off as 'Mary Highsmith' with no valediction, 'sincerely', 'faithfully' or otherwise.

The cool composure exhibited in the letter would prove temporary. Neighbours noticed that lights remained on during the night and that sometimes doors were left swinging on their hinges while she was out shopping. On 6 August 1975 she went for coffee in the local diner and it is thought she left her cigarette burning in the ashtray at home. The house was burnt almost to the ground, all of her clothes and furniture destroyed, and her pet dog was killed. It might well have been an accident, but her doctor advised Coates that she was effectively incapable of looking after herself. She spent the subsequent sixteen years, until her death, in a Fort Worth nursing home, gradually beset by what appeared to be Alzheimer's.

Highsmith sometimes mentioned her to friends and in her *cahier* of 28 May 1985, when she knew that Mary's condition was well advanced, she wrote, 'My mother would not have become semi-insane ... if I had not existed.' This should not, however, be taken as a contrite response to Mary's final letter, albeit a private one. Ten years later she composed an unsympathetic short-story account of a woman called Naomi, which is based unashamedly on the life of Mary Highsmith. The story ends with Naomi in a home, barely conscious and kept alive by drugs. In an unpublished 1990 sequel, 'The Tube', the same woman has become a brain-dead channel for administered liquefied foodstuffs. Both pieces are vividly realistic in terms of what awaits human beings who lose any sense of their physical presence long before it ceases to function. Their consistent feature is a lack of anything close to sympathy or compassion. Coates informed Highsmith in 1984 that for some years Mary had ceased to know who he was – and not once before or after that did Highsmith send her a letter, though given her taste for noir humour she might have considered it.

14

HER LAST LOVES

Edith's Diary (1977) is kept by the eponymous housewife Edith Howland, married to the journalist Brett and mother of Cliffie, who is ten when they relocate from New York City to small-town Pennsylvania. Things begin to go wrong when Brett leaves her for a younger woman and Cliffie turns into an alcoholic delinquent, cheating and failing his exams for Princeton which, in his mother's opinion, is his deserved destination. On top of things, she is left in charge of Brett's senile uncle, George. Edith's life is persistently ruined by fate or the bad behaviour of those closest to her and she repairs the damage by rewriting it in her diary, correcting the faults of Brett, Cliffie and others and turning horrible actuality on its head. Cliffie, for example, does spectacularly well at Princeton, becomes a hydraulic engineer, marries and has children, while his actual counterpart, the dropout, spends his spare time masturbating into a sock while fantasising about girls who in reality treat him with derision. The closest he comes to sex is with a rubber-doll facsimile of a woman called Luce. He abandons the project only out of fear that his mother might discover the half-constructed inflatable. Perhaps she did; hence his imagined manifestation as a specialist in hydraulics.

Edith's diary, her book of lies and alternative truths, is her bastion against depression, possibly insanity. It enables her to create a private world, the one she prefers over the version in which she exists.

There are few direct parallels between Edith's dismal story and her author's life – Highsmith was not married, nor lumbered with a deranged son. At the same time, we can see how she might have extrapolated aspects of her emotional condition to the novel. Although she would never openly admit to it, Cliffie's anarchic, debauched existence is a version of the way her own mother, Mary, thought about her. It is not quite a moment of contrition but when we look at the letters in which Mary despairs of her daughter, confessing to being unable to understand why she seemed so determined to ruin their relationship through her behaviour, the similarities are striking.

Edith, now middle aged, looks back on the departure of Brett with a sense of weary finality. She knows that this is not just the end of this particular relationship but that the future has no alternatives in store. By the mid-1970s Highsmith had not quite given up on affairs. Indeed, she began one with the journalist Marion Aboudaram just as she completed the novel and would dedicate the book to her. But throughout their time together Marion was under the impression that what they had was more a memorial to the irretrievable past than the beginning of something new. Brett's Uncle George, senile and apparently destined to a condition of hardly knowing who he is, seems rather superfluous to the rest of the narrative. He is a depressing supplement to everything else. Yet the question of why Highsmith invented him can be answered in terms of a relative of her own suffering from a similar state of mental decay, whom she had preferred to leave with her cousin and a Fort Worth nursing home rather than care for herself, let alone write to.

The novel was greeted with mixed reviews. The *Times Literary Supplement* and the *New York Times* praised Highsmith as a figure who had abandoned her home territory of populist crime and suspense fiction for an attempt at the literary mainstream, a work which tackled the travails of middle-class failure and disappointment, from the point of view of a woman. This allowed them to overlook its sometimes leaden prose and a conclusion which suggests that Highsmith ended the story because she despaired of taking it further.

Apart from three or four of Highsmith's closest friends no one would have been aware of the book's most intriguing feature. In later life Highsmith's *cahiers* and diaries were not always complete falsifications of the truth, but they enabled her on some occasions to reshape the actualities of her existence, and on others to tarnish the more comforting or bearable aspects of her life. One of her earliest *cahiers* contains the story of her first meetings with her biological father, Jay B. Plangman, who allegedly shows her pornographic photographs and kisses her in a way that is neither amicably familiar nor quite lascivious, but with just enough intention to cause her to wonder about the true nature of his feelings towards her. She picks up on this in 1970 more than three decades later when she mentions Plangman and that 'the word incestuous is a strong one' in a letter to her stepfather Stanley Highsmith. No evidence exists of Plangman's sexual inclinations nor of whether the meetings during which these alleged events occurred actually took place. She was not, like Edith, attempting to improve upon her comfortless existence in the routine sense but it is clear enough that Highsmith was spinning out a legend for herself involving events that marked her out as faintly exotic.

Typically, when she began a relationship she thought would be unique, perhaps even permanent, she recorded her thoughts in her diaries without speaking to another human being, least of all the particular woman involved. With Ellen Hill her first entry opens with enchanted hyperbole. 'O the benevolence! O the beautiful world! O the generosity of the heart as I go walking down the street ... today I am vaster ... How could it be? Isn't she like Titanic charmed into loving the donkey?' We should note that she had done it several times before, beginning with her first 'true love' in 1944, Virginia Kent Catherwood, who gave her a 'oneness' and a 'timelessness' and continuing with Caroline Besterman: 'I am nearly sick ... and must get hold of myself or crack up ...'

These are three among many of her visions of where each new affair would lead, and in every instance it is clear that by constructing the idyll she knows she is guaranteeing its destruction. Her description of Ellen Hill's physical characteristics – for example, 'small, quite chic, very good-looking ... very feminine' – are generous to say the least. She was not a plain woman but in the *cahier* Highsmith is determined to create a fantasy based on these exaggerations of her waif-like attractions. Ellen's discovery of Highsmith's diaries contributed to the collapse of their relationship but Ellen was not dismayed so much by her partner's disparaging remarks about her – she had heard many of these directly – as by the web of fantasy that Highsmith had spun around the two of them from when they had first met. Ellen felt that their actual lives had been appropriated by her lover to build a preferred world of her own.

It was even more complicated than this because Highsmith's *cahiers* and notebooks are sometimes more like a dialogue than an alternative reality. Often she remonstrates with herself for allowing fancy to overrule common sense. In 1968, for example, she wrote to her former girlfriend Ann Clark informing her that she was the real love of her life and as she posted the letter she entered in her *cahier* a question: 'I wonder if anything will ever come of it?' and answered: 'It is obvious that my falling in love is not love ... but a necessity of attaching myself to someone' (7 August 1968).

Similarly, Edith's diary is made up of fantasies and remonstrations against herself for indulging them. Rarely does she reread her versions of the past, because she is aware that comparing what she knows to be true with what amounts to a work of fiction would be unbearable, and comments, 'Isn't it safer, even wiser, to believe that life has no meaning at all?' This maxim is repeated dozens of times in Highsmith's notebooks and Edith continues: 'She felt better after getting that down on paper.' She knew that her entries would not alter anything in the real world but after she creates a particularly fantastical version of Cliffie's successful life after Princeton she notes that 'the entry was a lie. But after all, who was going to see it? And she felt better, having written it, felt less melancholic, almost cheerful, in fact.' Rereading the diaries, for both women, would serve only as a reminder that they preferred delusion to a confrontation with fact. Within a few days of beginning the novel she entered in her *cahier* that 'Today I have the alarming feeling that fantasy alone keeps me going...' (12 July, 1974).

Many writers and figures who have achieved esteem in other fields have kept diaries and notebooks as a means of influencing their legacy, particularly for biographers who would compare and contrast their subjects' records and observations with empirical evidence from the real world. A classic case is W. H. Auden's journal entry for 1 September 1939 in which he refers to a dream in which 'C was unfaithful'. 'C' was Chester Kallman, his most recent lover. Homosexuality was illegal in 1939 but he might, like Edith, have reflected that 'after all, who was going to see it?' – at least during his lifetime. He also refers a few days later in the journal to what would be one of his most famous poems, 'September 1, 1939', on which he was working, and refers to the events that inform it, principally the onset of the Second World War. What actually happened in September 1939 both to Auden as a private individual and within the world as a whole provides the framework for his subjective impressions and speculations, and the dynamic between the journal and its context offers the literary biographer vital raw material for a portrait of Auden at the close of the 1930s. What impression would he have left if, say, two weeks later he had expressed his relief that Germany had not invaded Poland and the war in Europe had been avoided? The more sympathetic would treat him as having created a parallel universe, perhaps because he was unable to face up to the likely consequences of another world war, though a larger number would probably regard him as having succumbed to madness.

Edith does the equivalent of this by rewriting the story of her family as she preferred it to be, but as a suburban middle-class housewife rather than a globally acclaimed poet, she could console herself that no one was going to see it. But fate, or rather Highsmith, had other ideas. Her ex-husband and other members of her family become concerned about her psychological condition and she becomes terrified that while she can as an individual present herself as sane the discovery of the diaries will mean a one-way ticket to a mental institution. The novel ends with her desperate attempt to collect and destroy them. She trips on the stairs and dies from head injuries.

In her early twenties, when fame was only a distant prospect, Highsmith treated her diaries as works of fiction, often inventing people and events for which there is no empirical evidence. Later, when she became aware that her private documents would influence perceptions of her as an individual and writer after her death, she stopped making things up, factually at least, but she continued to enter observations and reflections by parts fantastical, unhinged and sometimes unpalatable. Like Edith, she began a conversation with her alternative self. All of Highsmith's papers survive for inspection in the Bern archive. We have a record of when she decided to offer them to Switzerland but we can only speculate on the point at which she became content that her legacy would involve aspects of her personality that most would prefer to be lost from scrutiny for ever. It seems likely, however, that when she created the scenario of Edith panicking at the prospect of her secrets being disclosed Highsmith was considering what people would make of her, post mortem, after reading her diaries. Irrespective of how we feel about her as an individual we might also imagine a dark smile forming as she decided to do the opposite of the fearful Edith.

In December 1974, Highsmith was contacted by Marion Aboudaram, a writer and translator based in Paris who told her that she had been commissioned by the French edition of *Cosmopolitan* to do an interview, which was a lie. They did, however, speak briefly at an art exhibition in the city in January 1975 to make further arrangements for a meeting. Marion had made notes on Highsmith's likely return journey, and followed her by taxi to the Gare du Nord, boarding the same local train to Montcourt while making sure that she took a seat in a different carriage. Answering the door to Marion, Highsmith was beguiled and invited her in, and Marion confessed that she had been obsessed with her, from afar, for some time and asked if they could go upstairs to her bedroom and sleep together immediately. 'I could be your mother,' Highsmith replied, 'I'm too old.' The age difference was around twenty years – Marion was in her mid-thirties – but after phone calls they met again in Montcourt and began an affair, one that was as bizarre as any that featured in Highsmith's fiction.

Marion told Schenkar that their first sexual encounters were in Montcourt and that on every occasion Highsmith, after allowing her in, insisted that she strip naked, which had nothing to do with sex. 'She washed my clothes all the time. When I came in, she took off my raincoat, my trousers … she put the clothes in the bathtub and washed them' (Schenkar, p.404). To Wilson she stated that 'before we went to bed, she summoned me to the bathroom where I had to have a bath to wash off my perfume … she said the smell made her feel sick' (Wilson, p.352). Marion was puzzled by this behaviour. She was also fascinated by Highsmith's preoccupation with what had happened in Paris during the German occupation. Highsmith asked for photographs of her parents and questioned her on the length and smoothness of her legs, her facial bone structure and her skin tone. Marion's mother was one of the native French Jews of the capital who had evaded deportation and extermination by the Nazis. Marion remained confused by the fact that Highsmith insisted that they should visit only one place other than Montcourt and her apartment in Paris. 'I'm Jewish and you know I hate Germany because of that. And the only place Pat ever invited me to go was Germany!' (Schenkar, p.405).

After a few months Highsmith agreed to stay for longer periods with Marion in Paris. 'We made love a lot – the best love we made was at my place in Montmartre, where there are a lot of prostitutes on the streets and I think the prostitutes excited her. But we also used to make love in a little shack in the garden, where she had placed a little bed' (Wilson, p.353). Highsmith came to prefer Marion's little shack to her own house in Montcourt, and not just for sex. She even turned the small terrace between it and the main building into a version of her enclosed walled garden. From various discarded pots and pans she built small artificial ponds for a frog that had taken up residence. She fed the creature regularly and named it Dorothy. 'We laughed a lot,' recalls Marion, 'but underneath it, I was anxious because she was an alcoholic.' At the beginning of their affair Highsmith would come up with spurious tasks she needed to undertake in the kitchen or other ground-floor rooms of the Montcourt house where she had hidden bottles of spirits. In one letter to Marion in Paris she wrote, 'Poor dear, you're married to an alcoholic … Bring your ass and your typewriter but especially your ass.'

Their affair lasted almost three years and ended in 1978, if not quite by mutual consent then without bitterness. Compared with Highsmith's other relationships it might appear casual, even trivial, but for each it seems to have been suffused with a special kind of happiness. Leaving aside Highsmith's preoccupation with Jewishness and Germany, Marion implies that their enjoyment of each other's company and their mutual sexual attraction resulted from their both being slightly abnormal. Highsmith's various eccentricities often caused friction between her and her friends and sometimes she even regarded their tolerance as a licence to cause offence, but with Marion she had for once met a woman who had no concern with how she looked or behaved. Although she mentioned the affair to others, notably in letters to Blythe, Highsmith's descriptions of it and Marion were relaxed, casual and at no point did she resort to the ecstatic hyperbole of her time with Virginia, Ellen, Caroline et al. Marion was her amiably whimsical alter ego and it seems a pity that what they had should have ended as soon as it did.

The cause of their separation was principally Highsmith's obsession with Tabea Blumenschein. The two women had met several times before, but it was during the 1978 Berlin Film Festival that Highsmith declared that she wanted to take things beyond their mutual interest in the arts. Highsmith was fifty-seven and Tabea, a German avant-garde film producer and director, was twenty-five and a fan of the newly fashionable punk mode of dress and hairstyle. Her loose denims were ripped and paint-stained, her make-up colourfully garish and her hair blonde, carefully spiked. Once more Highsmith resorted to building up a private verbal account of the affair as something spectacularly unique, while conveniently forgetting that she had done this on numerous occasions before.

Despite apparent similarities between Marion and Tabea – young, rebellious and radical in their behaviour and outlook – Highsmith was drawn to the latter for perverse reasons, as a means of ruining her relationship with Marion. Just as she had done with her doomed affairs of the previous thirty-five years she wrapped herself and Tabea in a web of verbal grotesquery. In April 1978, for example, she sent Tabea a poem in which she compared the intensity of her love for her with a sudden desire to throw herself into a deep lake and drown, adding that 'This isn't blackmail ... I'd do it with a smile,' which must have comforted her new lover greatly. She took her to London and introduced her to Arthur and Cynthia Koestler in their house in Montpelier Square. Tabea, despite her radical bravado, felt completely out of her depth and returned to Berlin two days later. Shortly after that Highsmith wrote a poem about the episode opening with 'your kisses fill me with terror' and after she returned to Montcourt she sent a number of Tabea's (confidential) letters to Alex Szogyi, who, aside from his respectable literary persona, claimed to be able to discern the true nature of a person's character from their birth signs and handwriting. Szogyi, without having met Tabea, replied to Highsmith with a full character profile on a woman who had a '"big" personality ... and is used to a great deal of lebensraum'.

Highsmith eulogised the close of their affair with a poem, to herself, which includes the lines:

I realise that any sorrow I may know
Will come from 'wanting',
Desiring what I cannot have...

The statement that she only now 'realises' that sorrow comes from wanting what she cannot have is absurd in that she had experienced this on numerous occasions over the previous three decades. She was not so much confessing to amnesia as admitting to herself that she was addicted to the experience she describes. It is intriguing that nothing resembling this, either in verse or prose, records her feelings about Marion, either when they met or when the affair collapsed. Even in her letters to her she prefers an endearingly rude transparency over affection. Evidently, she enjoyed her years with her greatly but something vital was lacking: pain.

Highsmith met Monique Buffet when Val (who prefers not to disclose her surname), a London-based journalist, visited Montcourt in August 1977 and asked if she could bring a friend, an English teacher who lived in Paris. Monique was twenty-seven, blonde, petite and pretty, and she stated to Schenkar that all she recalls of this first encounter was that she was 'petrified ... I didn't say one word.' Nonetheless just before she and Val left Highsmith asked Monique for her telephone number and address. She contacted her nine months later shortly after she had broken up with Tabea, they agreed to meet in Paris a week after that, and immediately became lovers.

Apart from her relative youth Monique differed from Marion and Tabea considerably. Before they met, she was in awe of Highsmith as a writer, though not a dedicated fan, and she described herself to Wilson as androgynous, bisexual, happier with women than men, not overly promiscuous, and unexceptional in terms of her lifestyle. For Highsmith, this seemed an invitation to turn her, despite herself, into a hybrid of Marion and Tabea. Their second date, for example, Highsmith proposed 'Why not give the old clip joint ... a try.'

Following the Revolution, the French Penal Code was adopted in 1791 and contained a clause decriminalising homosexual acts. The law has remained largely unchanged since then, save for a discriminatory law that existed between 1960 and 1980 called the Mirguet amendment, and at various points when reactionary and church-affiliated bodies have done their best to make it socially unacceptable to be openly gay. The worst period was during the Nazi occupation where gays effectively had to go underground to avoid being singled out and sent to concentration camps. Later the Mirguet amendment ruled against public displays of homosexuality, most obviously sexual acts, but did not criminalise what people chose to do indoors or in private clubs. France was the European country where gay life was most tolerated, especially within the more liberal cosmopolitan districts. So, although the Katmandou had since the 1950s cultivated a louche, even debauched image, it was free to do so, markedly unlike the clubs in New York where she had met Marijane Meaker. Indeed the club, on the rue du Vieux-Colombier, profited financially not as a hiding place but rather as a hangout where customers would pay vastly inflated drinks prices as the cost of celebrity. Lesbianism was its trademark but being gay was not a necessity for women who wanted to display their independence by mixing with those of the same gender and excluding others. There was even a row of seats next to the dance floor known as the 'royale' section, given that it was often occupied by princesses from oil-rich Arabian states who wanted to enjoy evenings doing as they wished before returning to the patriarchal regimes of their Muslim homelands.

Highsmith proudly introduced Monique to the club as her guest, only to be told by the girl who checked coats that the place was packed. The author, disappointed, said they could repair to a rather less salubrious gay club less than half a kilometre away but as they left one of the co-owners, Elula Perrin, charged outside and ran after them down the road shouting, 'Pat Highsmith! No, no, no – we've got places!' Elula ushered them back in and ordered one of her waitresses to bribe two occupants of the 'royale' seats to make room for a prestigious client and her guest. Highsmith was delighted and her new girlfriend was suitably impressed. It was the beginning of her attempt to build a fantasy as lover and benefactor. According to Monique, 'She wanted to offer me everything – a flat in Paris, a car, trips around the world – but I never accepted anything from her' (Wilson, p. 370).

The affair lasted around two years, until Highsmith bought a house in Switzerland and divided her time between the two countries, but the two women corresponded regularly until Highsmith's death and met on several occasions.

Shortly before she met Monique, Highsmith was just over fifty pages into her next Ripley novel, *The Boy Who Followed Ripley* (1980). It was not that she was uncertain of where to take the narrative – there was nothing resembling a story, not even an opening. Highsmith had absolutely no idea of what she would do next with her most enduring literary creation, but as her brief encounter with Monique became an affair she began to see why she had come upon the only element of the opening part of the draft that hinted at a theme.

A boy, specifically a teenager, would be involved and as she looked more closely at her own experiences over the previous three years,

Billy, whose real name is Frank, became a more clearly defined literary presence. He is American, sixteen but precocious – he could have passed himself off as a twenty-year-old – and he arrives without warning in the village adjoining Ripley's house, contacts Ripley and asks for a job. His true motive soon becomes clear in that he has read of Ripley in the international press as a figure of wealth and esteem who was suspected of gaining his position by unvirtuous and allegedly criminal means. He eventually admits to Ripley that he has murdered his father, a wealthy industrialist, and has come to Europe, to Ripley, in the hope of finding fake identity documents and continuing his life underground as someone else. He is a youthful version of Ripley and there are even physical and temperamental similarities.

It is an intriguing scenario, especially since Highsmith had all but exhausted new variations on what her long-serving creation might do next. Now, he is faced with something that goes against his Machiavellian ability to control what occurs in his life. He is confronted by an embodiment of his past and for a while at least is not sure how to react. The inspiration came from two similar visitations experienced by Highsmith, first with Marion and more recently with Monique. Marion's arrival, like Frank's, involved subterfuge – first with her invention of a contract to do an interview for *Cosmopolitan*, followed by her pursuit of Highsmith from Paris by train to arrive, spectre-like, on her doorstep. Something similar occurred with Monique, brought to Highsmith's house by Val as a shy dumbfounded enigma who would soon become the elemental feature of the author's life. Both women, along with Tabea, saw Highsmith from a distance much as Frank does with Ripley. Like others with an interest in literature they saw her as both eminent and inscrutable and aside from her reputation as a writer they had heard from the underground circles in which they mixed with other women that her non-conformist inclinations went beyond her work. It never becomes apparent either to Ripley or the reader why exactly Frank killed his father but it is implied that Frank knows something of Ripley's past and hopes to learn how to create a new identity for himself. Frank is kidnapped in Germany, rescued by Ripley and after his return to America commits suicide, perhaps out of a sense of repentance. Or not. Highsmith appears to have given up completely on all conventional notions of motive. Instead the book seems to be a case of disorderly fiction jumbled with aspects of autobiography.

Highsmith saw in each of her three recent lovers versions of herself from three decades earlier: compulsive and unaffiliated (Tabea), unselfishly hedonistic (Marion) and a woman who was by degrees compassionate and apprehensive (Monique). What stays in the mind from *The Boy Who Followed Ripley* is a fatherly affection shown by Ripley towards Frank and the gradual sense of two men drawn together by a homoerotic mutual attraction despite, or perhaps because of, their age difference. The more striking scenes occur in a gay bar in Berlin, of the sort where Highsmith provoked the attention of others: a conventionally dressed middle-aged woman enjoying the attention of a well-known punk actress and film-maker of the city, less than half her age.

15

'I'M SICK OF THE JEWS!'

On 15 January 1980 Highsmith was working alone in the Montcourt house, leaning over her typewriter, when she began to notice that the paper on her desk and the machine itself was spotted with blood. She was puzzled because she had not, as far as she knew, injured herself but within a few minutes she found that the spots were the prelude to a flood. A neighbour phoned the local doctor who claimed he had more serious cases to deal with but the more helpful local *sapeurs-pompiers*, the part-time fire service, rushed her to Nemours hospital. It seemed for several days as if the effusive loss of blood from her nose would be impossible to control. The hospital specialised in the treatment of children, and young patients who were mobile were kept away from her bed for fear that they would be traumatised from something that looked like a battlefield dressing station. Transfusions kept her alive until it was found that for seven years, following the discovery of several clots in her legs, she had been overdosing on blood-thinning drugs. The clots had been cured but her overuse of the medicines and the principal cause of her thrombosis, excess alcohol, were diagnosed as the reason for her massive bleeding.

The hospital remedied the problem and prescribed a new regime of drugs, but in March she was again admitted for more detailed examinations. She was found to have seriously narrowed arteries in her femur at the top of her leg and in her iliac region in her lower stomach. A month later in London she booked herself into a private hospital for bypass surgery to normalise the blood flow in both parts of her body. She was advised that the operation was urgent, given that she was in imminent danger of suffering a heart attack.

On the night she was admitted to the hospital she made a note that she would later enter in her *cahier*: 'How appropriate, to be bleeding in two places.' When the nosebleed began she had been putting together records of her income from publications over the previous few years and typing up a comprehensive account for the French tax authorities. Since 1974 the Giscard d'Estaing presidency had been desperately attempting to resolve the economic crisis brought about by the increase in the price of oil from the Gulf states. Major corporations were badly hit but tax on average incomes and various forms of wealth tax levied on individuals had also been increased by between 15 and 20 per cent. By 1979 tax inspectors had been encouraged to act like policemen involved in criminal investigations, especially with expatriate French residents who might be receiving income from abroad and hold accounts in more generously taxed states. This was the other 'nosebleed'. Tax officials had visited her house and sent her demands on what they expected her to declare and the interest that would be imposed on unpaid taxes.

In early March 1980 she was told that a warrant was soon to be issued by the *impôts*, the tax office, to allow officials to enter her house and seize all available documents for inspection. Two days later she took a train to Bern and then local transport to the canton of Ticino and eventually the tiny village of Aurigeno. It was not a random gesture. She had contacted Ellen Hill who was now living near Ticino and asked her to find a suitable house in the region. She stayed only two days and put a deposit on a property that had an asking price of $90,000 and needed slight refurbishment. It was a stone house built in 1682 with low ceilings, small windows and one-metre-thick walls as security against the freezing winters. Ten days later, after she had returned to France, the Montcourt house was raided by two tax officers and a policeman. They seized all available documents, even her chequebook, to look at how potential outgoings corresponded with her records, and she described the incursion to her friend Christa Maerker as 'Nazi Style'. She was told that as a French resident, though not a citizen, she was forbidden from having an overseas bank account and in October 1980 informed threateningly that if she agreed to pay a fine of 10,000 francs further investigations would be suspended, for the time being.

She planned to avoid the most stringent French tax laws by becoming a non-permanent resident. Those permanently resident in the country, including expatriates, were forbidden from keeping bank accounts abroad as a means of securing their savings in countries with lower tax rates than France; i.e. virtually everywhere. Highsmith hoped to make use of a potential loophole whereby persons who lived outside France for at least 180 days a year were exempt from the status of permanent residents. She had obviously been taking uninformed advice, as six months after she bought the Aurigeno house the tax penalty on expatriate residents was overturned. Two years later she sold Montcourt and left for Aurigeno for good.

In January 1981 she flew from Paris to New York and lunched with Larry Ashmead, who as editor at Simon & Schuster had bought *Edith's Diary* and was now with Lippincott & Cromwell, who had brought out *The Boy Who Followed Ripley*. She said she was there to do research for her forthcoming novel. Specifically, she wanted to pick up on the mood of her native country, which had elected a right-wing Republican, ex-Hollywood actor to the presidency two months earlier. Highsmith arrived roughly at the time of Ronald Reagan's presidential inauguration, though this might have been a coincidence. For much of her life her interest in politics had been random and quixotic. She gave the impression that she cultivated radical opinions – right or left – for the sake of it, as a means of provoking a response, while in truth holding no sincere commitment to anything. Even her now notorious antisemitism, which became more conspicuous during the 1980s, was more a brand of gesture politics than a reflection of a heartfelt contempt for Judaism.

She was astute in her reading of the America that had brought Reagan to the White House. The press had presented him as a kind of B-movie John Wayne, the man who would restore a 7th Cavalry pride to an America humiliated in Vietnam and not prepared to back down against the Soviet bloc. He was the tough-guy opposite of his predecessor Jimmy Carter, who favoured liberal social policies and seemed to be shifting the country towards a European-style welfare state. Highsmith suspected that one of the reasons for his victory had been overlooked in press coverage: evangelicalism in particular, and religious fundamentalism in general.

From New York she flew to Indianapolis, the state capital of Indiana, where she stayed with her friends from the Lot, Charles Latimer and Michel Block. The largest single Christian denomination in the state was Roman Catholicism, represented mostly by second-generation immigrants from Western and Central Europe, but the Catholic Church, though conservative by its nature, did not significantly influence local politics. Far more outspoken were clergymen from the various groups that owed allegiance to the Puritan settlements of the East Coast in the seventeenth and eighteenth centuries: Baptists, Methodists, extreme Lutherans, Presbyterians and Evangelical Protestants. Many supported figures such as Robert Grant and Jerry Falwell who had through the 1970s campaigned to roll back the attempts by the Supreme Court to turn the US into a more secular state. They wanted federal laws that made prayers and Bible readings compulsory in state schools and they campaigned against the legalisation of same-sex activity, abortion and the abolition of the death penalty.

Reagan, following his political advisers, promoted all of these issues on the assumption that the Midwestern states would swing radically towards a restoration of social conservatism. He and they were proved right and Highsmith spent several months in disguise, posing as someone visiting relatives, talking to people in Bloomington, Indiana, attending church services and afterwards making notes. She found that even if right-wing politicians such as Reagan did not openly invoke scripture, voters in Bible Belt states would recognise parallels between his promises and what they had heard from the pulpit.

In February she flew back to Europe and went straight to her Aurigeno house which, in her absence, Ellen Hill had redecorated and furnished tastefully though not extravagantly. There were two bedrooms upstairs and rooms with sofas and chairs on the ground floor, and a writing desk. Within a week of her arrival she began *People Who Knock on the Door* (1983), based on her impression of how the Moral Majority – a blanket term for the alliance between right-wing politics and Christian fundamentalism – now controlled the destiny of America.

As in some of her previous novels this one was patently her attempt to unshackle herself from the classification as a 'genre' writer – suspense, crime, thriller, whodunnit or whatever – and once more she had difficulty in overcoming an addiction.

Chalmerston, the setting, is Bloomington thinly disguised, and the plot is concerned with the Alderman family. Arthur, the elder son, embodies the ambitions of the new America of his generation. He plans to go to Columbia University, New York, and become part of the liberated culture of the East Coast. Indeed, the novel opens with him reflecting on his afternoon of sex with his girlfriend Maggie Brewster as, in part, an act of rebellion against the hidebound religiosity of his hometown. Maggie eventually becomes pregnant and the parties involved – the two of them and their families – enter a conflict between the moral question of whether sex outside marriage is a sin, and expediency, principally the opportunity for an abortion.

Meanwhile Arthur's younger brother, Robbie, recovers from what seems to be a terminal illness and their father Richard, convinced that his period of dedicated prayer saved him, becomes committed to fundamentalism and creationism. He also, however, has an affair with and impregnates Irene, a born-again ex-prostitute and fellow member of Richard's church.

Heinemann accepted it for publication in the UK, though several on the editorial board expressed their reservations, and it did not come out in America until 1985, having been rejected by three publishers. Ashmead, the editor to whom she had first spoken of it when she arrived in America, thought it was unpublishable, by anyone.

Clearly the novel was intended as a literary polemic, with religious fundamentalism as its principal target but for a number of reasons it goes horribly wrong. Richard's shift towards extreme religiosity might have been based on what Highsmith had encountered in Bloomington. Preachers regularly reported on examples of individuals who had been 'born again' because they apportioned some life-changing event to the direct intervention of the Almighty. But in the novel the tension between the newly evangelistic Richard and Arthur plays out as a contrast between robotic abstractions rather than human beings who add interest to life and fiction. Highsmith obviously expects the reader to identify more with Arthur than with his father – Arthur embodies imperatives such as the desire for freedom of thought, for example – but as a literary character he is two-dimensional and fails to prompt anything close to sympathy.

Highsmith was exploring a genre, specifically the novel of ideas, that she had previously attempted and failed to master, and as we move towards the close of the novel, we become aware of her being drawn towards her natural home. Robbie discovers that his father has impregnated Irene but instead of confronting him with evidence of his hypocrisy he shoots and kills him. The act is described by Highsmith in a manner that reflects her sense of relief at no longer having to deal with the commonplaces of life.

> His [Richard's] jaw and neck were red with blood, as was the top
> part of his striped shirt … the front part of his father's throat
> looked torn away and also part of his jaw. Blood flowed into
> the green carpet. Spatters of blood on his father's desk caught
> Arthur's eye as he straightened … Now Arthur noticed that his
> father's blue trousers were damp between the legs.

As each grisly detail is laid out, clause after clause, one can almost hear Highsmith exhaling, 'I'm back!' She even implies that Arthur is quietly complicit in the murder as he privately savours details of the blood on the desk and the humiliating urine stains on Richard's trousers.

The conclusion is bizarre. Without even a token display of grief for Richard, Arthur and his brother visit their neighbour Norma for a party, alcohol included. Arthur revives his relationship with Maggie and heads for Columbia and Lois, the mother, sells the house to move east and escape the claustrophobic religiosity of the area. It is as though the death of Richard has provided an escape route for the rest of them and as they, and we, leave Chalmerston, Highsmith delivers a grotesque coda. Irene's baby, presumably Richard's, will be brought up with the fundamentalist church and, we are left to assume, become the heir to his worst characteristics by virtue of genetic inheritance and brainwashing.

Reading the novel is illuminating, at least if we look behind the words on the page to the state of mind of the woman who wrote them. For around 80 per cent of the book she is uncomfortable with what she is doing but once the real Highsmith takes over – the inventor of murderous psychopaths with no apparent moral compass – a strange mixture of excitement and contentment informs the prose and what is left of the story.

Before *People Who Knock on the Door* was published in Britain Highsmith was already two chapters into her next novel, *Found in the Street*. The books are very different except both grew out of

Highsmith's research visit to America in early 1981. Before flying to Indiana she had spent several days wandering around Greenwich Village and other parts of New York where she had lived in the 1940s and early 1950s. She took notes on the appearance of buildings in which she or her friends had lived, tried to remember if, say, doors were painted differently, and effectively attempted to recreate her earlier life. She walked the same streets she'd once taken to and from college and work, took meals, coffees and drinks in cafés and bars she recalled, or at least those that still existed. Alongside her notes she drew maps and she used this topography of her twenties as the setting for the characters of her novel. Buffie Johnson, who Highsmith knew almost four decades earlier, was socially well connected and cultivated the image of a self-supporting bohemian, despite her affluent family background. She was a widely acclaimed painter who owned an apartment in Greene Street, and Elsie Tyler, the magnet for all the male characters in *Found in the Street*, moves there shortly before the novel closes.

Ralph Linderman is a perverted, reclusive, antisemitic racist who is obsessed with protecting Elsie from the debauched city. Jack Sutherland, a successful thirty-year-old graphic artist, is married with a wife and daughter and he too is fascinated by her. Highsmith wrote to Barbara Ker-Seymer that 'half the characters in it are gay or half-gay' (16 September 1984), meaning that Linderman and Sutherland fixate upon Elsie not only because she is elusive and beautiful but because a woman such as her would reassure them of their heterosexuality. Before either can turn their speculations into tangible proof, one way or another, Elsie is murdered.

Many reviewers found the book fascinating, but a number were puzzled by it being caught in a time warp. Supposedly it occurs in the present day, the mid-1980s, but in terms of atmosphere – the way people socialise, use bars, etc., and the particulars of behaviour and conversational idiom – it seems to take us back at least thirty years. Highsmith began it within a year of her return from America.

It was her memoir-in-fiction, a an echo of the time in which, for most of the people she knew, sexuality was by varying degrees hidden and fluid. And once more we are back to the morbid trope of her twenties and thirties: love was coterminous with a kind of murder.

It is intriguing that all but one of the characters in the novel are housed in buildings adjacent to or facing the ones she recorded in her notes or on the map as once lived in by her friends, lovers, parents – even herself. It is as if she wanted to present her fictional inventions as neighbours of the people and places of her remembered life, individuals and events that echoed her past but were not exact representations of it, with the exception of Buffie Johnson and Elsie Tyler, who share a floor in the same building. There are other similarities between them: both are ethereally beautiful, and rather enigmatic in that those who know them compete for an intimate knowledge of their true selves. Buffie spun her sphinx-like persona from her growing reputation as a painter who seemed impossible to classify, shifting between abstract modernism and more conservative representational works, while Elsie bewitched people, men especially, by seeming to possess magical qualities that belied her ordinary background. She supported herself as a waitress while pursuing her career as a model. Buffie told Schenkar the story of when she first met Highsmith:

> I was aware from her attention that she wanted to become my friend. When I was about to leave she asked if she could see me again and I said yes. But when I gave her my telephone number I noticed she didn't write it down. I mentioned this and she laughed saying 'I'll remember.' To my surprise, she did and I was impressed by this trick of memory. (Johnson to Schenkar, November 2001)

Johnson goes on to state that Highsmith was keen to know her better not as a social climber but to see if they were both lesbians. Buffie was heterosexual, but for some, sexuality is nuanced and open to interpretation. In the novel Highsmith divides her memories of herself, specifically her fascination with Buffie, between Ralph and Jack. For both of them the most beautiful woman they've ever seen is not so much sexually alluring as an experiment in self-obsession. And so it was with Highsmith and Buffie. When they first met in 1941, Highsmith had wanted to have sex with women but was confused by the nature of her desires, caught between what she had been told she ought to be and what she suspected she might be. Buffie herself did not offer her an answer to this question, at least not directly. However, it was through her Highsmith met her first serious lover, Rosalind Constable.

What occurred afterwards, with her many affairs with women, is now a matter of record. Though she never had sex with her Buffie had shown her, albeit inadvertently, who and what she was. The two women did not meet again and in the novel Elsie is murdered before she can answer questions for Jack and Ralph that are almost identical to those faced by their author in 1941. Perhaps Highsmith was admitting that even when we think we know who we are we might be deceiving ourselves.

After she completed the novel Highsmith would never again have sex or an affair with a woman. It seemed to be her goodbye note from the life that had effectively begun when she met Buffie in 1941 and that now had become a kind of limbo. For the remainder of her time in Switzerland she met and socialised regularly with Ellen Hill, who lived less than an hour's drive from the Aurigeno home and the house she later built for herself. Their original relationship was the most complex and painful of Highsmith's life and for the next ten years, until her death, the two women lived out a pantomime version of the affair: sexless, without any pretence to affection or mutual respect but with an apparent addiction to mutual fractiousness.

When they met for meals or journeys through the country that was imprinted on each as a memorial to something that might have been, Ellen continually remonstrated with Highsmith on everything from her sloppy habits of dress to her ability to find stashes of alcohol at virtually all times of the day. Monique Buffet remarked that 'Pat knew it would be hell on earth living near Ellen Hill, but she went ahead and did it anyway.' Christa Maerker, the film-maker who knew both women, recalled that at a railway station Highsmith, self-parodically, proclaimed 'let's have some coffee', ordered beer for herself instead and was shouted at by Ellen in the manner of a governess: 'Pat, not in the morning!'

The parallels between her seemingly masochistic attachment to Ellen and *Found in the Street* are striking. In both she revisits her past without a hint of nostalgia but with a blend of contrition and self-loathing.

In April 1987 Highsmith travelled to Lleida in Catalonia to attend a literary conference. She was the principal interviewee and had agreed in advance to respond to questions on all aspects of her career. In reply to an enquiry on whether or not writers should indicate their political opinions outside their work, or more importantly, in it, she replied that 'If a writer, or painter, starts preaching, consciously, in his work, it is no longer a piece of art.' While she did not refer to *People Who Knock on the Door*, we might read this as an involuntary explanation of the book's flaws. Clearly she had researched it and begun writing it as a political polemic and soon realised that she could not realise her objective.

She went on to admit that she did hold political opinions but avoided the interviewer's query on their nature, stating vaguely that she was willing to 'boycott and be boycotted in return'. There was a detectable murmur in the audience because at the time political boycotts were directed primarily at three countries. There was the embargo on the 1980 Moscow Summer Olympics led by Jimmy Carter's US administration in protest against the Soviet

Union's violations of human rights, and the longer-term political and economic boycott of the South African apartheid regime. Less prominent was the campaign mounted by a number of Western intellectuals, academics and writers that Israel should be boycotted for its treatment of the Palestinians, which was implemented officially only by member states of the Organisation of Islamic Cooperation and the Arab League.

One member of the audience read out the dedication of *Found in the Street* published only six months earlier. 'To the courage of the Palestinian people and their leaders in the struggle to regain a part of their homeland. This book has nothing to do with their problem.' The second sentence is presumably an assurance to the reader who comes first to the dedication that the novel will not involve or address itself to affairs in the Middle East. Her interviewer asked if her statement was a personal message to organisations dedicated to attacks on Israel, specifically the Palestine Liberation Organization (PLO). She answered that 'Yes, it is addressed to the leaders, singular or plural, of the Palestinian people, who must choose their own leaders ... If they choose the PLO, as 96 per cent do as I state this, then my dedication is to the PLO' (Record of Lleida interview, 26 April 1987).

The interview was not widely reported at the time, but it was Highsmith's first public declaration of her political opinions and affiliations. Indeed, even among her conversational exchanges and correspondence there is little evidence of anything close to consistency in terms of who or what she supported. As we have seen she had no affection for Reagan, but she was aggrieved more by the spectacle of a B-movie actor who cultivated the votes of religious fundamentalists and blue-collar Midwesterners rather than by anything the president claimed to profess. At the same time, she wrote to Barbara Ker-Seymer in 1987 expressing her praise for Reagan's ally Margaret Thatcher. Ker-Seymer assumed initially that they shared a begrudging admiration for her as the first woman to rise to prominence in Western politics, but Highsmith corrected her and stressed that she supported Thatcher because of her tax-cutting policy, irrespective of the ideology behind it. The actor and director Nicolas Kent confessed that 'I could never work out Pat's politics', and Bettina Berch expanded, 'Although she was, later, anti-Bush, she could just as well come out thinking some right-wing ideologue cool because he happened to say something that struck her fancy' (Wilson, p. 374).

One factor that went against her erratic and faddish attitudes was her long-term antisemitism. In 1963 she was invited by Caroline Besterman to a dinner party in London hosted by a married couple, one a medical professional, the other an academic, whose families had moved to Britain from Central Europe in the mid-nineteenth century. The wife was Jewish, but secular, and hardly ever drew attention to her ethnic background. Nonetheless, Highsmith spent the evening seemingly intent on provoking an argument. Those present succeeded in turning the conversation elsewhere until there was an uncomfortable lull when Highsmith slapped the table, turned to her hosts and announced, 'I'm sick of the Jews!'

In 1988, ten months after the Catalonia conference, she wrote in her diary that she had 'spent a lot of time composing letters I think may be useful to peace and stopping the deaths … 72 Palestinians so far dead, no Jews' (28 February 1988). This might seem a commendable enterprise, an attempt to urge reconciliation rather than a specific attack on Israel and Jews. However, she leaves out the fact that since the mid-1960s the letters she had composed and sent to mostly left-leaning mainstream newspapers in America, Britain, France and Germany were signed by more than forty different individuals, none of which was 'Patricia Highsmith': her particular favourites were Edgar S. Sallich of Locarno, the Americans Isabel Little, Maria L. Leone, Janet Tamagni, Eddie Stefano and Elaine Dutweiler, and the London-based Englishwoman Phyllis Cutler. Each condemned Israel for its annexing of land from Palestinians and its policies following the wars of the late 1960s and early 1970s with neighbouring Arab states. Her pseudonymous letter writers shared the opinion that the only equitable solution was the abolition of Israel.

In a rare instance of speaking for herself she stated in an interview with Ian Hamilton in 1977 that 'I think the Jewish lobby, on the Middle East, is pulling Congress around by the nose ... these little Congressmen are afraid of losing their jobs, frankly, if they don't send money and arms to Israel ... I don't know why America supports a country that is behaving like that.' This sounds like a candid condemnation of Israeli policy, but it should not be seen as Highsmith joining the public debate.

Ten years later she wrote to Gore Vidal, expressing her support for him in an embittered exchange that had erupted between Vidal and two pro-Israel writers, William Safire and Norman Podhoretz, both Jewish. She asked Vidal to read a recently published letter in the *International Herald Tribune* condemning supporters of Israel as either Americans who wanted a colonial outpost in the oil-rich regions of the Middle East or Europeans who were attempting to salve their conscience for the Holocaust, at the expense of the Palestinians. She also confessed that while she had written it, it was signed by Edgar S. Sallich of Switzerland. There is no record of a reply from Vidal. She had stated in her letter to him that 'I don't care to use my own name too often, so I invent names. I could have said that many Jews in the USA seem to like America as a safe berth and source of money for Israel. But would such a letter get printed?' (Letter from Highsmith to Vidal, 9 June 1986). She also asked him not to disclose to the media that she had written to him.

In 1992 she wrote an essay which laid out how, in her view, the recent history of the Middle East had led to the present conflict and the injustices being meted out to the Palestinians. She treats the two major conflicts between Israel and neighbouring Arab states – the Six-Day and Yom Kippur Wars – as part of the Cold War played out by proxy nations. The Arabs were backed and armed by the Soviet Union, she argues, while Israel could make use of far more deadly and efficient air power and armour supplied by America. Israel triumphed in both instances and enabled the US to continue to treat it as its ally, or military outpost, in the eastern Mediterranean and within the oil-rich regions of the Red Sea, the Persian Gulf and the Indian Ocean. In return, the US expressed no objection to what amounted to Israel's colonisation of the West Bank, Jerusalem and other areas from which Arab troops had retreated.

> Americans and the world know that America gives too lavishly to Israel ... because the United States wanted Israel as a strong military bulwark in the Cold War. Now that the Cold War is over, America has cut none of its aid ... I blame my own country for the majority of injustices now being inflicted on what they consider Greater Israel.

As a military historian, Highsmith's expertise is flawed. Few would dispute that during both wars the Israelis had often come close to defeat. Indeed during the Yom Kippur conflict it seemed at the opening that Egyptian, Syrian and Jordanian forces were making irreversible inroads into territories declared as parts of the state of Israel in 1948. She was not, however, making use of impartial accounts to back up her version of events. During the essay she quotes from, amongst others, Vidal, Alexander Cockburn, Noam Chomsky and Edward Said and it is clear that her view is a cut-and-paste version of their polemics arguing that Israel was a US colonial outpost established both as an anti-Soviet airbase and as a means of bullying the countries on which the West depended for much of its oil. She pledged her support for each of these thinkers and writers and the essay is clearly her first detailed statement of allegiance, or it would have been, had she not decided to place it in an unmarked file and not attempted to get it into print.

The topic of the Israel–Palestine conflict has, especially in Western democracies, provided some individuals with the opportunity to divide themselves between their private and public personae. Those with a visceral loathing for Jews can disguise this in the media as a measured opinion on the politics of injustice. The British Labour Party has presented a recent example, with a large number of members, some of them MPs, carelessly expressing on social media a contempt for Jews, alongside quasi-Nazi sympathies and doubts about the nature and magnitude of the Holocaust. Those exposed claimed that their statements had been read 'out of context', and in defence directed their accusers to their publicly expressed opinions on a fair solution to the problems in the Middle East.

Fortunately for Highsmith, social media did not come into being until the late 1990s, but there is conclusive evidence that she cautiously divided her comments on Jews between recorded statements that might be acceptable as part of a broader discourse and her far more disturbing private inclinations. In her public statements she expressed sympathy for the Palestinians, while in conversations and correspondence – the equivalent of social media, which some foolishly regard as guaranteeing confidentiality or anonymity – she disclosed the true nature of her feelings: she hated Jews and wanted Israel to be destroyed. In 1989 on a publicity trip to Italy she sometimes wore a '"Palestine PLO check" sweater', which indicated support for the organisation whose then leader, Yasser Arafat, was known worldwide for his distinctive keffiyeh headdress. By the end of the eighties this had become an enormously popular fashion accessory for those who wanted to display some connection with radical chic, most of whom had little or no interest or knowledge of affairs in the Middle East. She recorded in her notebook that she had spoken in several interviews in Italy on US involvement in the region but there are no surviving records of such statements in the media. All of which places her within the cadre of left-leaning artists, intellectuals and celebrities for whom support for the seemingly oppressed or dispossessed was at the time a public obligation, and therefore something that hardly made them conspicuous. This was the manifest version of Highsmith; the real one was more unsettling.

Her friends became distressed and disturbed by what she said to them. During the 1970s she became an outspoken fan of the author Douglas Reed, at least in the sense that she recommended him enthusiastically to virtually all of her acquaintances. She never mentioned him in public. Before the Second World War Reed had worked for *The Times* and resigned because of, in his opinion, misrepresentations of Nazism in the press. After 1945 he became one of the most prominent Holocaust deniers in the West, writing in his book *Far and Wide* that 'Jewish losses' during the conflict were 'irresponsibly inflated' and come nowhere close to the six million claimed in the years after the liberation of the concentration camps: 'No proof can be given,' he declared. From 1948 he lived in South Africa, claiming that the indigenous population of the country were intellectually and morally incapable of governing themselves. His enduring legacy is *The Controversy of Zion*, completed in 1956 but rejected by all publishers until after his death and brought out in 1978 by Bloomfield Press. In it he repeated his statement that details of the Holocaust were largely fraudulent and went on to claim that the false narrative of the Nazi Final Solution had been invented by Jews themselves and that the creation of Israel was symptomatic of a 'semi-secret priesthood' of Zionism set upon controlling the world by infiltrating all of the centres of trading and finance outside the communist bloc.

In December 1989 Highsmith wrote to Vidal, recommending the book to him, and stating that she had sent three copies to her closest friends praising it as a source of 'enlightenment'. To Vidal she wrote that their lying about the Holocaust was evidence that Jews 'love to be hated' and that they enjoyed being targets by Palestinian activists, notably at the Munich Olympics of 1972, because they could present this as a 'second Holocaust'. In her view 'Holocaust' was a misnomer. It should be renamed either as 'Holocaust Inc.' in recognition of its role as a means of generating income for Israel in particular and Jewry in general, or 'Semicaust' given that the Nazis had managed to exterminate less than half of the Jews on earth, which disappointed Highsmith greatly. Again, Vidal did not reply to her. Kate Kingsley Skattebol had received one of the Reed volumes and later admitted that it reflected something in her friend that appalled her utterly.

Shortly after she finished her unpublished essay on Israel and Judaism in 1992 she flew to America, first to visit her cousins the Coates in Texas and then to stay for four days with Marijane Meaker, her lover from the 1960s, in Meaker's pretty colonial-style house in East Hampton, New York. Later in interviews and in her own memoir Meaker said that the experience was bizarre, as if she had been visited by a grotesque apparition. Some of Highsmith's more tolerable idiosyncrasies persisted but these had been edged aside by something quite horrible.

When they went for coffee in a local restaurant, she noted that America had become far more multi-racial since she had lived in the country permanently in the early fifties. The majority of the customers in the diner were African American and Highsmith remarked that there were probably so many present because of their 'animal-like' breeding habits, that black men became physically ill if they did not have sex 'many times a month' and were in any event too 'feckless and stupid to realise that unprotected intercourse led to pregnancy'. Worse still, apparently, was the tendency for blacks, men and women, to be improvident with money; hence their poverty-stricken condition was a burden upon the state.

This was a rehearsal for her principal rant, involving 'Yids' who she blamed for inciting virtually all forms of post-Cold War discord as part of a plot for global domination, though she did not offer a detailed explanation of how they would bring this about. According to Meaker her contempt for Israel was virulent and personal rather than based on anything resembling rational political opinion. She even avoided using the term 'Israel'. Preferring to refer to the region as Palestine and citizens of the 1948 state as 'Jews' rather

than 'Israelis', she seemed, like many pro-Palestinian activists, to
have already abolished Israel, in her mind at least. She berated
Meaker for maintaining friendships with New York 'Yids' and even
treated Jews as being responsible for the disappearance of ham
sandwiches from business-class menus on transatlantic flights. This
was, she contended, further evidence of the 'Yiddish' objective of
world control. Meaker was disturbed particularly by Highsmith's
confession that she enjoyed living in the Ticino region of Switzerland
because it seemed like a realisation of the Final Solution: Jews,
according to Highsmith, neither existed there nor were spoken of
by Swiss residents. Meaker asked her, 'Do you live in some little
Nazi coven?' (Meaker, pp. 183–98).

Eighteen months earlier Highsmith had submitted a screenplay for a
series running on German state radio called 'Impossible Interviews'.
As the title indicated, a figure from the present day, usually a writer
or intellectual, would create a fictional dialogue between themselves
and, typically, someone from history. Highsmith chose to speak
with a present-day figure, Yitzhak Shamir, then prime minister of
Israel. She tried to rectify the anomaly by making it clear during
the conversation that Shamir, and most other Israelis, were intent
on using the past as a means of advancing their local and global
interests. According to her every time they provoked the Palestinians
to act against them, they could claim this as a perpetuation of the
Holocaust and raise money, mostly from America, to fund their
own plans to expand. Christa Maerker and the production editor
at the radio station, who had suggested the project, were appalled
by what they read and more importantly astonished that Highsmith
might assume that a German radio network would broadcast what
amounted to a pro-Nazi drama in 1990.

Highsmith knew they would reject it, but it was part of the weird
exchange between her execrable true self and the one that the
media and the publishing industry thought they knew and found
acceptable. The screenplay confirmed for Maerker a suspicion

that she had nurtured since her visit to Highsmith in Switzerland. Five years earlier Maerker and others at dinner with Highsmith had become involved in an acrimonious exchange on Nazism, antisemitism and the creation of Israel. In the middle of the dinner Highsmith rolled up the sleeve of her sweater, slowly inscribed a number on her forearm with a ballpoint pen, and then laughed. She was mocking the experience of concentration-camp inmates and inviting her guests to condemn her. Instead, according to Maerker, they left the house.

Phyllis Nagy, who had known Highsmith since the mid-1980s, tells of how in 1990, shortly after the screenplay had been rejected by German radio, she played host to her during a week-long visit to New York. Nagy, twenty-eight and already earning a considerable reputation as a theatre director in the US, arranged an evening out in the city and asked Highsmith if she could bring along a woman, a poet, with whom she'd gone to college. Highsmith said she would be pleased to meet the young woman, known only as 'Barbara'. By this time Highsmith's obsessive concern with and loathing for Judaism was common knowledge among her friends and acquaintances, though no one spoke of it in the presence of the media. Nonetheless, Nagy felt it wise to warn her friend of what she was about to encounter. Both women were from left-leaning backgrounds and had come to generally regard manifestations of political extremism, racism included, as grotesque curiosities rather than as serious threats to the new liberal consensus. 'That's all right,' said Barbara, 'you don't have to mention that I'm Jewish.'

Highsmith had requested they meet at the door of the Duchess, a Manhattan lesbian club, now renamed, which she remembered from the late 1940s when its status and the activities of its clientele were clandestine. Her nostalgic exercise in time travel would take a further twist when Nagy and Barbara arrived to find that Highsmith too was accompanied by a college friend, Kate Kingsley Skattebol. The age difference between the two couples was more than forty years, which was accentuated once they entered the club whose clientele were mostly in their twenties. Nagy commented that their two companions looked both puzzled and out of place, as if they were pensioners who had wandered into a college discotheque. Skattebol broke the silence by commenting on the number and muscularity of black women on the dance floor. Highsmith agreed and added, once they reached the bar, 'Well at least we made it through *THAT*!' referring to the heaving crowd of well-built African Americans. She looked around and declared that 'Well, there certainly are a lot of blacks in here … [but] at least there are not a lot of Jews around.' Her three companions were initially silenced by her implication that physically Jews were as easily recognisable as African Americans, but Barbara chose what she thought was a telling rejoinder, stating, 'Excuse me, but I'm a Jew.' Highsmith turned to her, stared her up and down and observed, 'Well, you don't *LOOK* like one' (Interview between Schenkar and Nagy, 26 June 2002).

Some might take this as Highsmith's attempt to lighten the mood, coming across as a version of Wilde's Lady Bracknell, the mistress of involuntary irony. But given our knowledge of her unremitting antisemitism from her school years onwards this seems a little too charitable. Stereotypical representations of Jews in Western culture from the thirteenth century onwards emphasised supposedly defining racial characteristic such as large hooked noses, curly hair – often red – and a swarthy complexion. These supposedly genetic physical characteristics were usually accompanied by indications of reprehensible activity that meant Jews were fully deserving of their status as scapegoats for the worst ills of society. The visual stereotypes would thus be shown as practising various forms of greed and usury. When Highsmith informed Barbara that she did not '*LOOK*' Jewish she was also telling her that she was lucky in being able to disguise the 'innately vile' features of her race, which beneath the surface she might share.

We cannot ignore the fact that three of the women to whom she declared her undying love, notably Ellen Hill and Marion Aboudaram, were Jewish. Even after their relationship was over Highsmith maintained an addictive, masochistic attachment to Ellen which lasted almost until the end of her life. With Marion she showed an unusual interest in her anatomy, particularly her bone-structure, hair distribution on her legs and arms, and the survival of her mother in Paris during the Nazi occupation. Was this due to some twisted form of prurience? More likely, I suspect, was that Highsmith as the foul antisemite was in part an invention. Like Ripley she shifted between a personality that was seemingly charming and another presence that was utterly ghastly. Highsmith knew that those closest to her were appalled by her views and her expressions of them, which is why she continued to do so.

16

THOSE WHO WALK AWAY

Ripley Under Water (1991) was the fifth and final novel of the so-called *Ripliad* and indeed the last full-length work of fiction to go into print during Highsmith's lifetime.

The plot is another variation on an enduring theme. Ripley's quasi-aristocratic existence near Fontainebleau is once more disturbed by outsiders variously obsessed with him or intent on exacting a form of vengeance – this time, a thoroughly unappealing American couple, Janice and David Pritchard. The latter claims to have knowledge of Ripley's involvement in the death of Dickie Greenleaf, whom he murdered in *The Talented Mr. Ripley*, and more recently of his responsibility for the disappearance of the art collector Thomas Murchison (*Ripley Under Ground*). Pritchard photographs Ripley's house and arranges for local canals to be dredged for Murchison's corpse. He finds a skeleton which he leaves outside Ripley's front door and which Ripley then dumps in a pond adjacent to the Pritchards' house. In an attempt to drag it out with a garden rake the Pritchards fall into the water and drown.

One might suspect that such a brief synopsis does an injustice to the nuances and complexities of the work, but no. It is as ponderous and fatiguing as it sounds. It seems that Highsmith was making a rather despairing attempt to keep Ripley alive for another excursion into the gruesome and sadomasochistic, but her notes for the first draft suggest that she initially considered this to be his final outing. In her notebook she writes that 'He escapes into another person ... A form of schizophrenia', and in the draft she sometimes has him refer to himself in the third person, as though he had become two people simultaneously, one watching the other. At various stages in the early planning of the novel she looked at how Ripley might slip into an irreversible state of insanity, sometimes participating with the Pritchards in acts of violent sadomasochism, even involving ritual murder. Had she proceeded with these scenarios it would have meant the end of Ripley but obviously she changed her mind.

In 1986, a year before she began her notes for the novel, Highsmith had an operation in the Royal Brompton Hospital in London to remove a cancerous tumour from her lung. Later, X-rays showed that the original growth had disappeared and had not spread to other tissues. This was her third near-death experience, following two bypass operations for severe cardiovascular disease. Perhaps she felt it appropriate to export her own precarious state to her most long-standing creation and there is evidence that she wondered if she, and he, might survive for a while yet.

Shortly after her X-ray she was informed by the architect Tobias Ammann that a site had become available in the southern Swiss village of Tegna, surrounded by mountains and overlooking the Centovalli valley. Planning permission was available and she calculated that the cost of the land, design fees (she would use Ammann) and prices for labour and material would come to around half a million Swiss francs, roughly the amount she would obtain from the sale of the Montcourt and Aurigeno houses, plus some withdrawals from her American savings account. By the time she completed *Ripley Under Water*, with her anti-hero returning to his manor without being pursued by the police, she was settled into her own recently constructed version of Belle Ombre. Aside from being retreats from the outside world the two residences had absolutely nothing in common. Ammann was a devotee of the Le Corbusier concretist-modernist school but with a passion for even more impersonal brutalism. His plan for Highsmith was a masterpiece of architectural inhumanity, something that might provoke debate as an 'installation' but which none of the debaters would choose to live in. It can best be described as characterless, and from the outside it reminds one more of a Second World War bunker than a domestic residence.

Her Swiss publisher, Daniel Keel, drove to the house regularly from Zurich, Vivien De Bernardi was an occasional guest, Kate Kingsley Skattebol tried as often as she could to cross the Atlantic to stay with her old friend and the Hubers lived close by. Ellen Hill drove or took a train to Tegna every two weeks when the house was being finished. Soon after moving in Highsmith invited a number of her closest neighbours to a drinks party but after that she became politely reclusive, conversing with locals when she met them in shops or on the street but retreating to the fortress-style house whenever she could.

Irma Andina and Ingeborg Lüscher lived in the village and recalled the contrast between the figure they knew of from newspaper accounts and media appearances and their new neighbour. The real Highsmith was inoffensive and polite but always seemed determined to flee back to her house, never shook hands or looked you in the eye, and as Lüscher put it, 'didn't know how to react; she didn't like to breathe other people's air' (Wilson, p.437). Lüscher vividly recalls Ellen Hill as 'not only full of poison for Pat, but full of poison for the whole world'. Peter Huber said that 'one day Ellen arrived and dashed in like a rugby player ... Pat told her to leave. She did not want anything to do with her' (Wilson, p.428). As far as we know that was the last time they met.

By the end of 1993 it was clear from Highsmith's various health problems that it would be unsafe for her to continue to live alone. Bruno Sager's daughter worked for Highsmith's publisher, Diogenes Verlag, in Zurich and Daniel Keel recommended Sager to Highsmith as a full-time carer. He was recently divorced and had worked for local theatres and orchestras. Sager stayed with and looked after

Highsmith for six months and his later accounts of the experience carry an air of tragedy and very black comedy. He cleaned the house, did the shopping and cooking and took care of the garden. When he arrived it was wildly overgrown, except for the lawn which had been burnt brown during the previous hot summer. It took some time for him to persuade her to let him water it. She was making complaints against the local water company because of, in her view, its extortionate billings. She was, he observed, extremely mean but he did not complain about being paid only 400 Swiss francs a month. He had already decided that at the close of his time with Highsmith he would join a monastery, though he insisted that there was no connection between the two. When she died, eighteen months later, her estate came to more than three million dollars.

Sager also looked after the only other resident, Charlotte, a wild orange-coloured cat who spent much of her time outside, and Highsmith instructed him on the upkeep of her now diminished colony of snails in the garden and demanded that when he cleaned the house he must be careful not to harm spiders and to transport them safely into the open. He professed not to be surprised by what most would see as bizarre eccentricities. There were two bedrooms – he used one and Highsmith the other – and they shared the large sitting room where there was a television. Her favourite TV programme, he reported, was the British soap opera *EastEnders*, of which he knew nothing.

There was only one telephone – 'she refused to pay for another' according to Sager – and Highsmith used it at least every other week to speak with Kate Kingsley Skattebol, 'her best friend', as Sager put it. At first Highsmith was cold and distant but eventually she talked with him about art, literature and politics. 'Her politics,' he reported, 'were very extreme, based on certain prejudices, not on analysis.' The most extreme element involved Jews and Israel, and she told him of how Jews had discriminated against her, notably her current US publisher Otto Penzler who, she insisted, had censored her by dropping the pro-Palestinian dedication to *People Who Knock on the Door.* In truth, her agent had asked Penzler to delete it for fear that it might damage sales in America. Sager told of how she would list all of the figures in publishing who had conspired against her: 'She was vicious. "Oh, he's a Jew, you know, he's a Jew," she would say about them' (Interview between Sager and Schenkar, 7 June 2003).

When speaking of his time with Highsmith Sager comes across as a meditative figure, willing neither to judge nor be shocked. He reflected that while she had no time for organised religion of any kind he felt 'She was not an atheist, not at all.' He was not ordained, and he certainly did not attempt to coerce Highsmith towards anything close to faith, but he served her during the period before her illness worsened irreparably as a kind of secular priest. When he left, he was replaced by a young woman, again recommended by the Keels, who was so terrified by her employer that she refused to leave her bedroom when Highsmith was out of hers. She left in less than two weeks. After that Highsmith willed herself to open her door to neighbours, notably the Lüschers and Hubers, who happily helped her with the basics of existence.

While Sager was with her, her novel *Small g: a Summer Idyll* (1995) was accepted by Bloomsbury. It is set in contemporary Zurich, focuses on the seedy Jakob's Bierstube-Restaurant and involves a variety of figures who pass through it, including: Rickie, a middle-aged graphic designer; Teddie, an aspiring journalist; Dorrie, a freelance window dresser; Renate, a 'club-footed' couturier; and Luisa, Renate's apprentice and tenant. Sometimes the plot is reminiscent of a Restoration comedy, or the more recent variation on the genre, the Whitehall Farces. Characters often become confused about their own sexual orientation or more frequently misinterpret someone else's or misjudge their behaviour in terms of whether they are, or are not, mutually attracted. But to Highsmith's credit she achieves a wonderful balance between the almost comedic and an adventurous brand of realism. Among the confusion there is a message: that we are comfortable with our gender and sexuality when all is fluid and uncertain. Also, we detect within it traces of all aspects of the life and experiences of the author, from her clandestine existence in the 1940s in New York onwards. She was offered her largest-ever advance by Bloomsbury – £20,000 – and while it was initially rejected by Knopf for the US, the publicity campaign in Europe was impressive. In November 1994 she was invited to stay in the Ritz Paris, ostensibly to speak at the thirtieth anniversary celebration of *Le Nouvel Observateur*, but when she arrived, she found that everyone involved in publishing and in the media wanted to talk only to her about her forthcoming novel, rumoured to be the most ground-breaking work so far on contemporary sexuality and most specifically on the AIDS epidemic, which features in the plot. Within six weeks of her death the novel had sold 50,000 copies in France alone.

The Paris visit would be the last time she was to leave the Tegna house voluntarily. When Sager first arrived, she appeared to him to be seriously underweight and after his departure she lost a further fifteen kilos. She regularly coughed up blood and the cause for this horrible affliction was a combination of her returned lung cancer and aplastic anaemia, which causes the body to fail to produce blood cells in sufficient numbers. She knew her condition was terminal and at various times in 1994 made arrangements to leave the bulk of her financial estate to the Yaddo community where she had written her first novel, *Strangers on a Train*. Her Swiss publisher, Diogenes Verlag, was already dealing with many of her financial and legal affairs; she appointed them as her literary executors and instructed Keel to sell her papers and correspondence to the Swiss Literary Archive in Bern, which agreed to pay her 150,000 Swiss francs. This was not paid until after her death and on 1 February 1995 she signed the final version of her will, including a statement that the Bern proceeds should also go to Yaddo.

Bert Diener and Julia Diener-Diethelm lived in Zurich and were only distant friends of Highsmith. Nonetheless it was to them that she made a telephone call on the evening of 2 February asking if they would come to Tegna to drive her to the hospital in Locarno. They did not hesitate and on the following day she was visited in hospital by her accountant Marylin Scowden, who would be the last person to see her alive. She died shortly before 6.30 a.m. on 4 February at the age of seventy-four, before the medical staff did their customary rounds.

Her cremation in Bellinzona was followed by a memorial service in the church in Tegna where her ashes were interred. Notably Ellen Hill did not attend the service. Following the completion of *Small g* she made entries on the closing page of her final *cahier* on the possible title of her next book. It would, yet again, involve Ripley. There are no details on the plot, only possible titles, and all but one of these is crossed out: *Ripley's Luck*.

PRIMARY SOURCES

FICTION

NOVELS (US PUBLICATION DETAILS)

Strangers on a Train (New York: Harper & Brothers, 1950)
The Price of Salt (as Claire Morgan; New York: Coward-McCann, 1952)
The Blunderer (New York: Coward-McCann, 1954)
The Talented Mr. Ripley (New York: Coward-McCann, 1955)
Deep Water (New York: Harper & Brothers, 1957)
A Game for the Living (New York: Harper & Brothers, 1958)
This Sweet Sickness (New York: Harper & Brothers, 1960)
The Cry of the Owl (New York: Harper & Row, 1962)
The Two Faces of January (New York: Doubleday, 1964)
The Glass Cell (New York: Doubleday, 1964)
The Story-Teller (UK title: *A Suspension of Mercy*; New York: Doubleday, 1965)
Those Who Walk Away (New York: Doubleday, 1967)
The Tremor of Forgery (New York: Doubleday, 1969)
Ripley Under Ground (New York: Doubleday, 1970)
A Dog's Ransom (New York: Knopf, 1972)
Ripley's Game (New York: Knopf, 1974)
Edith's Diary (New York: Simon & Schuster, 1977)
The Boy Who Followed Ripley (New York: Lippincott & Crowell, 1980)
People Who Knock on the Door (New York: Otto Penzler Books, 1985)
Found in the Street (New York: Atlantic Monthly Press, 1987)
Ripley Under Water (New York: Knopf, 1991)
Small g: a Summer Idyll (New York: W. W. Norton, 2004)

SHORT STORY COLLECTIONS (US PUBLICATION DETAILS)

The Snail-Watcher and Other Stories (UK title: *Eleven*; New York: Doubleday, 1970)

Slowly, Slowly in the Wind (New York: Otto Penzler Books, 1979)

The Animal Lover's Book of Beastly Murder (New York: Otto Penzler Books, 1986)

Little Tales of Misogyny (New York: Otto Penzler Books, 1986)

The Black House (New York: Otto Penzler Books, 1988)

Mermaids on the Golf Course (New York: Otto Penzler Books, 1988)

Tales of Natural and Unnatural Catastrophes (New York: Atlantic Monthly Press, 1987)

The Selected Stories of Patricia Highsmith (New York: W. W. Norton, 2001)

Nothing That Meets the Eye: The Uncollected Stories of Patricia Highsmith (New York: W. W. Norton, 2002)

NON-FICTION

Plotting and Writing Suspense Fiction (Boston: The Writer, Inc., 1966)

CHILDREN'S LITERATURE

Miranda the Panda is on the Veranda (Doris Sanders, illustrations by PH; New York: Coward-McCann, 1958)

OTHER

All uncited quotations above from correspondence, notebooks, diaries and *cahiers* come from the Patricia Highsmith Papers, Swiss Literary Archives (SLA), Bern, Switzerland.

SUGGESTED FURTHER READING

Atallah, Naim. 'The Oldie Interview. Patricia Highsmith'. *The Oldie*, 3 September 1993.

Birch, Helen. 'Patricia Highsmith.' *City Limits*, 20–27 March 1986.

Bloom, Harold, ed. *Lesbian and Bisexual Fiction Writers*. Philadelphia: Chelsea House, 1997.

Blythe, Ronald. *Akenfield. Portrait of an English Village*. London: Allen Lane, 1969.

Bradford, Richard. *Crime Fiction: A Very Short Introduction*. Oxford: Oxford University Press, 2015.

Brandel, Marc. *The Choice*. New York: Dial Press, 1950.

Brown, Craig. 'Packing a Sapphic punch.' [On the publication of *Carol* under Highsmith's name.] *Sunday Times*, 14 October 1990.

—. 'The Hitman and Her.' *The Times Saturday Review*, 28 September 1991.

Broyard, Anatole. *Kafka Was the Rage: A Greenwich Village Memoir*. New York: Vintage, 1997.

Buck, Joan Juliet. 'A Terrifying Talent'. *Observer Magazine*, 20 November 1977.

Calder, Liz. 'Patricia Highsmith'. *The Oldie*, March, 1995.

Campbell, James. 'Murder, She (Usually) Wrote.' *New York Times*, 27 October 2002.

Carter, Hannah. 'Queens of Crime'. *The Guardian*, 1 May 1968.

Clapp, Susannah. 'Lovers on a Train.' [On the publication of *Carol* under Highsmith's name.] *London Review of Books*, 10 January 1991.

—. 'The Simple Art of Murder.' *The New Yorker*, 20 December 1999.

Clarke, Gerald. *Capote: A Biography*. New York: Simon & Schuster, 1988.

Connolly, Cyril. *Enemies of Promise*. London: Andre Deutsch, 1988.

Cooper-Clark, Diana. 'Patricia Highsmith – Interview'. *The Armchair Detective*, Vol. 14, no. 4, 1981.

Dupont, Joan. 'The Poet of Apprehension.' *Village Voice*, 30 May 1995.

—. 'Criminal Pursuits.' *New York Times Magazine*, 12 June 1988.

Eisner, Will. *The Plot: The Secret Story of the Protocols of the Elders of Zion*. New York: W. W. Norton, 2005.

Fallowell, Duncan. 'The Talented Miss Highsmith.' *Sunday Times Magazine*, 20 February 2000.

Flanner, Janet. *Darlinghissima: Letters to a Friend*. Edited by Natalia Danesi Murray. New York: Random House, 1985.

—. *Paris Was Yesterday*. New York: Penguin, 1979.

Foster, Jeanette Howard. *Sex Variant Women in Literature*. Baltimore: Diana Press, 1975.

Garber, Margery. *Vested Interests: Cross-Dressing & Cultural Anxiety*. New York: Routledge, 1992.

Glendenning, Victoria. 'Forbidden love story comes out.' [On the publication of *Carol* under Highsmith's name.] *The Times*, 11 October 1990.

Gowrie, Grey. 'Why her place is secure.' *Daily Telegraph*, 11 March 1995.

Greene, Graham. 'Foreword', *Eleven*. London: Heinemann, 1970.

Guggenheim, Peggy. *Out of This Century: Confessions of an Art Addict*. New York: Universe, 1987.

Guinard, Mavis. 'Patricia Highsmith: Alone With Ripley'. *International Herald Tribune*, 17–18 August 1991.

Hamilton, Ian. 'Patricia Highsmith.' *New Review*, August 1977.

Harrison, Russell. *Patricia Highsmith* (United States Authors Series). New York: Twayne, 1997.

Herbert, Rosemary (ed). *Oxford Companion to Crime and Mystery Writing*. Oxford: Oxford University Press, 1999.

Hughes, Dorothy B. *In a Lonely Place*. New York: Feminist Press, 2003.

Jamison, Kay Redfield. *Touched with Fire: Manic-Depressive Illness and the Artistic Temperament*. New York: Free Press, 1993.

Jones, Gerard. *Men of Tomorrow: Geeks, Gangsters, and the Birth of the Comic Book*. New York, Basic, 2004.

Laski, Marghanita. 'Long Crimes, Short Crimes'. *Listener*, 20 November 1975.

Meade, Marion. *Dorothy Parker: What Fresh Hell Is This?* New York: Penguin, 1989.

Meaker, Marijane. *Highsmith: A Romance of the 1950s*. San Francisco: Cleis Press, 2003.

Menninger, Karl. *The Human Mind*. Garden City, New York: Garden City Publishing, 1930.

Mitchell, Margaretta K. *Ruth Bernhard: Between Art & Life*. San Francisco: Chronicle Books, 2000.

Osbourne, Lawrence. *The Poisoned Embrace: A Brief History of Sexual Pessimism*. New York: Vintage, 1994.

Packer, Vin [Marijane Meaker]. *Intimate Victims*. New York: Manor Books, 1963.

Plimpton, George. *Truman Capote: In Which Various Friends, Enemies, Acquaintances, and Detractors Recall His Turbulent Career*. New York: Nan A. Talese, 1997.

Robb, Graham. *Strangers: Homosexual Love in the Nineteenth Century*. New York: W. W. Norton, 2003.

Rzepka, C.J. and Horsley, Lee (eds). *A Companion to Crime Fiction*. Chichester: Wiley/Blackwell, 2010; includes chapter by Brian Nicol on 'Patricia Highsmith'.

Sanders, Marion K. *Dorothy Thompson: A Legend in Her Time*. Boston: Houghton Mifflin, 1973.

Schenkar, Joan. *The Talented Miss Highsmith: The Secret Life and Serious Art of Patricia Highsmith*. New York: Picador, 2009

Skelton, Barbara. 'Patricia Highsmith at Home.' *London Magazine*, August/September 1995.

Steranko, James. *Steranko History of Comics*. Reading, PA: Supergraphics, 1972.

—. *Steranko History of Comics 2*. Reading, PA: Supergraphics, 1972.

Symons, Julian. *The Modern Crime Story*. Edinburgh: The Tragara Press, 1980.

Thurman, Judith. *Secrets of the Flesh*. New York: Knopf, 1999.

Tolkin, Michael. 'In Memory of Patricia Highsmith.' *Los Angeles Times Book Review*, February 1995.

Torres, Tereska. *Women's Barracks*. New York: Feminist Press, 2005.

Vidal, Gore. *Palimpsest*. London: Penguin, 1995.

—. *United States (Essays 1952–1992)*. London: Abacus, 1993.

Watts, Janet. 'Love and Highsmith.' *Observer Magazine*, 9 September 1990.

Wertham, Frederic. *Seduction of the Innocent*. New York: Rinehart, 1954.

—. *A Sign for Cain*. London: Robert Hale, 1966.

Wilson, Andrew. *Beautiful Shadow: A Life of Patricia Highsmith*. London: Bloomsbury, 2003.

Wineapple, Brenda. *Genet: A Biography of Janet Flanner*. New York: Ticknor & Fields, 1989.

Wolff, Charlotte, M.D. *Love Between Women*. New York: St. Martin's Press, 1971.

Yronwode, Catherine, and Trina Robbins. *Women and the Comics*. Forestville, CA: Eclipse Books, 1985.

INDEX